Take-Home Leveled Readers

On-level

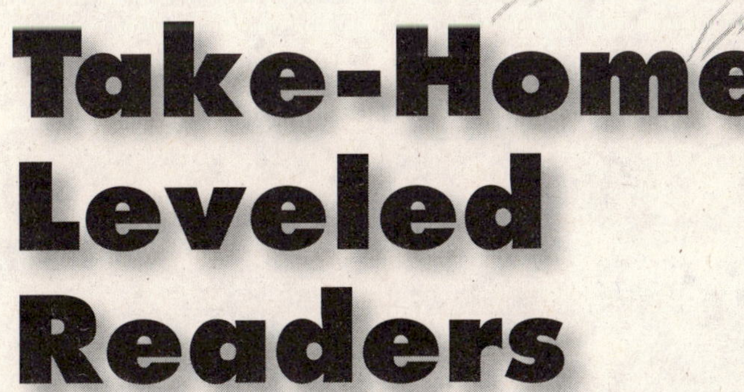

Science

PEARSON
Scott Foresman

Editorial Offices: Glenview, Illinois • Parsippany, New Jersey • New York, New York
Sales Offices: Needham, Massachusetts • Duluth, Georgia • Glenview, Illinois
Coppell, Texas • Sacramento, California • Mesa, Arizona
sfsuccessnet.com

ISBN: 0-328-19734-3

2 3 4 5 6 7 8 9 10 V004 13 12 11 10 09 08 07 06 05

Table of Contents

To the Teacher

Scott Foresman provides three Leveled Readers for every chapter of *Scott Foresman Science*, Grades 1–6: a *Below-Level Leveled Reader*, an *On-Level Leveled Reader*, and an *Advanced Leveled Reader*.

All three readers teach the same science concepts, same vocabulary, address the same target reading skill and contain the same graphic organizer as the corresponding student edition chapter, just at three different reading levels—providing access to important science content for all students. The On-level and Advanced readers also use additional examples to enrich the chapter and extend ideas

This book contains reproducible copies of the On-Level Leveled Readers for Grade 6. These are designed for you to reproduce and send home with your students as appropriate. Encourage students to share these books with parents or family members in order to practice reading skills and reinforce science content.

Online versions of these and other readers are also available through the Scott Foresman Leveled Reader Database.

CLASSIFYING LIVING ORGANISMS

by Mary Walsh

Genre	Comprehension Skill	Text Features	Science Content
Nonfiction	Compare and Contrast	• Captions • Charts • Glossary	Classifying Living Organisms

Scott Foresman Science 6.1

PEARSON
Scott Foresman

ISBN 0-328-13971-8

9 780328 139712

90000

scottforesman.com

What did you learn?

1. How do certain bacteria help people?

2. What are some ways fungi are harmful and some ways they are helpful?

3. How have people adapted to living in a very hot climate?

4. **Writing** in Science There are millions of living things on Earth. Write a short paragraph to explain the value of having a classification system for living organisms. Include a description of the system scientists invented and how it developed over time.

5. **Compare and Contrast** Species have to adapt to their environment. How alike and how different are birds and mammals? Support your answer with examples.

Vocabulary

adaptation
archaebacteria
bacteria
biosphere
classification
eubacteria
fungi
nonvascular plants
protists
species
vascular plants

Picture Credits
Every effort has been made to secure permission and provide appropriate credit for photographic material.
The publisher deeply regrets any omission and pledges to correct errors called to its attention in subsequent editions.

Photo locators denoted as follows: Top (T), Center (C), Bottom (B), Left (L), Right (R), Background (Bkgd).

3 Getty Images; 4 (R) Julie Mowbray/Alamy Images, (BL) ©Jerry Young/DK Images; 8 (BR) Getty Images;
9 (C) Nigel Cattlin/Alamy Images, (BR) Barry Runk/Stan/Grant Heilman Photography; 12 (CR) ©Jerry Young/DK Images;
13 (CLB, CBL, CBR, CRB) ©Jerry Young/DK Images.

Scott Foresman/Dorling Kindersley would also like to thank: 6 Linnean Society of London/DK Images;
8 (CL) Dr. Julian Thorpe/DK Images; 13 (TR) Natural History Museum, London/DK Images.

Unless otherwise acknowledged, all photographs are the copyright © of Dorling Kindersley, a division of Pearson.

ISBN: 0-328-13971-8

Glossary

adaptation a characteristic that enables an organism to survive and reproduce in its environment

archaebacteria group of bacteria made up of one-celled organisms

bacteria single-cell organisms that were once the only form of life on Earth

biosphere all living things and their environments

classification the process of grouping things according to common characteristics

eubacteria organisms that can cause diseases and can also be beneficial

fungi organisms that have no roots, stems, or leaves and cannot make their own food; so they have to live on other plants that can

nonvascular plants plants whose water and food get passed from cell to cell

protists mostly one-celled organisms, including some algae

species a group of individuals that are similar and can produce offspring that are similar

vascular plants plants whose water and food travel inside in tubes

CLASSIFYING LIVING ORGANISMS

by Mary Walsh

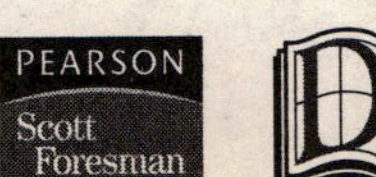

Where do organisms live?

The Biosphere

There are millions of living things on Earth we already know about. Scientists believe that there are still a large number that haven't been discovered yet. There are many living things around us, such as plants and animals. You know that there are also many living things in the ocean, in the desert, and even in the air. But if you could shrink Earth to the size of an apple, the area where you would find living things would be equivalent to the apple's skin!

The part of Earth that can support living things is called the **biosphere.** All living things and their environments together make up the biosphere. There are many types of environments in the biosphere: oceans, deserts, parks, yards, and even sidewalks in the middle of cities.

Scientists have already found nearly two million organisms in Earth's biosphere. They name about ten thousand new ones each year, and they think there are still millions more to be discovered.

Why are there still so many new types of organisms to be discovered? One reason is the size of our planet. The oceans are very deep and many areas of land have not been fully explored. Also, some organisms are very tiny and hard to find.

Each organism in the biosphere interacts with other organisms and their environment. Each one competes for the resources available. We also play an important role in the environment. Our actions affect the environment and the organisms living within it.

Phylum Chordata (Subphylum Vertebrata)
You can see that this gorilla is very different from the bird. The gorilla is in the class that feeds its young milk from the mother's mammary glands.

Phylum Chordata (Subphylum Vertebrata)
This bird is in the same category as the gorilla, but in a different class. Birds lay eggs, have lungs and feathers, and most have wings that they use to fly.

You might find a piece of bread with mold on it in a kitchen. The bread is part of the environment for a living mold.

Scientists often need to classify organisms into smaller groups than the kingdom, phylum, or class. Phyla can be divided into classes and classes can be divided into orders. Orders can be divided into families, and families into genera (the plural of *genus*) and species.

The number of organisms in a classification group decreases as the groups become more specific. As we move from broad groups like kingdom to more specific groups like family and genus, members of the group become fewer but more alike. Animals in the same genus share many characteristics, but only members of the same species can produce offspring.

This system of classification allows scientists to classify new organisms as they are discovered, and there are many species yet to be discovered. Perhaps one day you might be lucky enough to find and classify a new species!

More on Animal Classification

You saw the word *phylum* when we were talking about vehicles and dogs. In the Animal kingdom there are about thirty-five phyla (the plural of *phylum*).

Here are pictures from some of the phyla. Both the bird and the gorilla belong to the same phyla and have backbones. They are called vertebrates. The rest of the animals without a backbone are called invertebrates. More than 90 percent of the animal species on Earth are invertebrates.

Phylum Annelida
This peacock worm lives on the ocean floor. The feathers are tentacles that it uses to catch food. This phylum also includes earthworms.

Phylum Mollusca
Most mollusks have a soft body and a foot that they use to get around. The foot sticks out from the shell.

Phylum Arthropoda
Arthropoda is the largest animal phylum. More than a million species have been named. The tarantula has legs with joints, a complete digestive tract, and a body with segments.

Living Things Are Alike and Different

You can usually recognize a cat. Even if it's a different color or size or has a different kind of fur than another cat, you know a cat when you see one.

This is an example of a species. A **species** is a group of individuals that are similar and can reproduce to make more of themselves.

In the chart below you see an estimated number of known species for different groups of organisms. This chart shows the species that are alive today. Some scientists think that 99 percent of all species that were ever alive no longer exist.

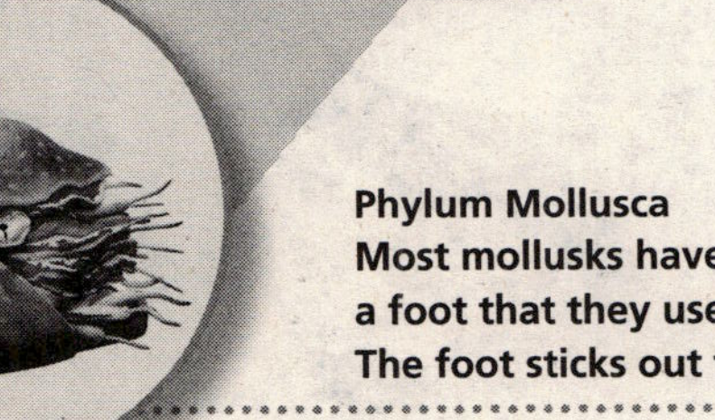

Even though these cats have different fur and a different shape, they are still members of the same species.

Group	Number of Living Species
Vertebrates	42,000
Mammals	4,000
Birds	9,000
Reptiles	6,000
Amphibians	4,000
Fish	19,000
Invertebrates	980,000
Plants	248,000

Sometimes Living Things Change

An **adaptation** is a characteristic that helps an organism survive or reproduce in its environment. Plants and animals whose adaptations fit an environment are more likely to survive than plants and animals whose adaptations do not. For example, giraffes eat leaves. But so do many other animals. The giraffe's long neck is an adaptation that allows it to reach leaves in the tops of trees that many other animals could not reach.

Another example is the redwood tree, *Sequoia sempervirens*. These trees are among the tallest and oldest living things. Redwoods produce a substance called tannin that repels insects, fungi, and many animals that would otherwise eat the tree's bark or leaves. They can also take in more than 2,000 liters of water in a single day. These are just a few of the adaptations that help the redwoods survive in their environment. Many live more than fifteen hundred years.

Sometimes environments change. When they do, plants and animals whose adaptations fit this change are likely to survive. There was a moth in Europe that was a light color until about the 1850s. That was when people started to build factories that sent a lot of black smoke into the air. The smoke would settle on the bark of trees and make them black. The predator of the moths could see the moths easily when they were a light color on black bark. Darker moths were better suited to survive in their environment. Over time, most surviving moths were darker in color.

Look at the organisms in these photos. Each one has an adaptation that makes it able to survive in its environment.

The monkey's long tail lets it swing from tree to tree.

Redwood trees are among the tallest and oldest living things.

Classes Are Not Just for School

Now let's look more closely at how scientists classify dogs, using a similar system. Look at the photos below to see what each category stands for.

Kingdom:	Animals
Phylum:	Chordata
Class:	Mammalian
Order:	Carnivore
Family:	Canidae
Genus and Species:	*Canis familiaris*

Order: Carnivore Carnivores eat animal flesh. They have large, strong teeth with sharp cutting edges.

Class: Mammalian Mammals are warm-blooded animals whose babies drink milk from the mother.

Phylum: Chordata This phylum includes birds, reptiles, fish, and mammals. They have a nerve cord that runs below their back.

Kingdom: Animals This kingdom is made up of all animals, including insects and fish.

Classifying Animals

The Animal kingdom includes many different kinds of organisms. They all have some things in common. They all ingest food. But they get it from somewhere else instead of making it like plants do. All animals have specialized tissues, except for the sponges. For example, most animals have a mouth to chew food and a stomach to digest it. Every living thing in the Animal kingdom can also move on its own at some point in its life and can reproduce, usually by mixing cells with another parent.

Before we look at subgroups in the Animal kingdom, let's see how we might classify things in a "Vehicles" kingdom. We could use a chart like the following:

Kingdom:	Vehicles
Phylum:	All vehicles with wheels
Class:	Vehicles with wheels that are used to transport people
Order:	Vehicles with two wheels that transport people
Family:	Small vehicles with two wheels that transport only one person
Genus and Species:	Street bike

You see that the groups keep getting smaller and smaller.

Genus and species: *Canis familiaris*
The dog that lives in homes with people is named with both its genus and its species. This is a convention that helps to identify any organism.

Family: Canidae
This includes various animals related to dogs. A fox belongs to the family of dogs.

The hummingbird has a long beak so it can suck up the nectar from inside a flower.

The spines of the cactus are actually leaves. Their shape helps the plant to conserve water.

The anteater's snout is long so it can slurp up ants on the ground.

The hard shell of this turtle protects its soft body.

Classifying Organisms in Categories

Scientists need a way to talk about the millions of organisms that we know about on Earth, so many years ago they invented a system to organize them.

Imagine that you have just completed washing and folding your clothes. But you need to put them in your dresser or your closet. Right now socks are mixed in with shirts, and jackets are mixed in with pants. So the first thing you do is group them. You put the things you wear when you go outside in the closet, and things that you wear in the house in the dresser. Things that you wear to bed go in one drawer, and things that you wear during the day go into another. Grouping things according to their similar characteristics is called **classification.**

Scientists also classify living things. Their system of classification is based on the structure of an organism, how it reproduces, and how it feeds.

Carolus Linnaeus was a doctor who worked with plants in the 1700s. He divided living things into two groups, or kingdoms: Animals and Plants. Animals are capable of moving themselves (locomotion), while plants are not. When a plant moves in the wind, the wind is moving it—it is not moving by itself.

Carolus Linnaeus classified organisms in two categories: plants and animals.

Classifying Plants

You know some characteristics that almost all plants have, such as making their own food. Some plants have other characteristics that make them different. One way they are different is how they move water inside.

Plants need water to make food. When the plant is very tall, as the redwood tree is, the water and food must travel inside in tubes. These are called **vascular plants.** There are more than 260,000 species of vascular plants.

Some plants must pass water from one cell to the next. These plants have no tubes, so they are called **nonvascular plants.** You can tell that these plants must be very small, because the plant has no easy way to move the water up or down. There are about 18,000 species of nonvascular plants.

Scientists divide vascular plants into two groups—those that make seeds and those that don't. You know plants that make seeds. For example, when you cut an apple or an orange, there are seeds inside. These plants are called angiosperms.

Many plants that make seeds also produce flowers. Some evergreens make seeds but don't make flowers. Pinecones hold the seeds the tree produces. These plants are called gymnosperms.

There are some plants without seeds, such as ferns. Ferns reproduce through spores and need a humid environment. Plants that have seeds can adapt to drier conditions than most seedless plants. That is why there are few plants without seeds. Ferns and horsetails belong to this group.

Here is a pinecone and some of its seeds.

Dandelions during and after flowering— the seeds are left after the plant has flowered.

How are plants and animals classified?

You are already familiar with many members of the Plant kingdom. From the massive redwood trees of California to the flowers you pass on your way to school, there are many types of plants. We find plants everywhere—from sidewalks to parks to bodies of water. They provide all of what we eat in some way. If we eat animals, they have eaten plants also. Even if an animal eats other animals, the other animals may have eaten some plants. If we don't eat animals for our food, then we eat plants directly.

Most plants take the energy from the Sun and convert it into food. They do this using chlorophyll, a substance in their cells, through a process called photosynthesis. Plants need sunlight, nutrients, and water to make food.

The larger the plant's leaves, the more chlorophyll it has and the more food it can make.

Our Lady's plant collects water around its leaves so it has water when it needs it.

The Six Kingdoms

Since Linnaeus, other scientists have added new groups to classify living things. We now have six kingdoms altogether. This has been possible because we now can see things that are not visible to the naked eye. With microscopes we can see organisms that Linnaeus did not know existed. For example, we now know that **bacteria** exist: single-cell organisms that were once the only form of life on Earth.

The six kingdoms of classification depend on how an organism gets its food, how it reproduces, and the kind of cell wall it has. Each kingdom is divided up into smaller and smaller groups based on organisms' specific characteristics.

The first kingdom, **Archaebacteria,** is a group of bacteria made up of one cell each, with unusual cell walls. Archaebacteria can live where there is no oxygen. Some live beneath the surface of the Earth, where temperatures are very high. Others make natural gas, which we can use to heat our homes.

The kingdom **Eubacteria** includes several different types of bacteria. One type takes nitrogen from the air and fixes it so plants can absorb it. Plants need nitrogen to make their own food. Without these nitrogen-fixing bacteria, many plants and animals would die.

Other members of Eubacteria cause diseases such as botulism and tuberculosis. Botulism can occur when food has not been canned properly; it can kill a person. Many of us carry the tuberculosis bacterium around with us, but we are strong enough that it doesn't make us sick.

Some Archaebacteria grow on undersea steam vents.

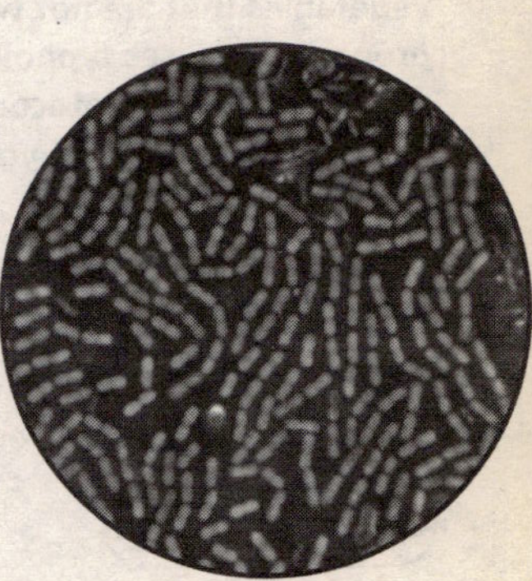

Eubacteria

The **Protists** kingdom includes many one-celled organisms, such as the amoeba and paramecium. There may be more than two hundred thousand protists that have only one cell.

The Protists also include some algae, which can make their own food, and some "slime molds."

The Six Kingdoms

Archaebacteria
These are the most ancient of all living things on Earth. They can use chemicals, such as hydrogen sulfide, to create energy. We can find them living in hot springs.

Fungi
Fungi lack chlorophyll, so they cannot make their own food. They resemble plants because of their appearance and because they have no locomotion.

Eubacteria
Some of these bacteria cause disease. For example, the *Salmonella typhi* sometimes comes from fruits and vegetables that are not washed properly; it causes typhoid fever. Another called Streptococcus can destroy the enamel on your teeth.

Plants
The Plant kingdom is the most abundant of the six kingdoms on Earth.

Protists
This kingdom includes red, brown, and green algae.

Animals
This kingdom includes organisms we normally consider animals, as well as some we might not. Sponges, which live in the ocean, are in this group.

Maybe you have been in the woods and seen mushrooms growing. Mushrooms are **Fungi,** the fourth kingdom. These organisms resemble plants but have no roots, stems, or leaves. Fungi (plural of *fungus*) have no chlorophyll, so they cannot make their own food. Instead, they have to live on other organisms that can provide food.

You have probably seen other types of fungi as well. For example, if you have ever had a piece of bread go bad, it got mold on it. That mold is a type of fungus.

Some fungi are very helpful to people. Penicillin, a medicine that fights infection, comes from fungi. We use yeasts to make bread rise and certain other fungi to make cheese.

Other fungi are not so helpful to people. For example, one causes athlete's foot. There is another called wheat rust, which is a fungus that can destroy millions of crops.

wheat rust growing on a wheat stalk

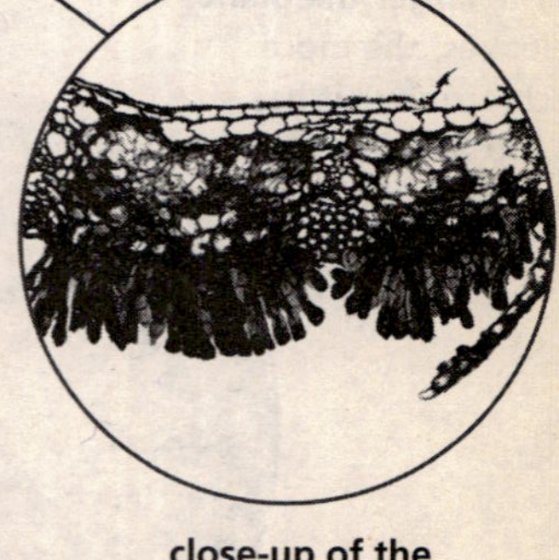

This fungus is sending spores into the air, which will create more fungi.

close-up of the wheat rust

Parts of Cells

by Mary McLean-Hely

Genre	Comprehension Skill	Text Features	Science Content
Nonfiction	Make Inferences	• Captions • Charts • Glossary	Cells

Scott Foresman Science 6.2

What did you learn?

1. What are cells?

2. What is an organelle?

3. What happens when a cell grows to be too large?

4. **Writing** in Science All living organisms are made of cells with similarities. Explain how a single-celled organism is different from a multicellular organism.

5. **Make Inferences** Review the concept of diffusion of water in cells. Make an inference to answer this question: When you see a plant with dried or wilted leaves, what can you say about the plant's cells?

Picture Credits
Every effort has been made to secure permission and provide appropriate credit for photographic material.
The publisher deeply regrets any omission and pledges to correct errors called to its attention in subsequent editions.

Photo locators denoted as follows: Top (T), Center (C), Bottom (B), Left (L), Right (R), Background (Bkgd).

Illustration
11 Robert Ulrich.

Photographs
Opener: Biophoto Associates/Photo Researchers, Inc.; 4 David Spears/Clouds Hill Imaging Ltd./Corbis;
6 (C) Science Museum, London/DK Images; 7 (T) David Parker/Photo Researchers, Inc., (CR) Dr. Jeremy Burgess/
Photo Researchers, Inc.; 14 Biophoto Associates/Photo Researchers, Inc.

Unless otherwise acknowledged, all photographs are the copyright © of Dorling Kindersley, a division of Pearson.

ISBN: 0-328-13974-2

Glossary

chromosomes	two DNA molecules joined together that contain information about how the cell will grow and develop
diffusion	a process in which a substance moves from an area of higher concentration to an area of lower concentration
DNA	a material that has coded information about how an organism will grow and develop
endoplasmic reticulum	a network of folded membranes that moves materials in the cell and helps to make proteins
mitochondrion	an organelle that converts food energy into a form that the cell can use
mitosis	a process in which a cell nucleus divides, creating two nuclei
organelle	a structure that performs specific jobs within the cell
osmosis	the process of water passing through the cell membrane by diffusion
ribosome	an organelle that begins to make protein

Parts of Cells

by Mary McLean-Hely

PEARSON Scott Foresman

DK

What is a cell?

You are already familiar with processes such as birth, growth, death, use of energy, and movement of water. They happen daily in your town. But did you know that they also occur in every cell of your body? If you look at your hand, you can see the skin and fingernails. But on a much smaller level that you cannot see, there is a world of activity.

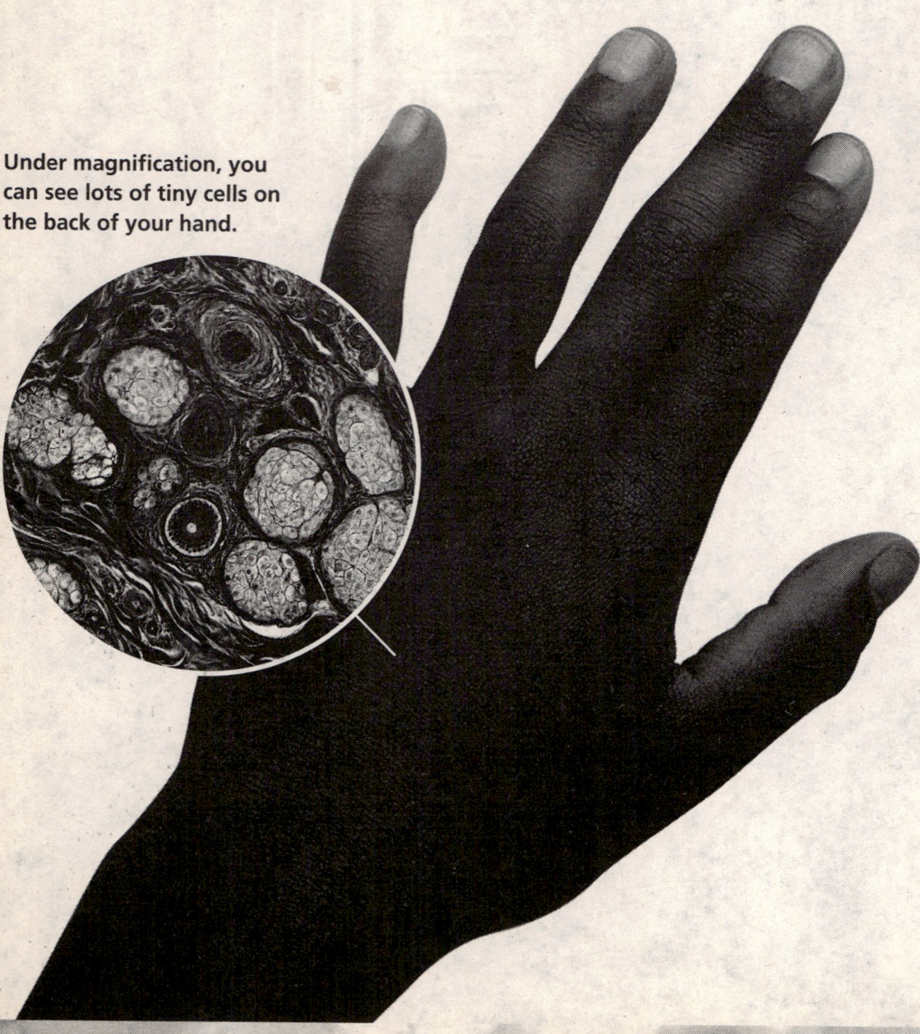

Under magnification, you can see lots of tiny cells on the back of your hand.

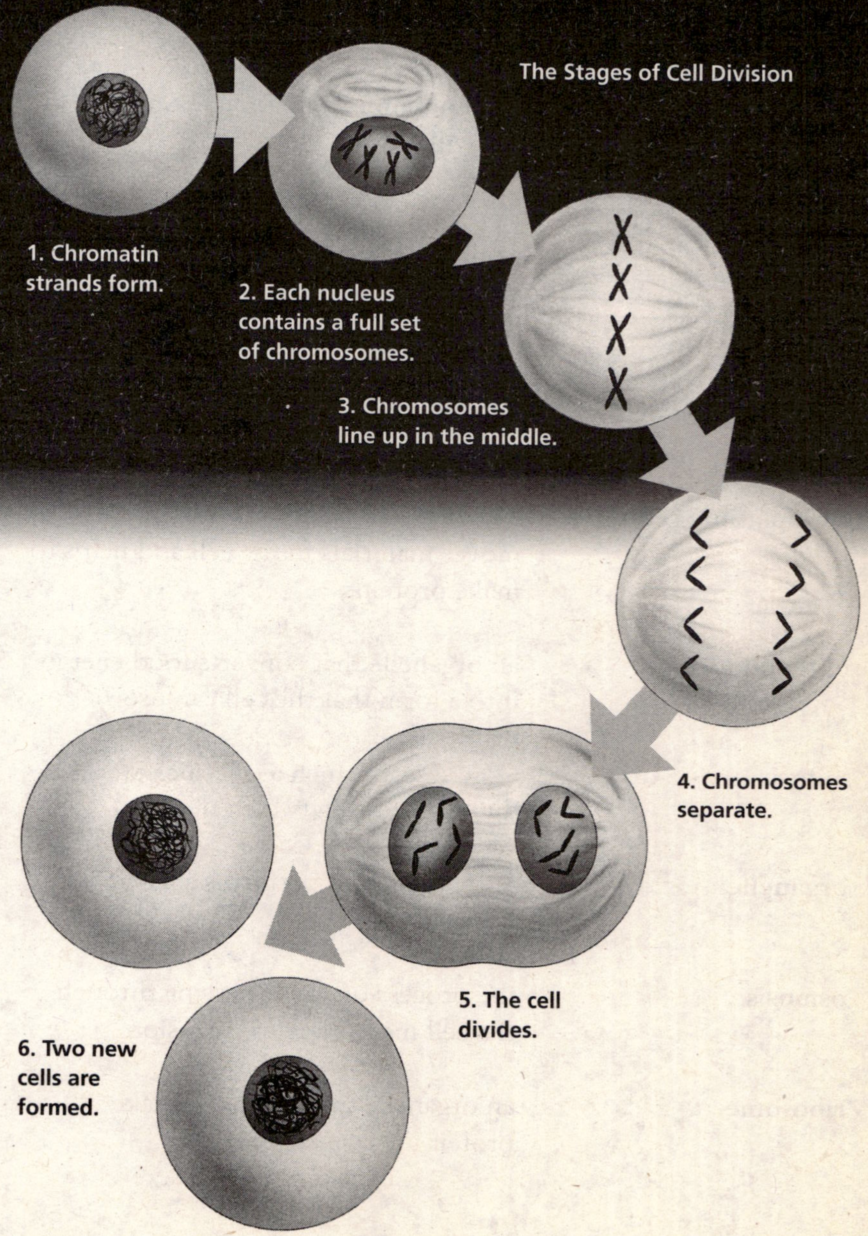

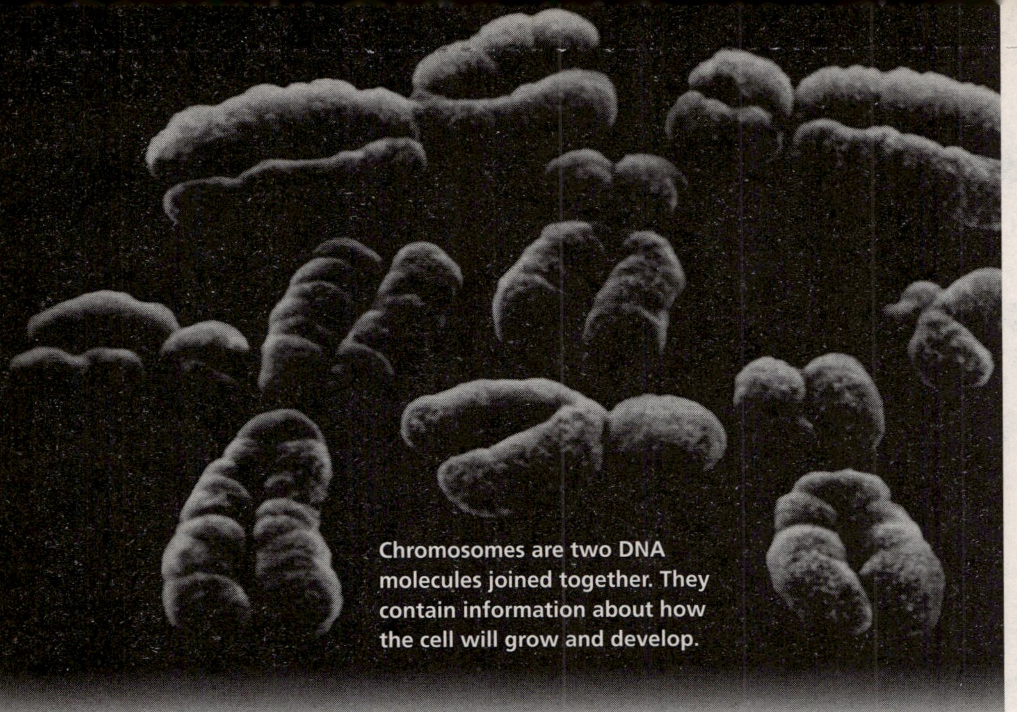

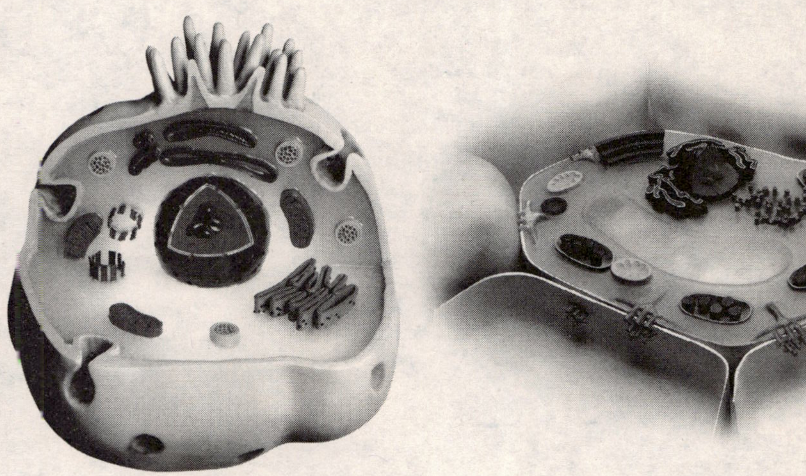

Dividing Nucleus

Mitosis takes place in a series of steps. In the first step, the cell gets ready to divide. First, it copies its DNA. Then the DNA becomes threadlike strands called chromatin.

Next, mitosis begins. The chromatin coils make short, compact chromosomes. **Chromosomes** are two DNA molecules that are held together. They contain a cell's operating instructions. Each cell must have a full set of chromosomes in order to grow and work properly.

Then, the membrane around the nucleus dissolves. Pairs of chromosomes line up at the center of the cell. Each chromosome splits into two identical halves. The two halves move to opposite ends of the cell. Each half is now an independent chromosome. The chromosomes uncoil, becoming chromatin. A new membrane forms around each nucleus, and mitosis is complete.

Finally, the cell divides. In animals, the cell membrane pinches inward, forming two identical cells. In plants, the new cell wall divides one plant cell into two.

Understanding Cells

You may not think that a watermelon, a ladybug, and a panda bear have much in common, but they do. Like all living things, they are made of cells.

Take a look at the pictures above. What do they have in common? That's right. They are both cells. Now, take another look. What is different about them? Right again! They come from different organisms. What are cells? Cells are the smallest units that can carry out the activities of life.

All living organisms have cells. They need cells to get energy, remove waste, reproduce, and repair.

Large organisms, such as humans, are made up of many cells, or are multicellular. There are different groups of cells. Each group of cells has a job. For example, in a tree, there are cells that carry water from the roots to the leaves. There are other cells that carry sugar from the leaves to other parts of the tree. In the leaves, there are cells that use water and carbon dioxide to make oxygen and sugar. All these different kinds of cells can exist in one tree.

Not all organisms are multicellular. Some have only one cell. They are called single-celled organisms. They are too small to see without a microscope.

Single-celled organisms are different from larger organisms that have many cells that do different jobs. A single-celled organism must do all the jobs itself. It needs to get energy, remove waste, and make new cells. Each part of the cell has a job. A single-celled spirogyra, as shown here, makes its own food in one part and also reproduces by dividing and making two cells.

a single-celled spirogyra

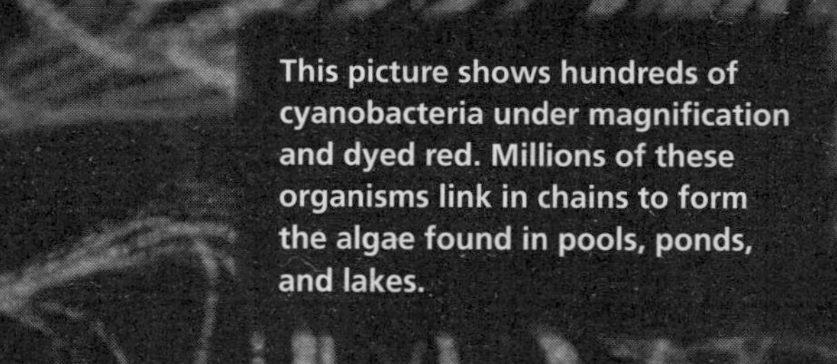

This picture shows hundreds of cyanobacteria under magnification and dyed red. Millions of these organisms link in chains to form the algae found in pools, ponds, and lakes.

Growing Cells

As you know, in the past people did not know about cells. They had other ways to explain what happened in the body. It took a microscope to show people that cells existed. That's because cells are so small that the human eye cannot see them without help.

All cells are very small, whether they are tiny single-celled algae or the skin cells of a huge elephant. What gives an elephant its size is the great number of cells that are in it. Large organisms have a huge number of cells.

Cells need to be small in order to carry out all of their jobs. A cell must take in oxygen and food and let out waste. All of these materials need to move through the cell membrane.

When a cell grows to a large size, the cell membrane and other parts of the cell also grow larger. Materials in the cell, such as food, have to move farther to reach where they are going. Waste also has to travel farther to leave a large cell. When a cell gets too big, it could take too long for all the needed activities to happen. If the important jobs are not done, the cell dies.

Dividing Cells

When they get too large, single-celled organisms divide into two new cells. Cells from multicellular organisms also divide, making new cells and causing the organisms to grow in size. When you grow, your body is making more cells. Cells also divide in order to take the place of old cells that are damaged or worn out.

Cell division is a continuous process. A cell starts to divide within its nucleus. This is called **mitosis.** Stored in the nucleus is **DNA,** which has coded information about how a living thing will grow and work. It helps the cell make proteins. It will be in both of the new cells that come from dividing.

Blanketweed consists of many spirogyra.

Developing Cell Theory

Scientists developed a theory about all cells. The cell theory has three parts:

- All living things are made of one or more cells.
- Cells are the basic units of living things.
- All cells come from existing cells.

It sounds pretty simple, but it took a long time for scientists to formulate cell theory. Today, we know a lot about cells. But there was a time when people didn't know that cells existed. Doctors could not help people as much as they do today because they didn't know that tiny cells they couldn't see could make people sick.

Cells were discovered by an Englishman named Robert Hooke. He made a simple microscope and was able to see the tiny cells in a layer of bark from a cork tree. He thought the structures looked like rectangular rooms. So he called them cells, and the name stuck.

Other discoveries followed. Each plays a role in what we know about cells today. Below and on the next page is a list of important discoveries that led to the cell theory and other things we know about cells today.

● In 1683, a Dutch scientist, Anton van Leeuwenhoek, built a microscope powerful enough to see blood and bacteria cells.
● In 1828, Robert Brown, from Scotland, discovered the cell nucleus.
● In 1838, Matthias Schleiden, a German scientist, found that all plants are made of cells. In 1839, another German scientist, Theodor Schwann, found that all animals are made of cells.

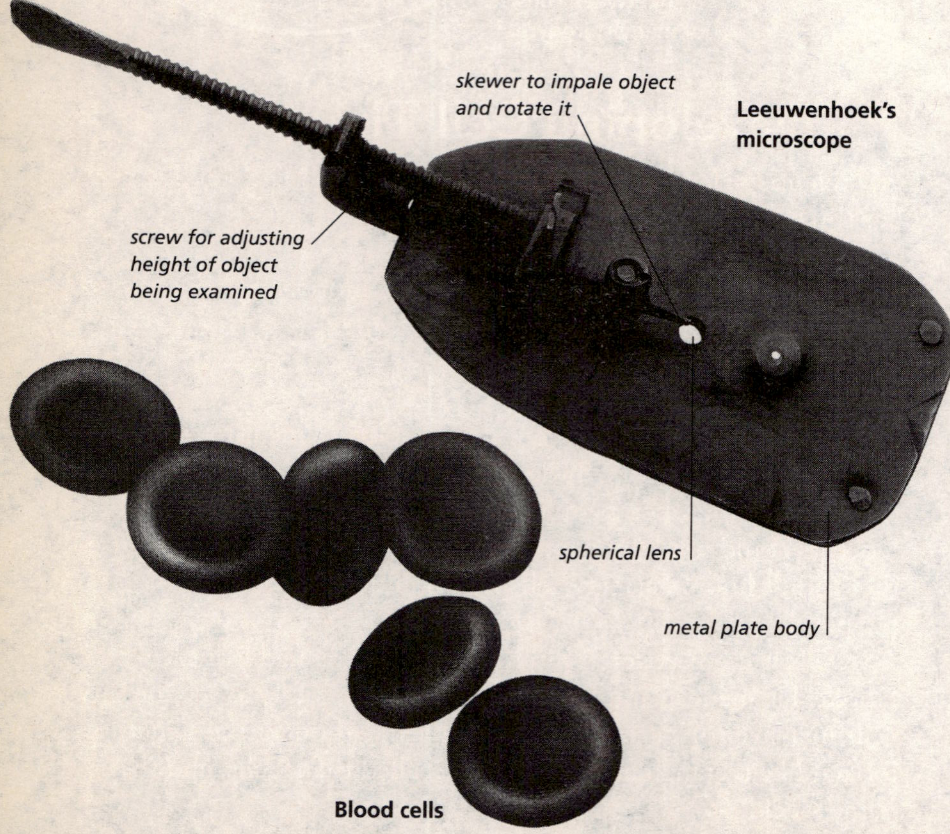

Moving In and Out of Cells

You may think you know a lot about cells now. But you haven't yet read about one of the largest parts of a cell. About two-thirds of the mass of a cell is water. There is a lot of water in the cytoplasm and in other places too.

Cells need water to dissolve substances such as nutrients that they use for energy. These substances come from outside of the cell in a process called diffusion. In **diffusion,** a substance moves from an area of higher concentration to an area of lower concentration. This allows substances to move in and out of cells.

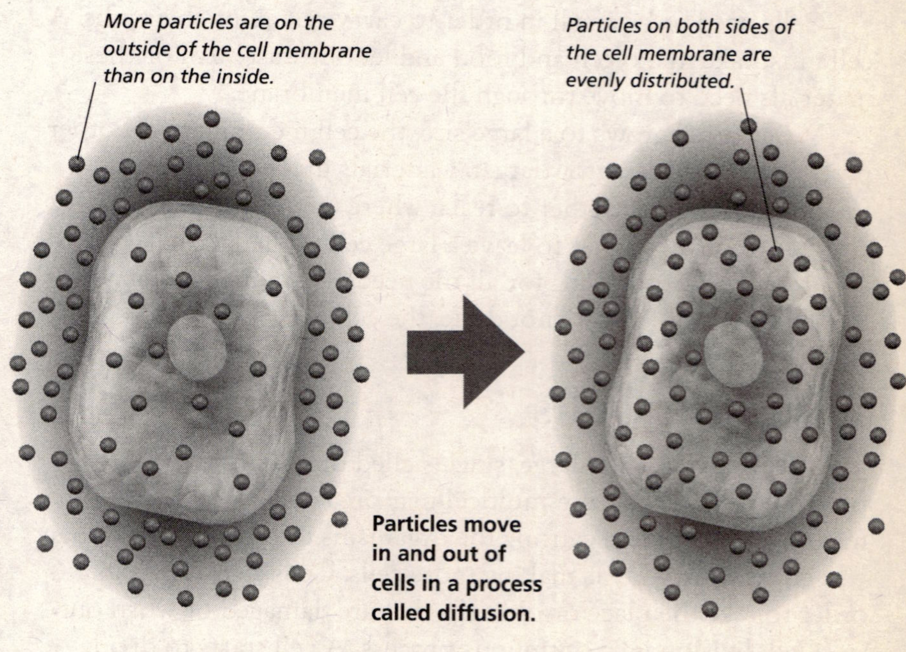

Only certain substances can enter or exit a cell by diffusion. The cell membrane controls what goes into and out of it. Water can pass through the cell membrane. Diffusion of water across a cell membrane is called **osmosis.**

Plant cells are different from animal cells in some ways. Most plant cells have one large vacuole, and animal cells have many smaller vacuoles. Plant cells also contain chloroplasts, the organelles that contain chlorophyll for photosynthesis. Plant cells also have a rigid outer wall that provides support, which animal cells do not have. However, both plant and animal cells have a cell membrane that holds together the internal environment of the cell.

In multicellular organisms, different cells perform different functions. Therefore, different kinds of cells may have different kinds of organelles. Or they may have a different number of a certain organelle. For example, in plants, the cells in the leaves will have more chloroplast organelles than cells in other parts of the tree. That's because it is the job of those cells to carry out photosynthesis.

Plant cell

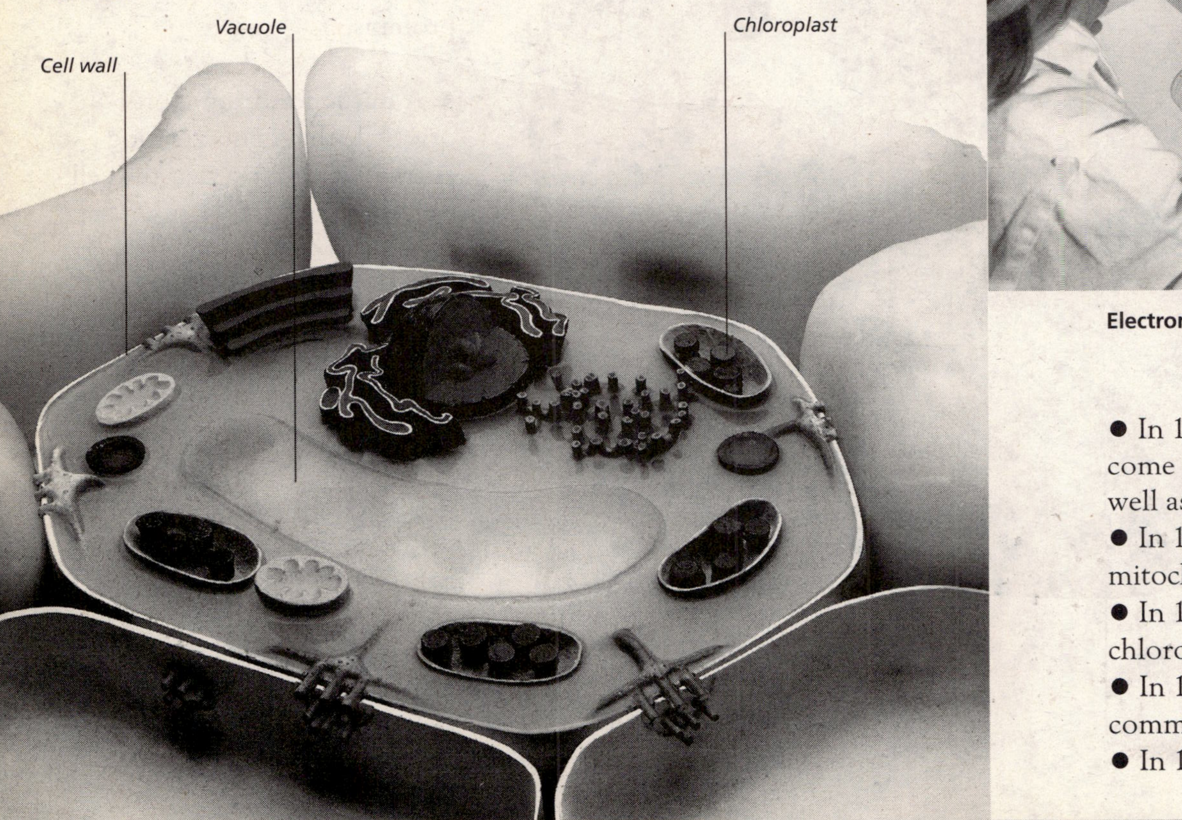

● In 1855, a German doctor, Rudolf Virchow, found that all cells come from already existing cells. The observations of Virchow, as well as those of Schleiden and Schwann, form the cell theory.
● In 1857, a Swiss scientist, Albrecht von Kölliker, found mitochondria in muscle cells.
● In 1865, Julius von Sachs, also German, showed that chlorophyll is located in chloroplasts.
● In 1875, microscopes similar to those used today were in common use.
● In 1931, the electron microscope was invented.

The Functions Of Organelles

Parts of a Cell

There are many different types of cells with different jobs, but they all share common features.

As you know, cells carry out the activities of life. All cells must get, store, and release energy. They also must remove waste and reproduce. Most cells have a control center that makes sure these jobs are done. The many jobs are performed by different structures in cells called organelles. An **organelle** is a structure that performs specific jobs within the cell.

Take a look at the animal cell you see here. The different organelles are labeled. The organelles are found in cytoplasm, which is a fluid inside of cells.

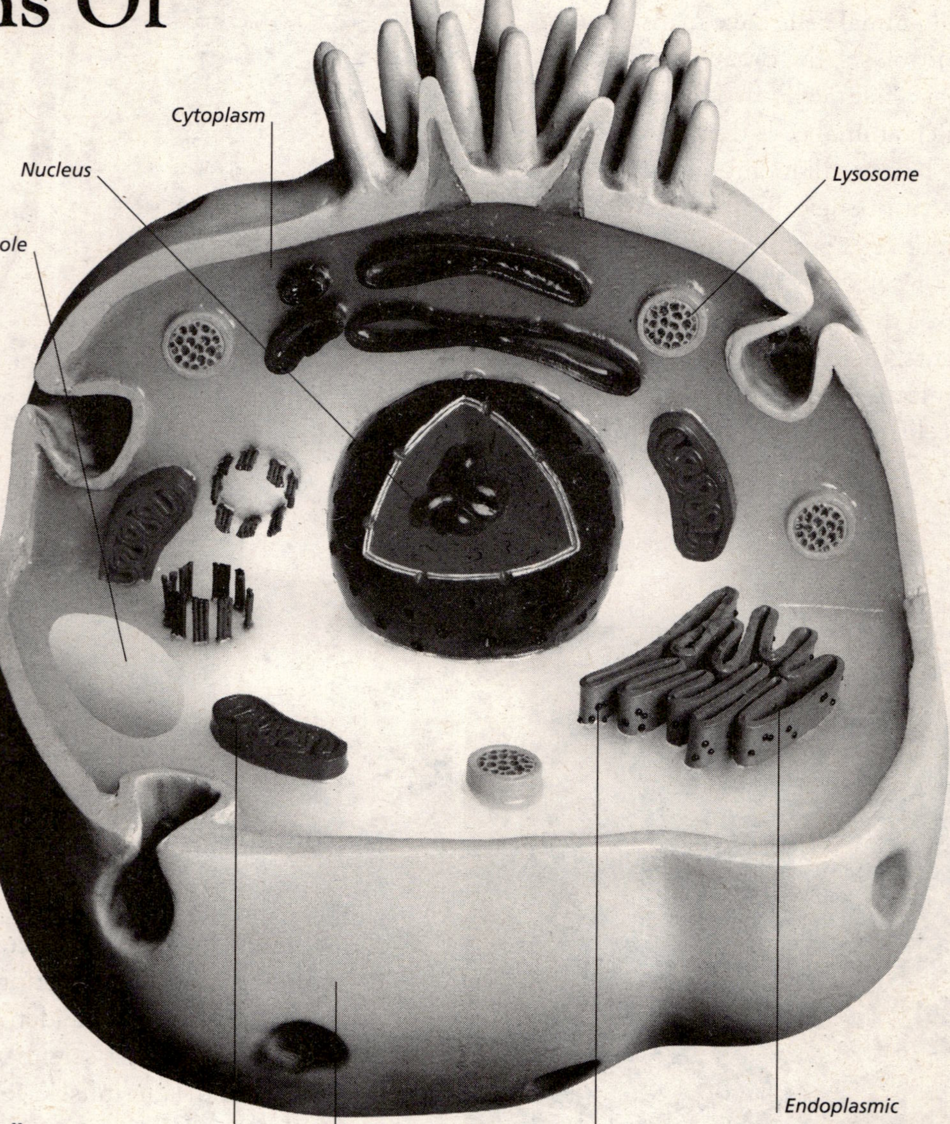

Below is a list of the organelles inside of a cell.

● The nucleus is an organelle that directs the cell's activities. It contains the cell's operating instructions and stores information that will be passed along to other cells.

● The **endoplasmic reticulum** (ER) is a network of folded membranes that moves materials in the cell and helps to make proteins.

● A **mitochondrion** is an organelle that converts food energy into a form that the cell can use.

● A **lysosome** is also an organelle. It has powerful chemicals that break down harmful molecules and recycle worn-out cell parts.

● A **vacuole** is an organelle that stores water and nutrients and helps the cell digest food.

● A **ribosome** is an organelle that begins to make protein.

Reproduction
of Species

by Jennifer Coates-Conroy

Genre	Comprehension Skill	Text Features	Science Content
Nonfiction	Sequence	• Captions • Charts • Glossary	Reproduction

Scott Foresman Science 6.3

PEARSON
Scott Foresman

DK

scottforesman.com

ISBN 0-328-13977-7

9 780328 139774

90000

What did you learn?

1. How are traits passed on from parents to offspring?

2. How does DNA make a copy of itself?

3. Some animals reproduce by sexual reproduction. What is the difference between internal and external fertilization? Give examples.

4. **Writing** in Science Explain how mutation could change the message a gene is sending.

5. **Sequence** Reread page 12 about fertilization. Make a chart to describe the sequence of events during fertilization in seed plants. What is the result of pollination in plants?

Vocabulary

asexual reproduction
egg cell
fertilization
gene
heredity
meiosis
selective breeding
sexual reproduction
sperm cell

Picture Credits
Every effort has been made to secure permission and provide appropriate credit for photographic material.
The publisher deeply regrets any omission and pledges to correct errors called to its attention in subsequent editions.

Photo locators denoted as follows: Top (T), Center (C), Bottom (B), Left (L), Right (R), Background (Bkgd).

Illustrations
12 Robert Fenn; 19, 20 Tony Randazzo

Photographs
Opener: Getty Images; 1 ©M. I. Walker/Photo Researchers, Inc.; 2 Getty Images; 3 (CBR) ©American Museum of Natural History/DK Images; 9 ©Gerry Ellis/Minden Pictures; 10 Getty Images; 13 ©Fred Bavendam/Minden Pictures; 14 ©American Images Inc./Getty Images; 15 ©M. I. Walker/Photo Researchers, Inc.; 23 (TL) Jerry Young/DK Images.

Unless otherwise acknowledged, all photographs are the copyright © of Dorling Kindersley, a division of Pearson.

ISBN: 0-328-13977-7

Glossary

asexual reproduction	a type of reproduction in which a single parent produces offspring
egg cell	a female's sex cell
fertilization	the union of the male and female sex cells
gene	the basic unit of inheritance that transmits a specific trait from parents to their offspring
heredity	the transmission of characteristics, or traits, from parents to their offspring
meiosis	a type of cell division that produces cells with half the number of chromosomes
selective breeding	the process of selecting organisms with desired traits to serve as parents, in order to improve offspring
sexual reproduction	a type of reproduction in which two parents are needed to produce offspring
sperm cell	a male's sex cell

Reproduction
of Species

by Jennifer Coates-Conroy

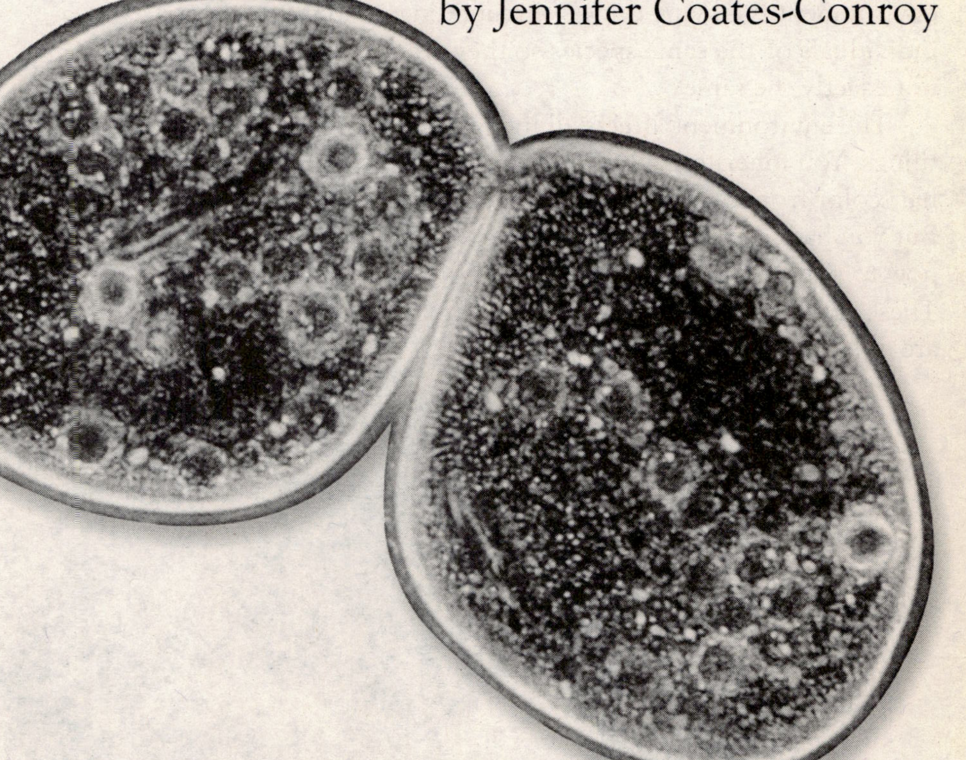

Heredity

Heredity is the passing of traits from parents to their young. All living things are the result of heredity because they are produced by earlier generations. Parents and offspring share traits and look similar. The mother and baby gibbon below look alike. Heredity is the reason why specific bacteria have a certain shape, lilac flowers have the same shade of blue as the parent plant, and strawberries share a similar flavor.

Not all the characteristics of an individual are inherited from its parents. There are some external factors to consider. Some traits are learned within the environment. The environment is a living thing's surroundings, and it can affect individuals of the same species so they are not exactly the same.

The environment affects all living things. You inherited your eye and hair color from one of your parents. But you had to learn how to swim or how to play the piano by practicing. These skills are learned traits. They are not passed on through heredity.

Seeing Eye dogs are a special breed of dog that are trained to help blind people. Selective breeding enhances not only physical characteristics, but also certain types of behavior in animals. Some breeds of dogs are selected because of their scenting abilities. These breeds are used to help police and airport personnel with security situations. Some breeds are even trained to alert people who suffer from certain life-threatening conditions. Today there are nearly four hundred recognized breeds that have been selectively bred for hunting, herding, protection, and companionship.

Dogs are closely related to wolves.

The many kinds of dogs that are common today were bred after 1850.

Many Breeds of Dogs

Dogs appear in archaeological records of almost all human cultures that lived thousands of years ago. Dogs were the first animals to be domesticated. Dogs are the distant cousins of wolves. Little by little, wolves and humans got closer to each other. Wild dogs, perhaps wolves, hung around early human settlements, eating scraps of food. Humans relied on dogs to warn and alert them to possible dangers.

Dogs have changed a lot since ancient times. Instead of being predators, dogs became domesticated and didn't have to look for food anymore. Dogs come in many shapes and sizes.

The bud growing on this hydra will separate to form a new offspring.

hydra

Asexual Reproduction

Many plants produce offspring through **asexual reproduction.** This requires only a single parent plant. Asexual reproduction is common in plants. Other organisms, such as bacteria, also reproduce asexually. A single-cell *E. coli* bacterium splits into two new cells. Some bacteria can double their number every twenty minutes. If conditions were right, a single bacterium might reproduce into millions in a matter of hours!

In asexual reproduction the plant makes replicas of itself. The process in which a cell's nucleus copies and divides is called mitosis. The new offspring has the same DNA as the parent plant.

Living things use many different processes of asexual reproduction. Some plants reproduce by growing buds. Other organisms reproduce by spores.

Mushroom Spores

cap

stalk

spores

gills

Asexual reproduction occurs in some flower species. In one type of asexual reproduction, stems arch over and take root at their tips, forming new plants. The strawberry plant reproduces above-ground in this way.

Duckweed grows in ponds and reproduces asexually through a process called budding. A parent plant will form many buds, each having the same DNA as the parent plant. The little buds that grow from the parent plant eventually drop off to start new plants. The new plants can cover a pond very quickly.

Another form of asexual reproduction uses spores. Most plants that do not make flowers, such as mosses and ferns, reproduce asexually using spores. Spores have stored food just like seeds. Under the right conditions, a plant spore develops into a new plant.

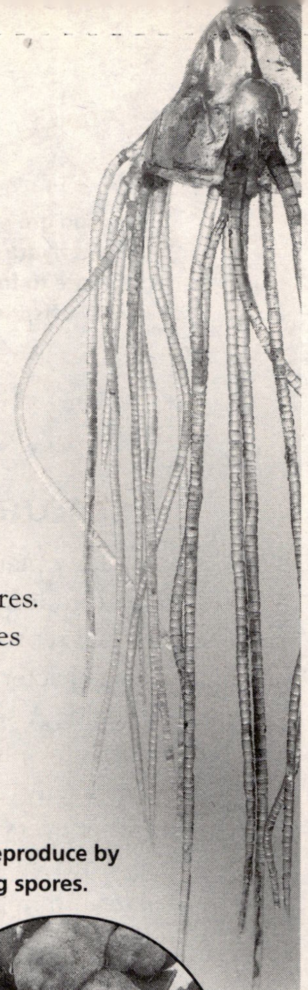

This strawberry plant reproduces by growing above-ground stems from which new plants will start.

Ferns reproduce by growing spores.

All over the world, people produce animals and plants with traits that they desire. Selecting a few living things with desired traits to serve as parents is called **selective breeding.** Selective breeding helps produce crops that yield more food per plant. This process is used not only for plants but also in the breeding of animals.

Today cows produce much more milk than they did in the 1800s, which was about 1,500 liters a year. Thanks to selective breeding and better nutrition, some cows can now produce as much as 10,000 liters of milk a year! Modern breeding techniques are applied every day to raising farm animals, such as cattle, hogs, poultry, and sheep. Many plants, such as potatoes, wheat, rice, and fruits, are now hardier and more resistant to disease thanks to modern breeding techniques.

Today some cows can produce as much as 10,000 liters of milk a year.

Choosing Traits

Corn has been around for a long time. But the corn we eat today looks very different from the wild corn grown thousands of years ago. About 8,000 to 10,000 years ago, the people in what is now Mexico began to change a grasslike plant they ate into corn. By choosing and planting seeds from the plants with traits they liked, they grew more plants with the traits they wanted. When those plants grew, they selected seeds from them. They planted these seeds, growing more plants like them.

The corn we have today is the result of the work done by breeders. In 1905 an American scientist, George M. Schull, began to experiment with the breeding of corn. Until then, farmers tried to improve their crops by using their best ears as seeds for the next crop. Their crops were of mixed quality and low yield. Schull, a geneticist, used techniques similar to the ones applied by Gregor Mendel, an Austrian scientist. He used pure breeding strains and artificial pollination. The hybrid corn he developed had more resistance to disease. The sweet taste of corn is also the result of hybrid plants.

The corn we have today is an example of the advantages of selective breeding.

Some animals, such as jellyfish, also reproduce asexually. Buds or other parts of the animal break away, and a new animal is created. In other species, such as corals, the buds remain attached to the parent. This results in colonies of animals.

Some species even grow a replacement for the lost part. Many starfishes can grow another arm if they lose one. If the part that falls off contains enough genetic information from the parent, it can grow into a new organism. Starfishes, also called sea stars, reproduce this way.

Some plants use their roots for asexual reproduction. The dandelion flower and some trees reproduce in this way. When the roots of a dandelion plant separate from the original root, these "fallen" roots send up new stems. In time, a whole patch of dandelions will grow! Potatoes grow sprouts through the same process of mitosis. Potatoes grow from pieces of the tuber. Each piece must have a bud, or eye, for a plant to sprout and develop into a new plant.

When buds of a jellyfish break away, a replica of the animal is created.

Each stem on this potato will become a new plant.

How are traits passed on?

The instructions for making a new organism are found in the parents' DNA. Parents pass on traits to their offspring.

Structure of DNA

You know that heredity is the passing of traits from one generation to the next. But how are traits passed from parents to their young? The answer is in the nucleus of the parent cell. Cells —the building blocks of all living things— are not so different in plants or animals.

The nucleus in a cell of any living thing contains its chromosomes. The chromosomes are spread throughout the nucleus in the cell. They are made up of proteins and two DNA strands tightly coiled, as seen in the picture here. The DNA stores the coded information about how an organism will grow and develop. This information makes one organism a cat and another a tree.

There is only one chromosome in the *E. coli* bacterium. This chromosome contains the DNA instructions shared by each new cell.

In the left table, the two purebred parents, one black *BB* and one white *WW*, led to four young chickens with mixed genes. With one gene from the mother and one from the father, all four possibilities have the combination *BW*. So the young had both black and white feathers. The offspring from these parents will all be Erminette chickens, or hybrids.

Observe the right table. What happens if both parents are Erminette chickens? The results are quite different. The four possibilities for mixes are one black chicken, two Erminette chickens, and one white chicken. There are similar examples in people. Two parents with wavy hair can have children with wavy hair, straight hair, or curly hair.

Punnett Squares

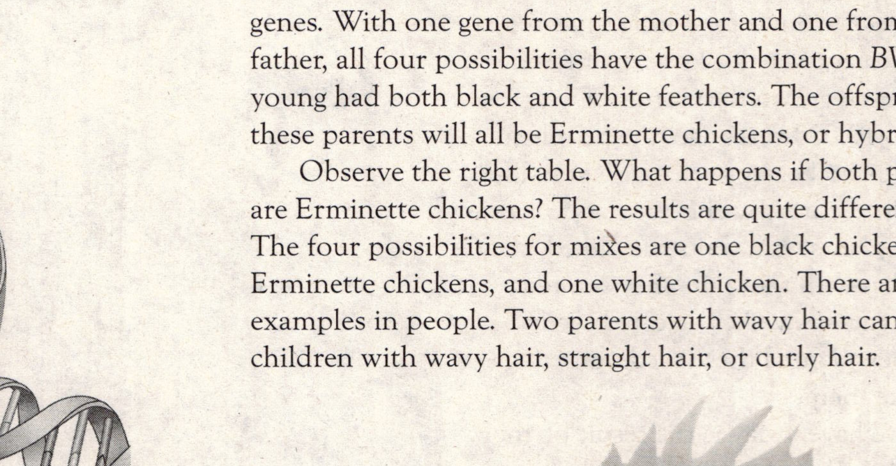

Before the 1950s, scientists could see chromosomes in cells, but the role of DNA was unknown. Now we know that DNA carries all the instructions for a cell. If you look at a strand of DNA, it looks like a twisted ladder. This "ladder" contains millions of rungs. The "rungs" are made of pairs of four materials called bases. The bases are known by the letters A, T, C, and G.

The DNA strand is divided into sections called genes. A **gene** is a series of base pairs, or rungs of a DNA ladder. Genes are what determine heredity. Each gene gives the instructions for making a substance that contributes to a trait. For example, a gene in your DNA determined the color of your eyes or hair. In the same way, a gene in a lilac plant decides the shade of color of its flowers.

The strands of DNA are tightly twisted inside the chromosomes.

Sharing Dominance

Genes do not always have dominant and recessive versions of a trait. The Erminette chickens you see here have genes for both black and white feathers, and neither version is recessive. The chicken has both colors. In this case the genes share dominance.

The tables on the next page are called Punnett squares. They can help you understand how each chicken got its feather color. The left table shows all the possible offspring gene mixes if both parents are purebred chickens. The right table shows the four possible combinations if both parents are Erminette chickens.

Copying DNA

Each rung on the DNA ladder is made up of a pair of bases. There are only four DNA bases from which each pair is made. Look at the DNA drawing on this page. Each of the four colors represents a base. The order in which the pairs are arranged varies from place to place on the DNA strand. The instructions each gene gives to the cell are hidden in this unique DNA's coded message.

The order and combination of the bases are very important. Base A and base T fit together, and base C and base G fit together. Pairing like this allows DNA to make an identical copy of itself when it divides.

The order of the base pairs varies along the strand of DNA.

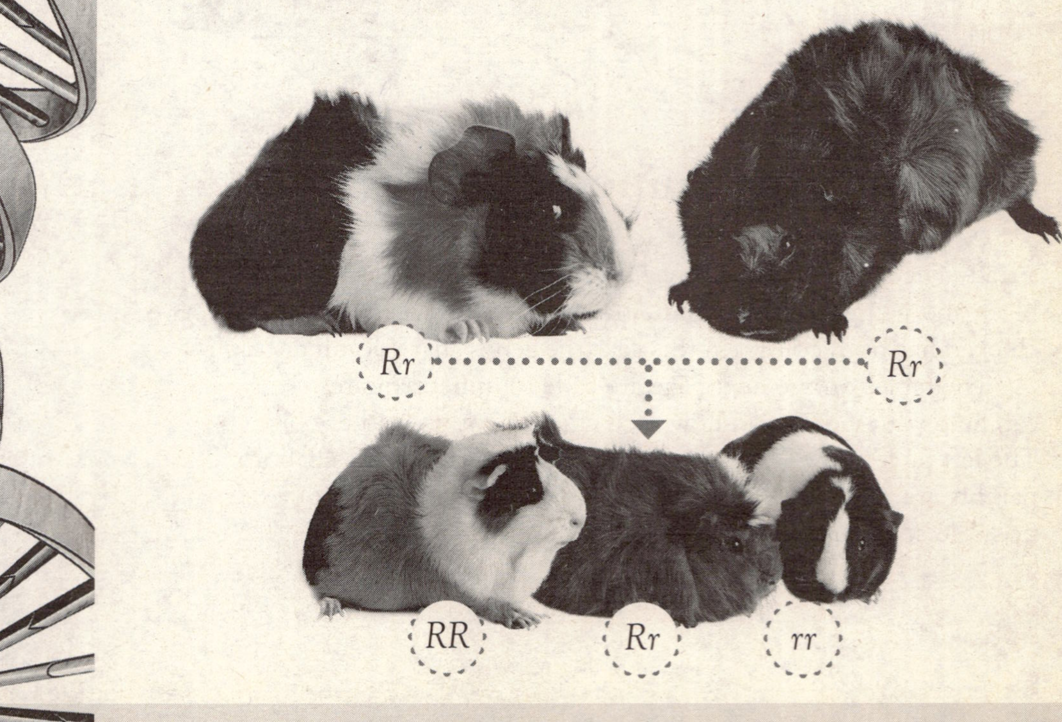

A parent could have two dominant or two recessive genes. For example, the mother guinea pig has two genes for rough fur. Both are dominant. They are written as *RR*. The father has two genes for smooth fur. These are recessive and are written as *rr*. When a living thing has two versions of a trait of the same type, it is called purebred for that specific trait.

What type of fur will the offspring of this mother and father have: rough or smooth coats? Each offspring will get one trait for fur from the mother, *R*, and one from the father, *r*. The offspring will have *Rr*. Because rough fur is dominant, all the young will have rough coats.

What happens if the parents are not purebred? What if each parent has an *Rr* gene? Their young can have three possible gene mixes: *RR*, *Rr*, or *rr*. Which of these will show up as a rough coat? All the offspring with a combination of *RR* or *Rr* will have a rough coat because the rough coat gene is dominant. Only the *rr* combination will show up as a smooth coat.

How do genes determine traits?

Genes are what determine traits in an individual. Scientists are continuously learning about the way genes work to better understand the reproduction of living things.

Dominant and Recessive Traits

You know that traits are inherited from each parent. Parents can have the same trait or a different version of a trait. How do genes decide which trait is expressed? For example, the guinea pigs you see here can have one gene for smooth fur from their mother and another for rough fur from their father. Why does a guinea pig with both of these versions have a rough coat? How can it have a smooth coat?

For each trait, an individual has a pair of genes—one from each parent. But genes can have different versions of a trait, such as in the case of these guinea pigs: rough coat and smooth coat. When an offspring has both versions of a trait, one may show up. The other one may not. A gene that masks another is called a dominant gene. The other gene is hidden and is called a recessive gene. For guinea pigs, rough fur is dominant and smooth fur is recessive. This means that the only way for a guinea pig to have smooth fur is to have inherited the trait from both its parents.

Guinea pigs can have rough coats or smooth coats depending on the combination of genes they inherit from their parents.

When the cell divides through mitosis, the base pairs in the DNA from the parent cell come apart. Free-floating bases within the cell's nucleus pair with the separate bases on the DNA strand. The process continues until there are two new strands of DNA. The two strands are identical to the parent's cell.

Sometimes, when this is happening, a mistake is made. The resulting DNA is not an exact copy. One base might take the place of the wrong base. A base might be added or removed. A change occurs in the DNA strand. This is called a gene mutation.

Sometimes a changed gene is passed to an organism offspring. The baby camel below is completely white due to a rare genetic disorder called albinism. The gene responsible for producing the substance that makes pigments is not present in its DNA. Albino animals are less likely to reach adulthood. The albino baby lacks the ability to blend in with its environment and is an easy prey for predators.

This baby camel has a very rare condition called albinism, a genetic disorder.

What is sexual reproduction?

Many living things inherit their genes from each one of two parents.

Reproduction by Two Parents

In **sexual reproduction,** living things get half of their DNA from one parent and half from the other. A male and a female sex cell join together. In mammals, a female sex cell, called an **egg cell** or ovum, joins a male sex cell, called a **sperm cell.**

Each sex cell has only half the chromosomes needed by the rest of the cells in an organism's body. Therefore, if a living thing has seventy chromosomes in all, each of its sex cells will have thirty-five chromosomes. **Meiosis** is a type of cell division that produces cells with half the number of chromosomes.

During sexual reproduction, the sex cells join in a process called fertilization. **Fertilization** is the union of the male and female sex cells. A new cell forms as a result of the fusing of the nuclei of the two sex cells. Now this new cell has a complete number of chromosomes, and it is called a zygote. The new cell will divide into more cells to make a complete organism.

This baby lion inherited its genes from both parents.

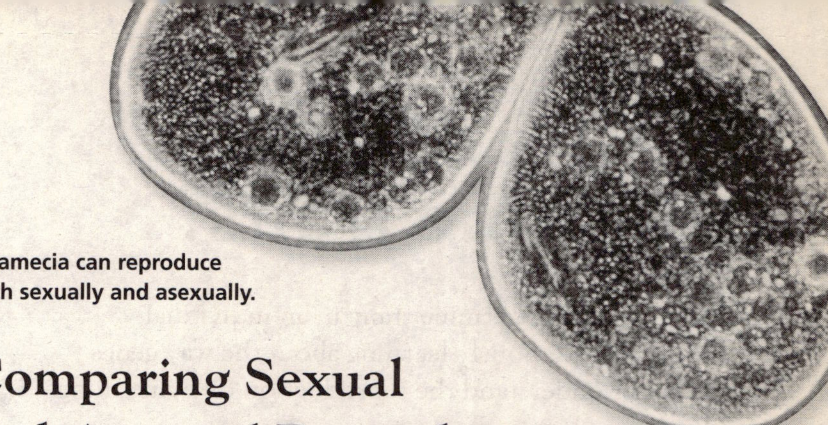

Paramecia can reproduce both sexually and asexually.

Comparing Sexual and Asexual Reproduction

Both sexual and asexual reproduction have advantages and disadvantages.

Asexual reproduction is simple, fast, and very efficient. It can produce a larger number of offspring in less time with less energy. Only one parent is needed. An individual can reproduce itself even if the closest member of its species is miles away.

Asexual reproduction starts with one cell. The offspring's DNA is identical to the parent's DNA. This can be an advantage when conditions in the environment are favorable. The individuals will continue to reproduce. But a change in the environment, such as drought or food scarcity, could have a negative effect on their survival. Under these conditions, an entire population could disappear!

Sexual reproduction requires more energy, and it is a slower process. Offspring always have two parents. The new offspring have a unique DNA. Under the right conditions in their environment, they will continue to reproduce. Any change that would affect their survival might affect only part of the population. Because of the differences in each individual, some of them will have some favorable traits—and a better chance to survive and reproduce. The surviving members will pass on those favorable traits to their offspring.

Individuals Differ

Observe the puppies on this page. They look pretty much like their parents, but none of these puppies are exactly the same. Remember that in meiosis, each sex cell receives only half of the DNA found in other cells of the individual's body. The fertilized egg that grows into a puppy is formed from an egg cell from the mother and a sperm cell from the father. The puppies look alike because they have the same mother and father. Still, each puppy looks slightly different because it grew from the combination of a different sperm and egg.

Meiosis

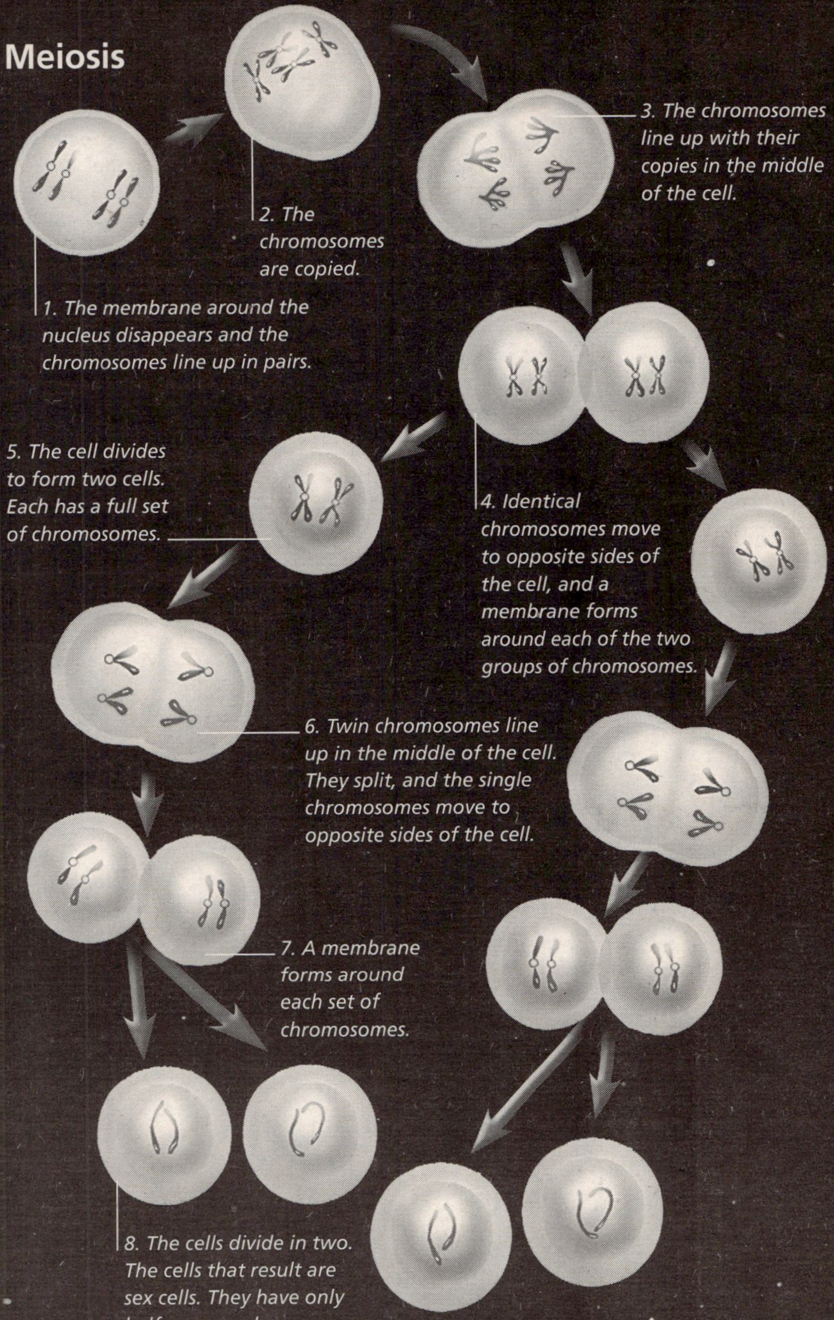

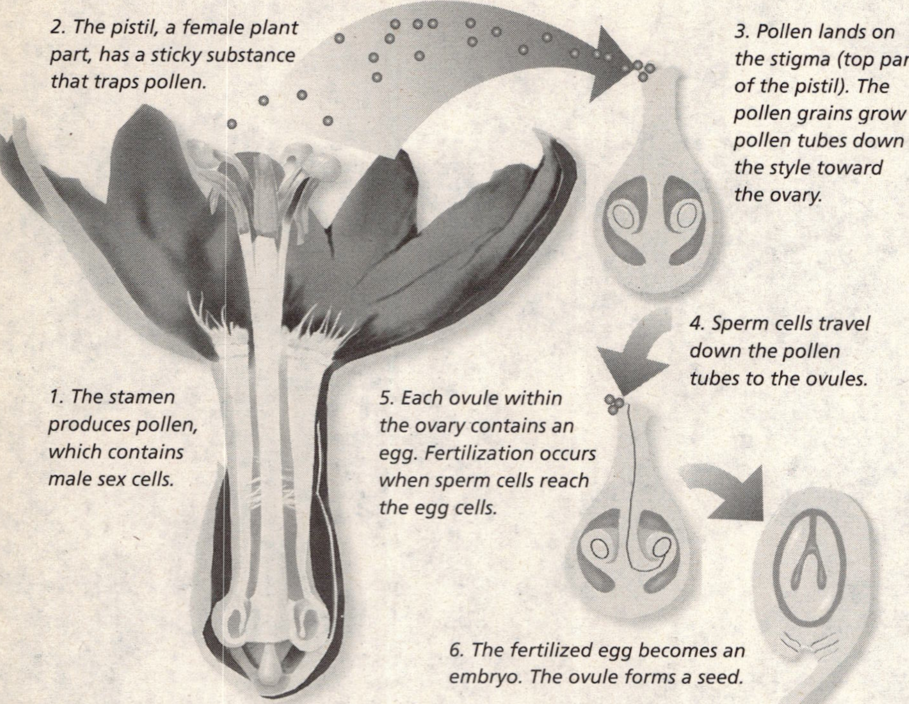

Fertilization in Seed Plants

Sexual reproduction starts with pollination. The organ of the plant where pollination takes place is the flower. Flowers produce pollen. If the pollen lands on the same plant, the process is called self-pollination. When the pollen is carried to another plant, it is called cross-pollination.

Flowers have male and female parts. The male part is the stamen, which produces the pollen; the female part is the pistil, which is often like a bottle with a wide bottom and a narrow neck. The egg cell lies at the bottom of the pistil.

Fertilization occurs within the flower when the male sex cell reaches an egg cell. A fertilized egg will grow and become a seed. This seed contains a plant embryo. The ovule ripens to form the fruit around the seed.

Follow the steps in the diagram to learn how fertilization occurs.

Fertilization in Animals

Each time a sperm and egg cell from animals unite, a zygote forms. The zygote cell divides into more cells to form a new organism. There are two methods of fertilization in animals: internal and external.

External fertilization takes place outside the female. Many animals that live in or near water use this process to reproduce. They release eggs and sperm cells into the water. The sperm cells swim to the eggs and fertilize them. The number of cells released in water is very large, to compensate for the environment and other animals that will eat them. Staghorn corals live in salt water and reproduce by external fertilization. In some places the number of colonies has been greatly reduced.

Internal fertilization takes place inside the female animal. A fertilized egg needs moisture and protection from the environment in order to develop. In some animals, the fertilized egg develops inside the female. Others lay eggs with shells that protect the fertilized egg.

Staghorn corals reproduce by external fertilization. Both sperm and egg cells are released into the water at the same time.

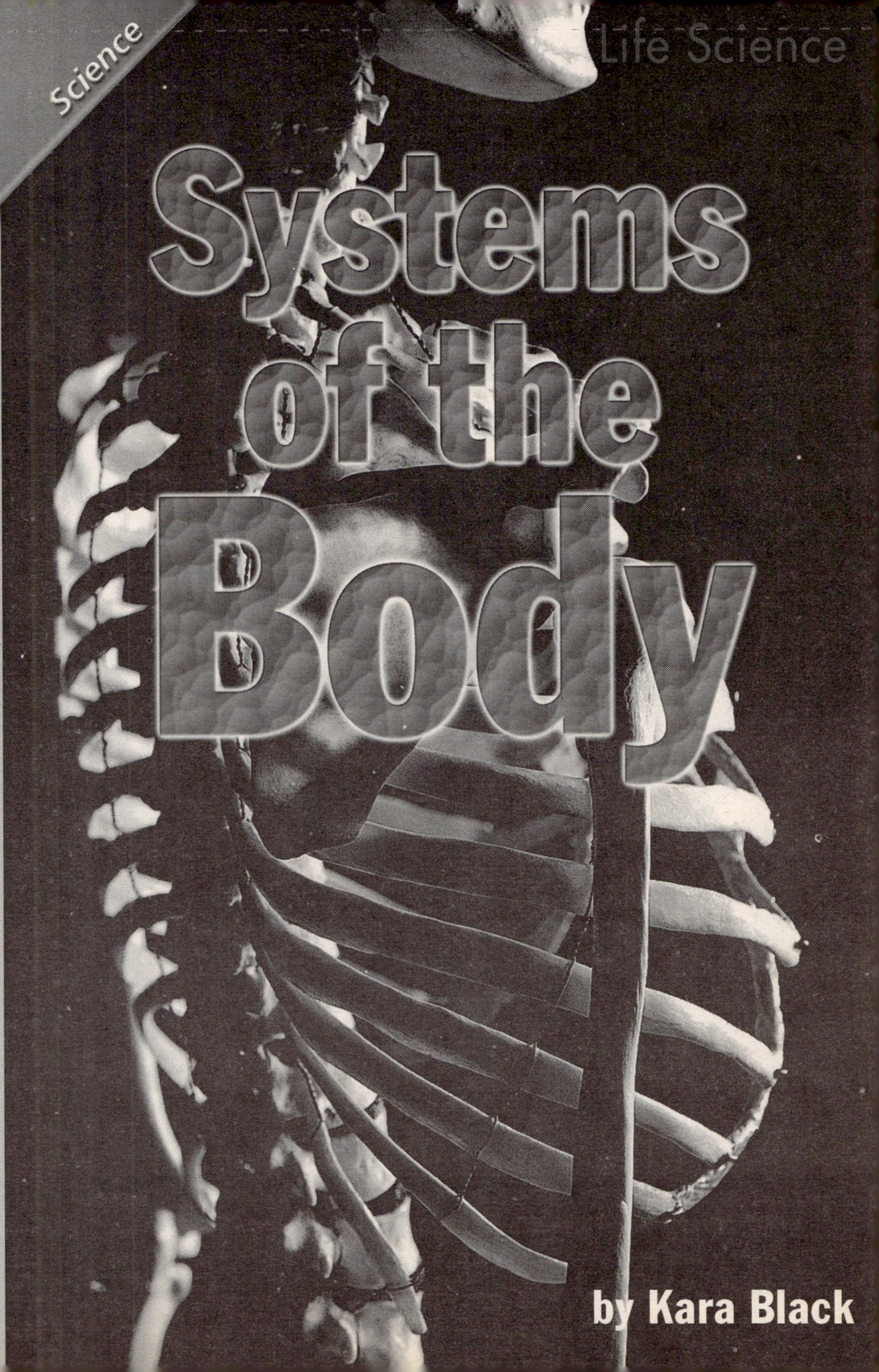

Systems of the Body

by Kara Black

Genre	Comprehension Skill	Text Features	Science Content
Nonfiction	Cause and Effect	• Captions • Charts • Glossary	Body Systems

Scott Foresman Science 6.4

PEARSON
Scott Foresman

scottforesman.com

What did you learn?

1. How can you help the cells in your body to work properly?

2. Starting with the heart, describe the route that blood takes through the body when moving to provide your body with oxygen and nutrients. Name the specific types of blood vessels.

3. Describe the way neurons communicate with other neurons.

4. **Writing** in Science Your endocrine system releases hormones in order to control many of your body's functions. Write to explain how a biofeedback loop mechanism works to regulate the release of hormones.

5. **Cause and Effect** When pathogens enter your body, they cause your immune system to react. Describe your immune system's response to the attackers.

Vocabulary

alveoli
antibody
endocrine gland
enzyme
hormone
impulse
neuron
pathogen

36

Picture Credits
Every effort has been made to secure permission and provide appropriate credit for photographic material.
The publisher deeply regrets any omission and pledges to correct errors called to its attention in subsequent editions.

Photo locators denoted as follows: Top (T), Center (C), Bottom (B), Left (L), Right (R), Background (Bkgd).

6 (TR) Gladden Willis, M.D./Visuals Unlimited; 7 (TL) VVG/Photo Researchers, Inc.;
10 (BR) Science Photo Library/Photo Researchers, Inc.; 20 SPL/Photo Researchers, Inc.

Unless otherwise acknowledged, all photographs are the copyright © of Dorling Kindersley, a division of Pearson.

ISBN: 0-328-13980-7

Copyright © Pearson Education, Inc.

Glossary

alveoli	tiny sacs at the end of bronchioles, where oxygen enters the blood and carbon dioxide is removed
antibody	a chemical produced by white blood cells that kills specific pathogens
endocrine gland	an organ that releases chemical substances directly into the blood
enzyme	a protein that breaks food down into nutrients that can be used by the body
hormone	substance released by the endocrine glands that control many of the body's functions
impulse	a message that travels from an axon of one neuron to the dendrite of another neuron
neuron	a nerve cell forming part of a network that passes messages throughout your body
pathogen	an organism that causes disease

Systems of the Body

by Kara Black

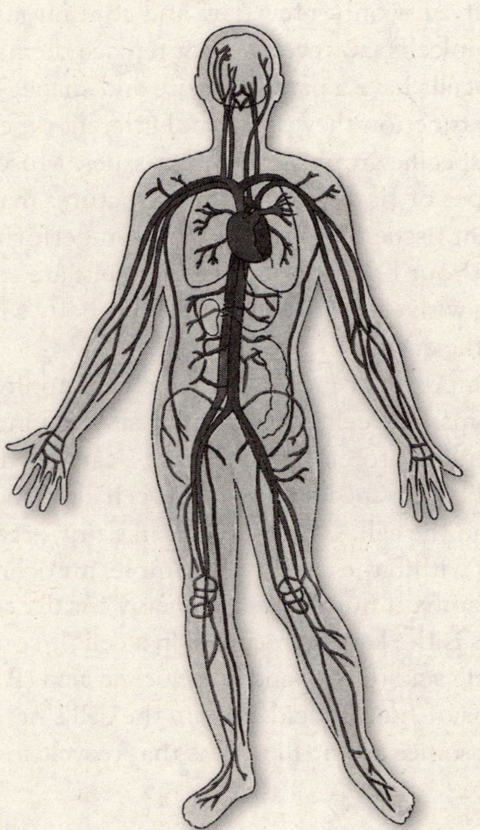

How is the body organized?

Cells Working Together

Your body is composed of more than 75 trillion cells, all working together to help your body grow and sustain itself. Each cell is a living unit that is capable of taking in food, getting rid of waste, and reproducing. Some cells, such as the cells in the liver and skin, live for only a few days and continuously replace themselves. Brain cells, however, do not replace themselves.

Specialized cells have a particular size and shape. Their form depends on the function they perform. Different types of cells are organized into specific groups known as tissues. Muscle and bone are different types of tissue. Organs are structures made up of two or more different tissue types, and each organ performs a certain function within your body's systems. Your cells are constantly communicating with each other to meet your body's needs and make it work efficiently.

A cell is composed of molecules, which are nonliving and made up of atoms. The cell is made up of several kinds of molecules, including proteins, nucleic acids, carbohydrates, and lipids. These all have a specific role in the cell's function and form organelles within the cell. Organelles are like tiny organs that do specific jobs within the cells. For example, mitochondria are organelles that convert nutrients into energy for the cell.

The nucleus is the largest organelle in a cell. It contains deoxyribonucleic acid (DNA) and ribonucleic acid (RNA). These two forms of nucleic acid contain the cell's hereditary information. Lysomes are small organs that recycle molecules and dispose of waste.

Good health habits start early in life. Developing good health habits now can help you stay healthy. Food is very important to keep your body nourished, so eat a well-balanced diet and drink plenty of water. Keep your body fit by exercising regularly. Rest and sleep enough so your body can recover.

When playing sports, protect yourself from physical harm by wearing the required protective gear. Practice good cleaning habits. Wash your hands often. Regular physical checkups can help your doctor to detect any potential health problems.

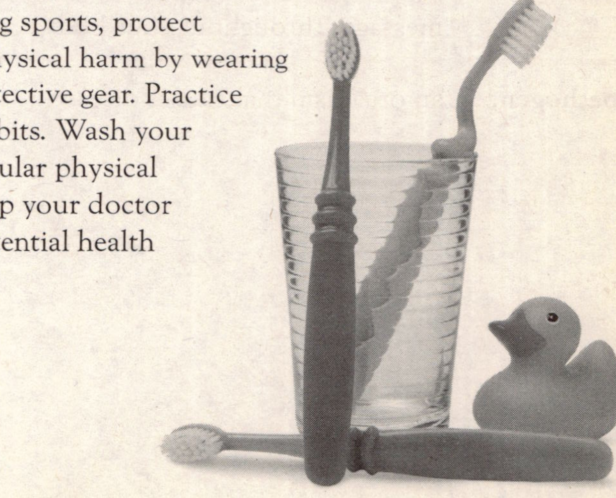

Systems Working Together

All the systems in your body work hard to keep you alive and healthy. When you are exercising, your respiratory and circulatory systems work harder. Your heart pumps faster to bring more nutrients and oxygen to the cells in your muscles.

Your amazing body runs without stopping every minute of your life. It does such a good job and runs so smoothly that you might forget that you also need to take care of it on a daily basis.

Your immune system works to rid your body of pathogens. White blood cells produce chemicals called antibodies in order to kill pathogens that enter your body. Still, you need to take responsibility for your own health.

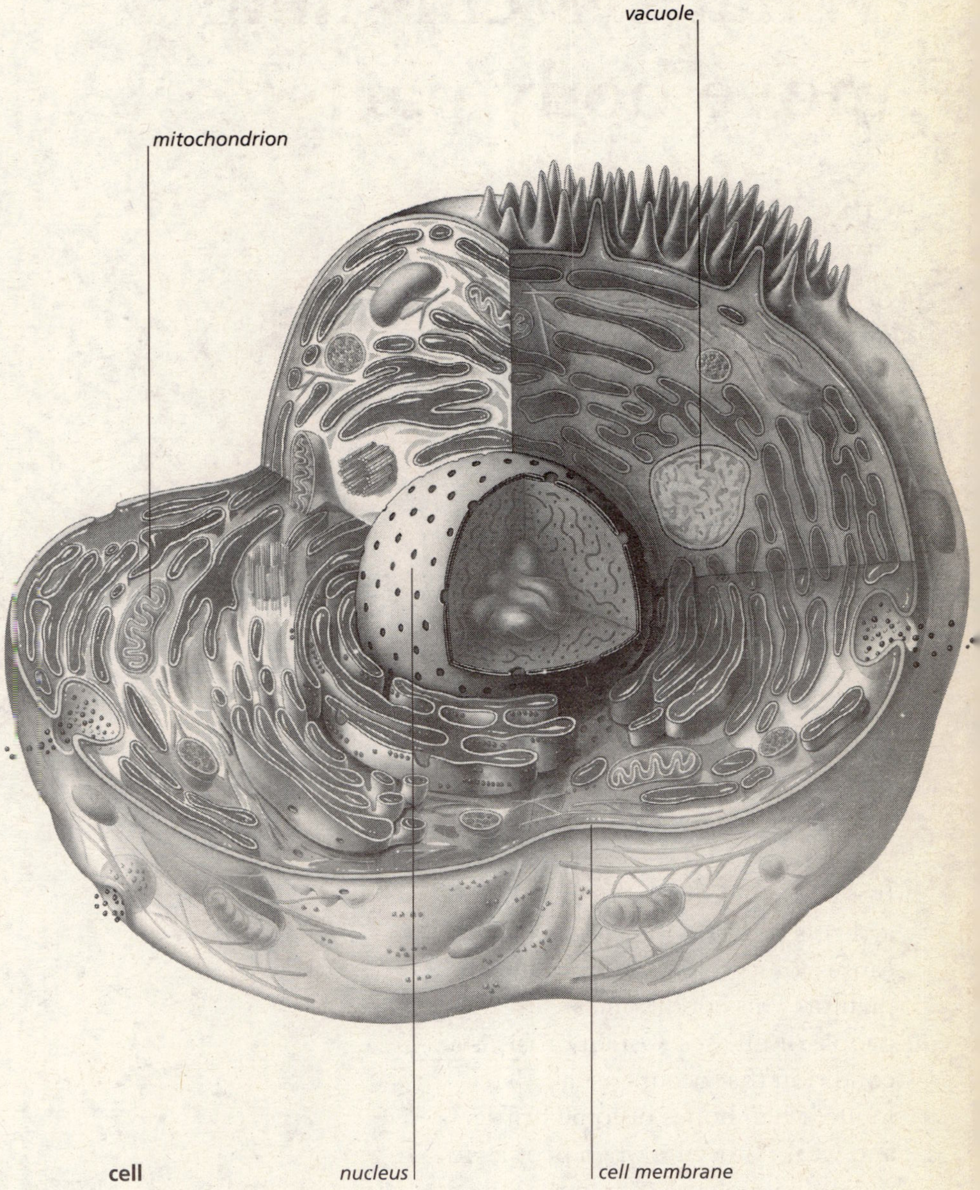

What systems help move body parts?

Skeletal System

Your skeleton is made up of 206 bones, and it works with muscles to make the body move. The largest bone in your body is the thighbone, and the smallest bone is the stirrup bone, found in your ear. Bones are composed of living tissues and nonliving substances. The inside of bones is soft and contains bone marrow, where red blood cells, white blood cells, and blood platelets are formed. Bones perform several functions. They support your body, protect your internal organs, and store minerals such as calcium.

Your skeletal system can suffer from different diseases, such as arthritis and osteoporosis. Arthritis causes joints to become swollen and painful. This condition can affect people of all ages. Osteoporosis is a condition that occurs usually later in life, when bones become brittle and weak. It occurs when people do not get enough calcium in their diet to keep their bones healthy.

This is why most people only get chicken pox once during their life. This same principle is at work when you receive immunization shots from your doctor.

After a pathogen enters the body, lots of white blood cells are created. Body cells that have been infected by the pathogen are attacked by the white blood cells. At the same time, other types of white blood cells are directed to produce antibodies. **Antibodies** are chemicals that destroy pathogens.

A white blood cell surrounds and destroys a group of pathogens.

How do systems keep the body healthy?

Immune System

Your body must defend itself against foreign bodies that may cause disease, such as bacteria, viruses, and fungi. These organisms are known as **pathogens.** Your body depends on its immune system to repel pathogens and keep you healthy.

There are two types of immunity: innate immunity and adaptive immunity. Innate immunity, also known as nonspecific immunity, works to keep pathogens from entering your body. Your skin prevents pathogens from entering your body. Tears wash pathogens out of your eyes and also have chemicals that kill harmful organisms. Your nose, mouth, and throat produce mucus that catches pathogens, and your stomach secretes chemicals that kill pathogens.

If harmful organisms happen to get past these defenses, your immune system develops specific defenses. This is known as adaptive immunity, because your body adapts to the threat to fight it.

Adaptive immunity only responds after a harmful organism is detected. It responds to each specific pathogen. Adaptive immunity also recognizes pathogens that have invaded the body in the past and protects your body against them.

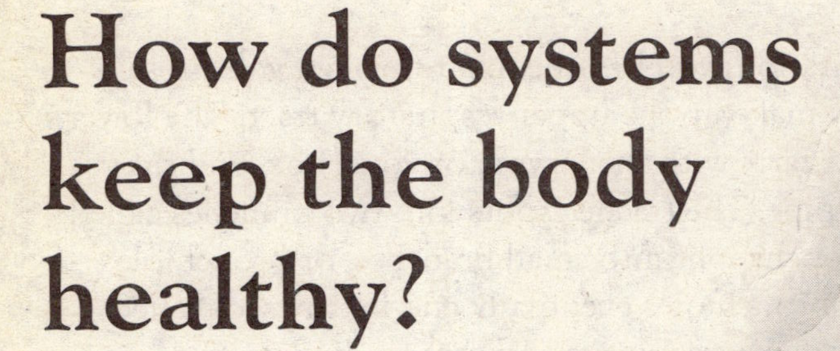

A joint is formed when two or more bones come together. There are three major types of moving joints: ball-and-socket joints, hinge joints, and pivot joints. Some joints, such as the ones in your skull, do not move. Joints that do move are connected by tough tissues known as ligaments. Another type of connective tissue is cartilage, which covers the ends of bones at joints. Cartilage is softer and more flexible than bone and protects bones where they rub together.

Muscular System

More than six hundred muscles form your muscular system and work with your skeletal system to make your body move and function. There are three kinds of muscular tissue: smooth muscle, cardiac muscle, and skeletal muscle. Your muscle tissue makes up 40 to 50 percent of your body weight.

Smooth muscles are involuntary muscles. They are found in the organs of the digestive system and in blood vessels. Involuntary muscles operate automatically to control parts of the body.

Cardiac muscle is another type of involuntary muscle. This muscle is located only in your heart and contracts automatically to move blood through the chambers of the heart.

Skeletal muscles are known as voluntary muscles because they are the only kind of muscle you can consciously control. Skeletal muscles are attached to the skeleton. They do the work of moving your body.

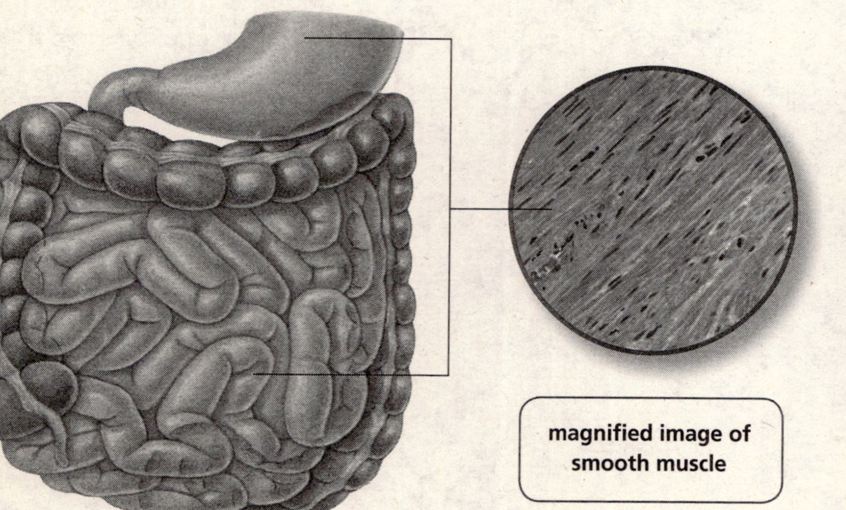

smooth muscle

magnified image of smooth muscle

During respiration, you breathe in air through your nose and throat. They make up the upper respiratory tract. The lower respiratory tract starts with the larynx, or voice box, and the trachea, or windpipe. The trachea splits into two branches called bronchi. The bronchi split into small branches, or bronchioles. In the lungs, the bronchioles eventually end in tiny sacs called alveoli. **Alveoli** are where oxygen and carbon dioxide are exchanged in the blood, and there are about 150 million alveoli in each lung. They are arranged in clusters, like grapes, and are surrounded by capillaries. Blood vessels move oxygen from the lungs to the heart. The heart pumps this oxygen throughout the body through smaller and smaller blood vessels. The same process happens in reverse to eliminate carbon dioxide from the body. Cells expel carbon dioxide into the bloodstream, and the carbon dioxide is carried to the heart, then the lungs, and finally exhaled.

Lungs are not made up of muscle tissue, so they cannot contract on their own. They rely on the diaphragm to help them. When your diaphragm contracts, your lungs fill with air, and when the diaphragm relaxes, you exhale.

42

Respiratory System

Your respiratory system brings oxygen to all parts of your body and carries away carbon dioxide. Cells require oxygen to release energy, and carbon dioxide is produced as waste. Your nose, trachea, bronchial tubes, and lungs make up your respiratory system.

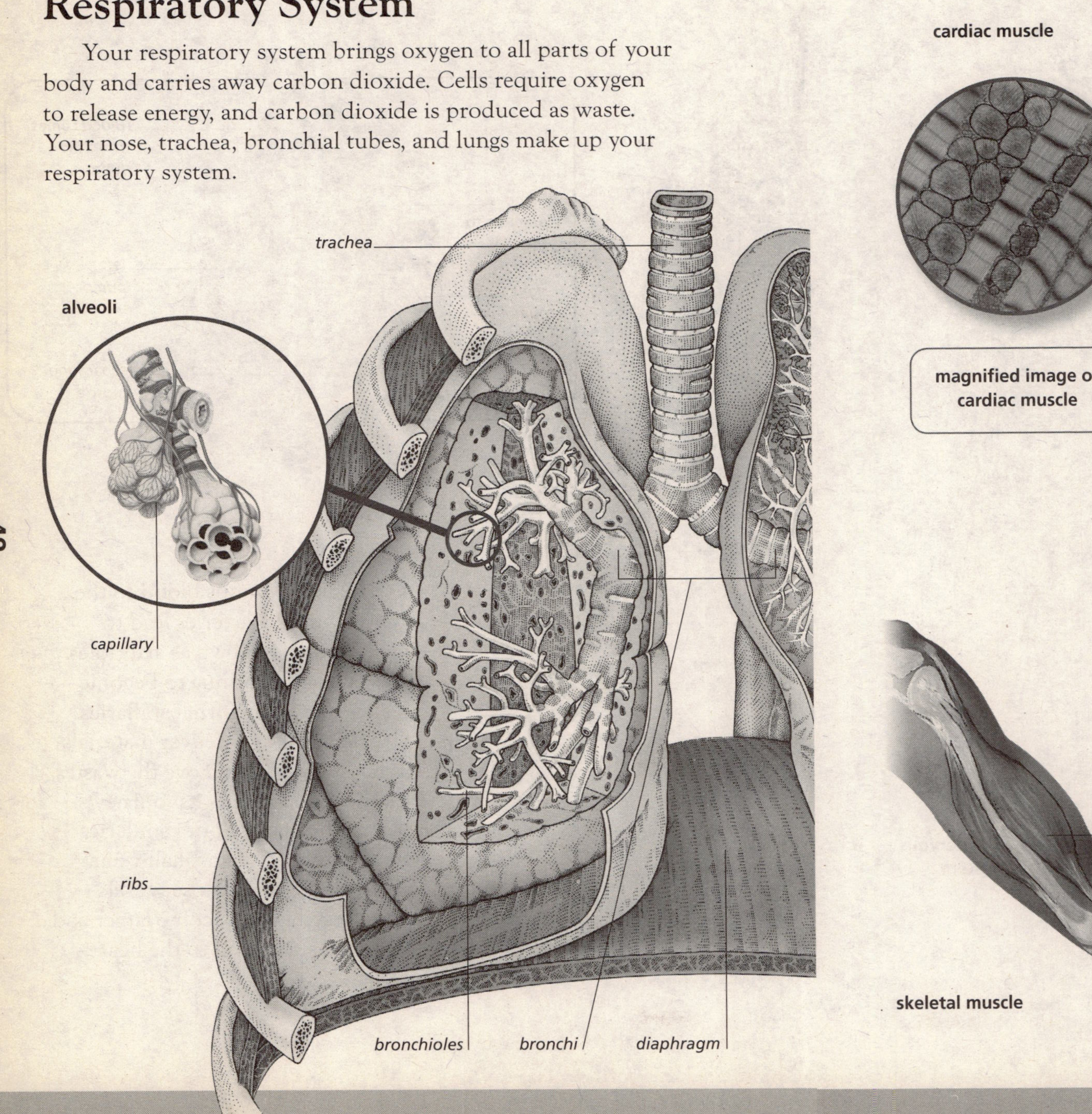

How do systems control the body?

Nervous System

Your nervous system includes the brain, the spinal cord, nerves, and sense organs. Information is constantly collected and processed by the nervous system, and your body responds consciously and unconsciously to this information. Your brain and spinal cord are connected to nerves that send and receive information from one body part to another.

Your brain has several parts that control specific functions: the brain stem, the cerebrum, and the cerebellum. The brain stem and cerebellum help regulate many functions of your body automatically. Your heartbeat, respiration, and digestion are maintained by the brain stem. The cerebellum controls your balance and posture. The cerebrum interprets information gathered by your senses and controls conscious thought.

The heart pumps blood to the arteries, and the arteries lead to smaller vessels known as arterioles. These vessels continue to become smaller until they form capillaries.

The capillaries deliver materials to the tissues and remove the wastes, and the blood begins its journey back to the heart. Your capillaries join together to form small veins called venules, and those vessels merge together to become larger and larger veins that lead to the heart.

44

Circulatory System

The circulatory system is made up of blood, the heart, and blood vessels. It transports nutrients and oxygen throughout your body and carries away wastes. Blood is made up of plasma and three kinds of cells: red blood cells, white blood cells, and platelets. Plasma is the liquid part of the blood that carries these materials, and it is mostly water. Red blood cells bring oxygen to parts of your body, white blood cells help your body fight diseases, and platelets help your blood clot if you get a cut.

There are three types of blood vessels in your circulatory system. Blood is carried away from the heart by arteries and is carried toward the heart by veins. The smallest blood vessels are called capillaries. These vessels are so thin that oxygen and nutrients can pass right through their walls and into body tissues. Carbon dioxide and other wastes are removed from tissues by capillaries in the same way.

The circulatory system helps to regulate your body's temperature. When your body gets too hot, blood vessels near the skin enlarge to get rid of heat. When your body is cold, the blood vessels conserve heat by contracting.

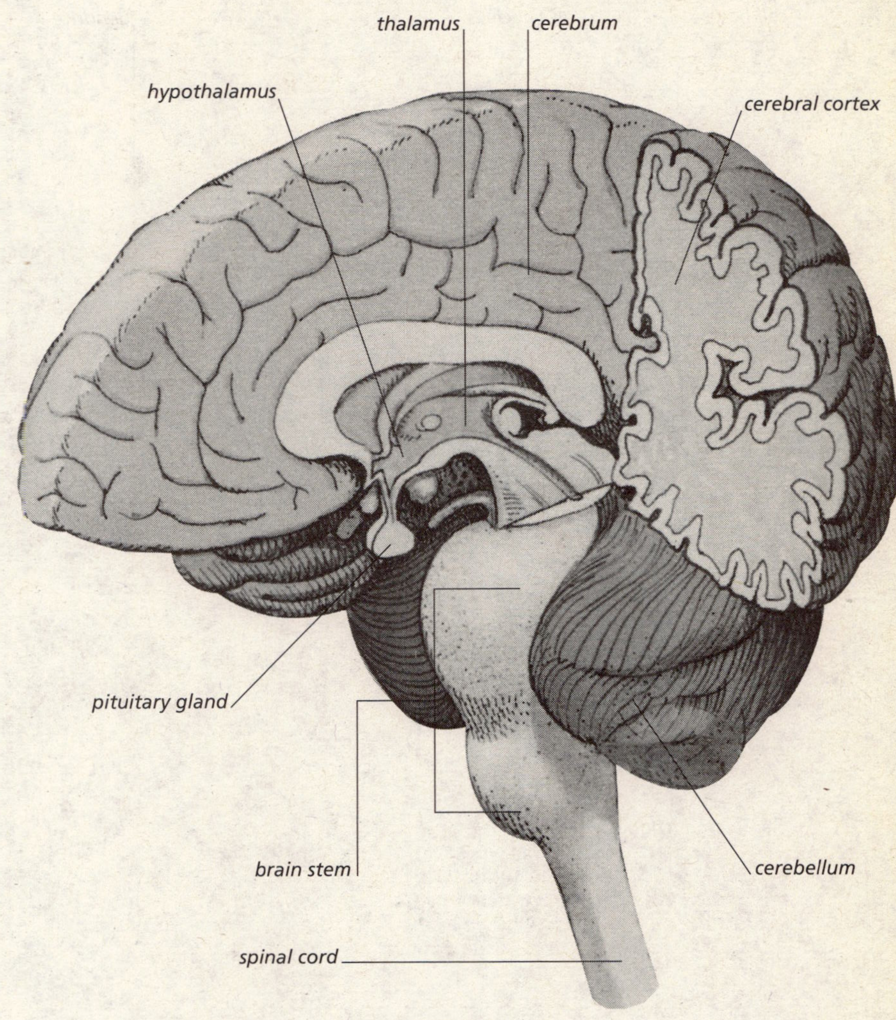

the brain

Your nervous system controls and regulates many of your body's systems, so it is important that you protect it from harm. You should always wear a helmet when riding a bicycle and wear a seatbelt when riding in a car. Certain sports, such as football and ice hockey, require players to wear special equipment to protect the brain. Your nervous system may also be affected by different kinds of bacteria, parasites, or viruses.

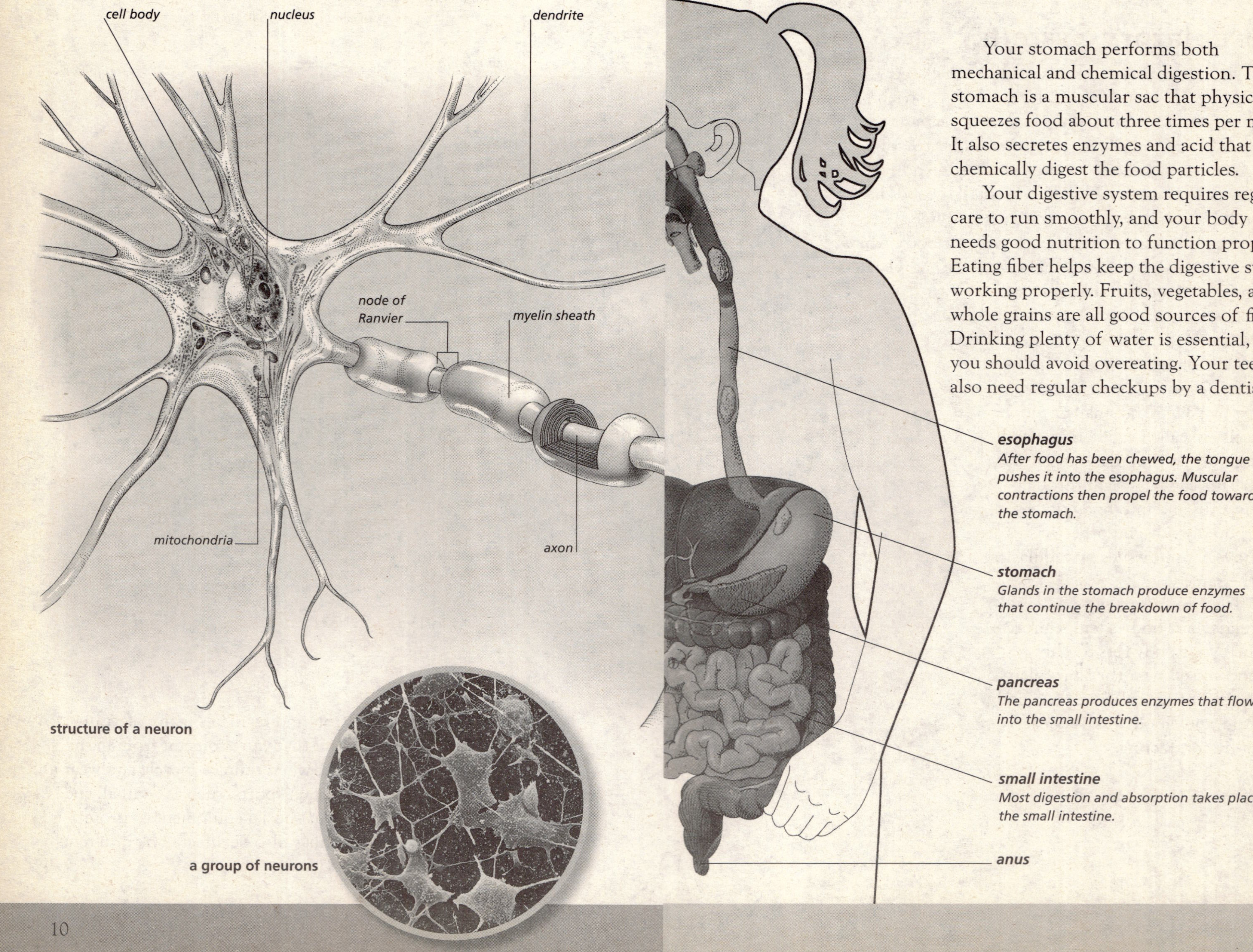

structure of a neuron

a group of neurons

Your stomach performs both mechanical and chemical digestion. The stomach is a muscular sac that physically squeezes food about three times per minute. It also secretes enzymes and acid that chemically digest the food particles.

Your digestive system requires regular care to run smoothly, and your body needs good nutrition to function properly. Eating fiber helps keep the digestive system working properly. Fruits, vegetables, and whole grains are all good sources of fiber. Drinking plenty of water is essential, and you should avoid overeating. Your teeth also need regular checkups by a dentist.

esophagus
After food has been chewed, the tongue pushes it into the esophagus. Muscular contractions then propel the food toward the stomach.

stomach
Glands in the stomach produce enzymes that continue the breakdown of food.

pancreas
The pancreas produces enzymes that flow into the small intestine.

small intestine
Most digestion and absorption takes place in the small intestine.

anus

How do systems transport materials?

Digestive System

Your digestive system breaks down nutrients from your food into a simpler form that can be used by your cells. Cells use these nutrients for energy to grow and repair themselves.

There are two phases of digestion: mechanical digestion and chemical digestion. During mechanical digestion, your teeth and mouth break food down into smaller pieces, but your body still cannot absorb them. An **enzyme** is a protein produced in cells that helps speed up chemical reactions. During chemical digestion, enzymes and acids break food down into molecules that can be absorbed into the bloodstream.

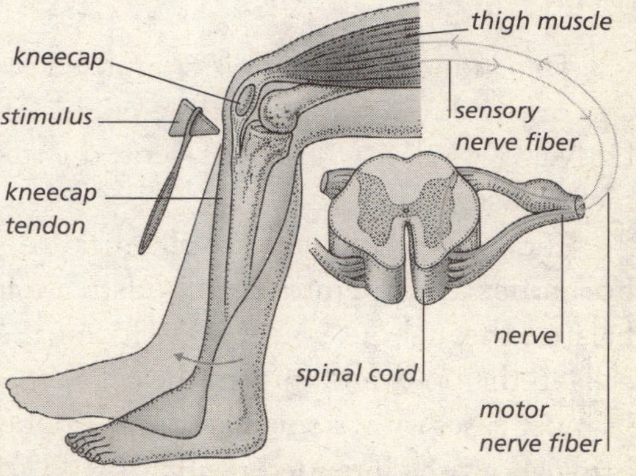

Nerve cells, or **neurons,** transmit messages throughout your body. Neurons consist of a cell body with branching parts. Dendrites are the short branches that receive messages from other neurons and carry them to the cell body. An axon is a long branch that transmits messages to other neurons. There is a chemical change, which triggers an **impulse.** Nerve impulses travel from the axon of one neuron to the dendrites of another neuron.

Most impulses are processed by your brain, which interprets this information and tells your body what to do. However, your body can automatically react to some things. This reaction, or reflex, helps protect the body from dangerous situations. For example, the doctor may check to see if your reflexes are working properly by tapping your knee lightly, making your leg kick out.

Tapping the kneecap tendon stimulates a sensory nerve in the thigh muscle, which transmits a signal to the spinal cord. Motor nerve fibers relay the signal back to the muscle, making the leg kick out.

Endocrine System

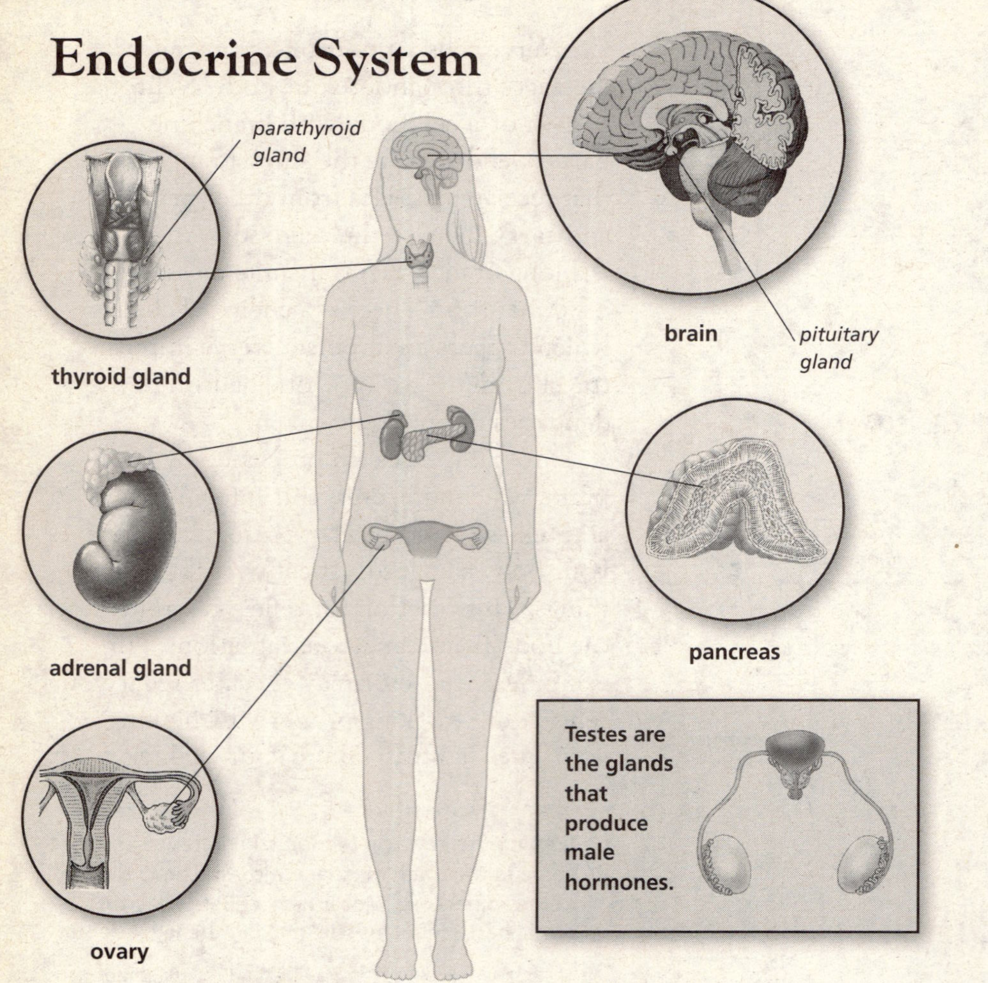

The endocrine system is composed of specialized body tissues and organs known as **endocrine glands.** These glands influence body growth, body reactions, reproductive functions, and metabolism.

Endocrine glands release chemical substances called **hormones** directly into the bloodstream in order to achieve balance throughout your body. Hormones travel to specific target cells in the body and inform the cells to carry out a certain task. In most cases only a small amount of a hormone is released to bring about the intended result.

Biofeedback Loop

Endocrine glands constantly regulate substances in the body to keep them in balance. The glands release more or fewer hormones, depending on the need.

Hormone levels are regulated by a biofeedback loop. A biofeedback loop functions by constantly sending information back and forth throughout the body. The endocrine glands release hormones when needed and stop releasing hormones when they are not needed. The thermostat in your home functions in a similar way. The thermostat is set to a specific temperature, and when it gets too cold, the heat turns on. When the temperature in your home reaches the temperature set on the thermostat, the heat turns off.

Endocrine Gland	Function
Pituitary	Controls development and body growth: controls the thyroid, ovaries, testes, and other glands
Thyroid	Controls how cells release energy
Parathyroid	Controls the amount of calcium and phosphorus in the blood
Adrenals	Control the body's reaction to anger, fright, or fear
Pancreas	Controls amount of glucose in the blood
Ovaries	Control female characteristics and the menstrual cycle
Testes	Control male characteristics

Life Science

Science

Plant Processes

by Jean Szeto

Genre	Comprehension Skill	Text Features	Science Content
Nonfiction	Compare and Contrast	• Labels • Captions • Diagrams • Glossary	Plants

Scott Foresman Science 6.5

ISBN 0-328-13983-1

PEARSON

Scott Foresman

scottforesman.com

What did you learn?

Vocabulary

cellular respiration
epidermis
guard cell
phloem
photosynthesis
stoma
transpiration
tropism
xylem

1. List the three main parts of a plant. Describe what they do.

2. Leaves make food. What is this food called?

3. Why are mitochondria called the powerhouse of a cell?

4. **Writing** in Science Seeds and spores reproduce in different ways. Write to explain how they reproduce. Use examples from the book to support your answers.

5. **Compare and Contrast** photosynthesis and cellular respiration? How are they the same? How are they different?

Picture Credits
Every effort has been made to secure permission and provide appropriate credit for photographic material.
The publisher deeply regrets any omission and pledges to correct errors called to its attention in subsequent editions.

Photo locators denoted as follows: Top (T), Center (C), Bottom (B), Left (L), Right (R), Background (Bkgd).

Opener: ©Comstock Inc.; 1 Dr Jeremy Burgess/Photo Researchers, Inc.;
5 (BL, BC) Dr Jeremy Burgess/Photo Researchers, Inc.; 6 (T) ©Comstock Inc.; 13 (T) Digital Vision.

Unless otherwise acknowledged, all photographs are the copyright © of Dorling Kindersley, a division of Pearson.

ISBN: 0-328-13983-1

Glossary

cellular respiration	the process by which cells break down food with the release of energy
epidermis	a thin outer layer of cells
guard cell	a cell that opens and closes a leaf's stoma
phloem	a group of cells that carry glucose, produced by the leaves, throughout the plant
photosynthesis	the process by which plants make glucose
stoma	the small hole in the epidermis of a leaf (plural: *stomata*)
transpiration	the loss of water from a leaf
tropism	the turning or bending movement of a living organism
xylem	a group of cells that move water and minerals from the roots to other parts of the plant

Plant Processes

by Jean Szeto

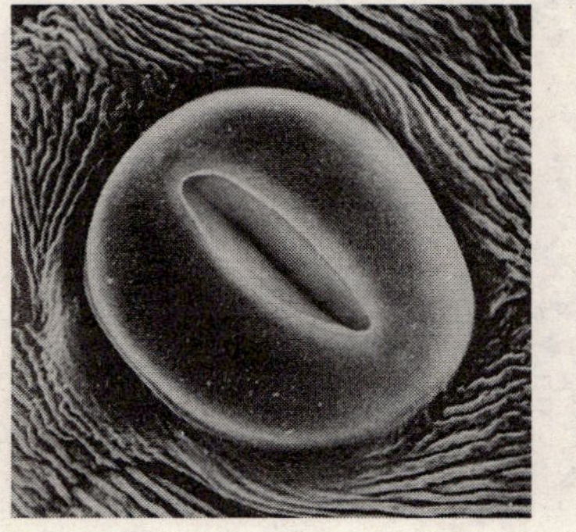

The Parts Of A Vascular Plant

What anchors a plant and absorbs minerals and water from soil? That is the job of the plant's roots. What do leaves do? The plant's leaves use water to make food in the form of glucose. Why is the stem important? A plant's stem supports the plant and transports water, minerals, and glucose.

A vascular plant has tiny tubes that transport liquids, such as water and glucose. The roots, leaves, and stems all contain these tiny tubes.

Roots

You have probably seen flowers moving when the wind blows. Why don't they blow away? The flowers are held in place by their underground roots. Roots help the plant stay secure in the ground. They start from the base of the plant and spread in the soil. There are many types of root.

Some plants have only one main root, with many tiny roots growing from it. This type of root is called a taproot. Dandelions have taproots. Other plants have many smaller roots that spread out like tiny arms.

Some plants do not grow from seeds. Mosses and ferns produce spores, not seeds. The table below shows how spores and seeds are different. Like seeds, spores can become plants only if conditions are right. Wet conditions suit most spore-producing plants.

Spore	Seed
contains a single cell that grows into a new plant	contains a multicellular embryo that develops into a new plant
does not contain stored food	contains stored food
is usually very small	can vary in size

Tropism: Responding To The Environment

Why do roots grow down and stems grow up? Plants, like all living organisms, respond to the environment. Although plant behavior is hard to see, it certainly exists. Have you seen plants that bend, turn, droop, or twist? This turning or bending is called **tropism.**

Plants do not have nerves to control behavior as animals do. Instead, the chemicals that plants make can cause different behavior. For instance, chemicals can cause cells in different parts of the plant to grow at different rates. Cells on one side of a stem may grow very quickly. Cells on the opposite side may grow very slowly. This uneven growth causes a stem to bend. Tropism is the plant's response to the environment.

The seed coat containing the plant embryo breaks open when it becomes too small to contain the growing plant. This allows more oxygen and water to reach the plant. When the plant cells have more oxygen, they grow larger and break apart to form new cells, helping the plant to grow. The extra water also helps the plant to grow. However, too much moisture can harm the plant, if there is not enough oxygen to balance out the dampness. Seeds with too much moisture may not grow. They may rot instead.

To protect the plant during poor growing conditions, some seeds become inactive. Inactive seeds often survive conditions that would kill a plant. For example, some seeds can survive droughts, freezing temperatures, and even forest fires!

When seeds germinate, roots grow downward. At the same time, the stem grows upward. New cells develop at the tips of the roots and stem, and plants get bigger. Branches on a plant's stem grow from side buds. Some plants increase in width too. To help with the growing process, cells divide to repair damaged tissue in the plant.

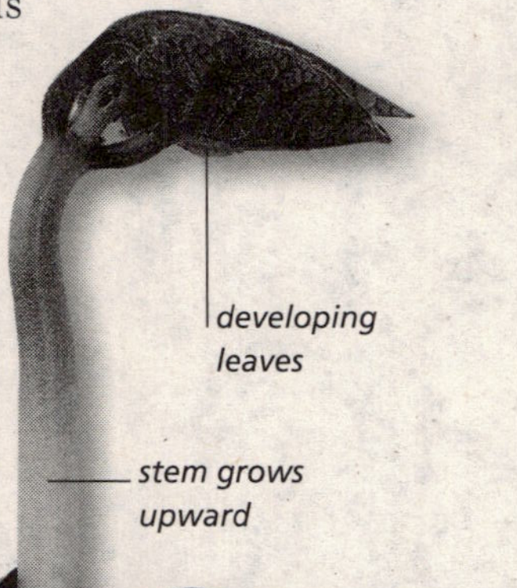

**germination of
a runner-bean plant**

Most roots are in the soil, which contains water and minerals. Water and minerals enter the root through a thin outer layer of cells called the **epidermis.**
The epidermis has root hairs that help the root absorb water from the soil. If the epidermis did not have root hairs, it would absorb less water. Nutrients move from the epidermis to the xylem.
The **xylem,** a type of vascular tissue, moves water and minerals from the roots to other plant parts.
Some plants, such as certain orchids, have aerial roots, which extract moisture from the air.
Plants make their own food. The leaves of a plant make a type of sugar called glucose. Another type of vascular tissue is **phloem,** which moves glucose to the different parts of the plant. Roots store some of this glucose in the form of starch. Beets are roots that store food.

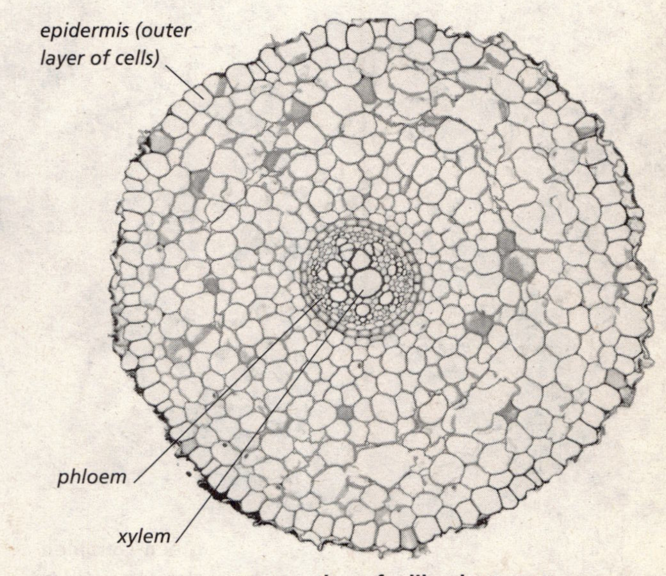

cross section of a lily plant root

Stems

Stems come in different forms. They can be tall or short, rough or smooth, curved or straight. Stems support plants. Like roots, they have xylem and phloem. The xylem and phloem move water, minerals, and glucose between the roots and the leaves of the plant.

Some stems are green and easy to bend. Plants with this type of stem are called herbaceous plants. The leaves and stems of these plants can die in cold weather, but their roots keep on living underground. Each year, these plants grow new stems. Strawberries, grasses, and weeds are herbaceous plants.

Other stems are strong and thick. Plants with this type of stem are called woody plants. These plants grow to be large and live for a long time. A woody plant may lose its leaves for part of the year, but its stem remains alive. Examples of woody plants are trees, shrubs, and vines.

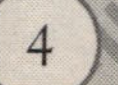

Jerusalem artichoke

**green-stemmed
strawberry plant**

**woody stem
of sycamore tree**

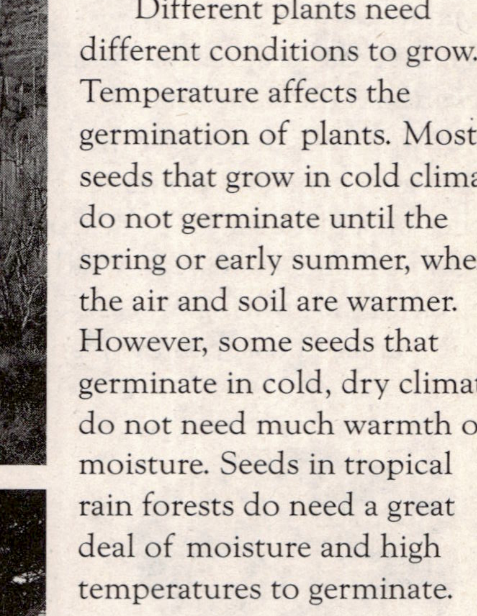

Germination
And Growth

A seed contains a tiny developing plant called an embryo. The seed coat protects the embryo. Before it can fully develop, the embryo must wait until conditions are suitable for germination. Germination is the process of growth from seed to plant.

Different plants need different conditions to grow. Temperature affects the germination of plants. Most seeds that grow in cold climates do not germinate until the spring or early summer, when the air and soil are warmer. However, some seeds that germinate in cold, dry climates do not need much warmth or moisture. Seeds in tropical rain forests do need a great deal of moisture and high temperatures to germinate.

Seeds can also grow inside cones. Gymnosperms are plants that produce their seeds in cones. Unlike angiosperms, gymnosperms do not produce flowers. Gymnosperms live a long time—even thousands of years!

One common type of gymnosperm is the conifer. Conifers are woody plants that often have long, thin leaves called needles. The Scotch pine is a type of conifer.

Conifers have two types of cones—male and female. Female cones have ovules with egg cells. Male cones make pollen that contains sperm. Pollen, often blown by the wind, moves from male cones to female cones. Sperm then fertilize the egg cells. Once it has been fertilized, the female cone closes up and develops seeds. It can take two years for seeds to mature fully. Then the cone opens and the seeds are released. There is no fruit to protect gymnosperm seeds.

Many products, such as wood, paper products, and paint, are made from gymnosperms. Oil from gymnosperms is used in everyday products such as air fresheners and soaps. Gymnosperm seeds are also a source of food.

The Scotch pine is a gymnosperm, which produces seeds inside cones.

There are also stems that grow under the ground. A Jerusalem artichoke is an underground stem called a tuber. Potatoes are another example of underground stems. Food stored in tubers helps the plant to survive. For example, if it does not rain enough or it is too cold, a plant may not make enough sugar. It survives because it has a store of food in its tubers.

Leaves

Leaves come in all shapes and sizes. But the function they all have in common is that they make food for plants. As leaves make a food called glucose, water and gases travel in and out of the plant through tiny holes in the leaf's epidermis. Each hole is called a **stoma** (plural: *stomata*). The cell that opens and closes a leaf's stoma is a **guard cell.**

Sunlight can cause guard cells to take in water. The water that is taken in through the guard cells puts pressure on their walls. This increased pressure causes the shape of the guard cells to become curved. Once the guard cells curve, the stomata open.

A guard cell usually closes a leaf's stoma at night.

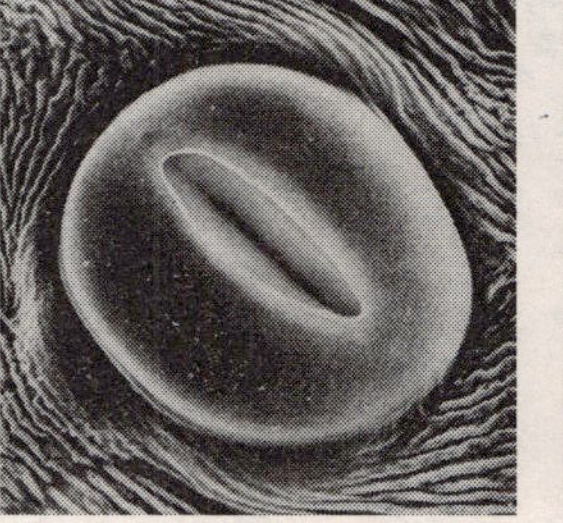

Then the guard cell opens the stoma during the day.

Transpiration

When stomata open, gases from the air enter the leaf and water passes out of the leaf. The loss of water from the leaf is called **transpiration.** The amount of water lost during transpiration depends on air temperature, wind, and the amount of water in the air and the soil.

To survive, the plant needs to replace the water lost during transpiration. As water exits a leaf, more water is taken into the leaf. This movement pulls more water up through the xylem in the stem. The plant can take in more water through its roots. If more water is lost by transpiration than is gained by the roots, the plant may wilt and even die.

How do seeds and plants grow?

Some seeds are made inside flowers. Other seeds develop inside cones. Different plants need different conditions in order to grow. Plants' behavior depends on the environment.

Plants with Seeds

In a plant that produces seeds, the first step of growth occurs when a tiny seedling emerges from a seed. Angiosperms are seed plants that produce flowers. Angiosperms are very common—scientists have found between 200,000 and 300,000 species of them! Only insects have more species than angiosperms. Apples and tulips are examples of angiosperms.

Angiosperms are vascular plants. This means they have special tissues—xylem and phloem—that move materials around the plant. Most angiosperms develop seeds inside a fruit. The fruit protects the seeds.

Humans use angiosperms in many ways. We use them as food crops and in medicine. Lumber, perfume, and some fabrics are also products made from angiosperms.

Flowering plants and apples are both angiosperms.

56

How do plants get and use energy?

Leaves make glucose, which contains energy. Cells break down this energy. The plant uses the energy to live and grow.

Photosynthesis

Different flowers have different colors, but most leaves are green at some stage in their life. Why are leaves green?

A chloroplast is a tiny structure found inside most plant cells. It contains a substance called chlorophyll, which makes leaves and other parts of plants green. Chlorophyll also allows a plant to make its own food in the form of glucose. Animal cells do not have chlorophyll, so they are usually not green and cannot make their own food.

Photosynthesis is the process in which plants make glucose. During photosynthesis, chlorophyll uses light energy from the Sun, carbon dioxide from the air, and water to form glucose and oxygen. Energy is stored in glucose, which plants use for life processes. When organisms eat plants, they use glucose as energy too. The process of photosynthesis is summarized in this equation.

$$\text{carbon dioxide + water} \xrightarrow[\text{chlorophyll}]{\text{light energy}} \text{glucose + oxygen}$$

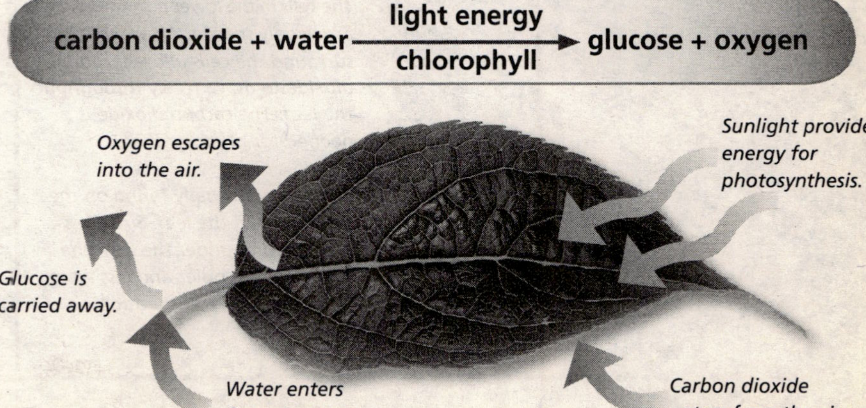

Carbon Dioxide–Oxygen Cycle

Have you noticed that the equations for photosynthesis and cellular respiration look similar? Let's look at the equations again.

Photosynthesis:

$$\text{carbon dioxide + water} \xrightarrow[\text{chlorophyll}]{\text{light energy}} \text{glucose + oxygen}$$

Cellular respiration:

$$\text{glucose + oxygen} \longrightarrow \text{carbon dioxide + water + energy}$$

The two processes are almost the reverse of each other! Photosynthesis uses carbon dioxide, water, and energy to produce glucose and oxygen. Cellular respiration uses glucose and oxygen to produce carbon dioxide, water, and energy. If one process ended, the other process would not happen. Photosynthesis and cellular respiration form a cycle, called the carbon dioxide–oxygen cycle.

Animals breathe oxygen from the air. Plants take in oxygen through leaves. During respiration, animals and plants use oxygen to change energy in food to energy they can use. Plants use the energy to produce more food and oxygen during photosynthesis. The carbon dioxide–oxygen cycle ensures that there is enough oxygen and carbon dioxide for each process to happen.

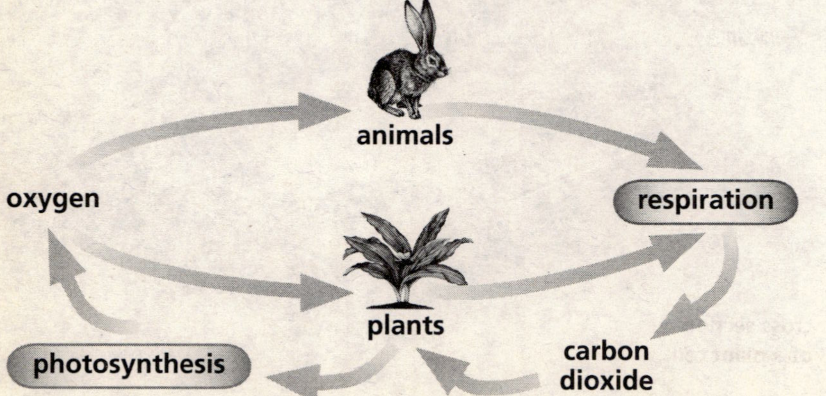

The Structure of a Leaf

The process of photosynthesis requires
light energy from the Sun.

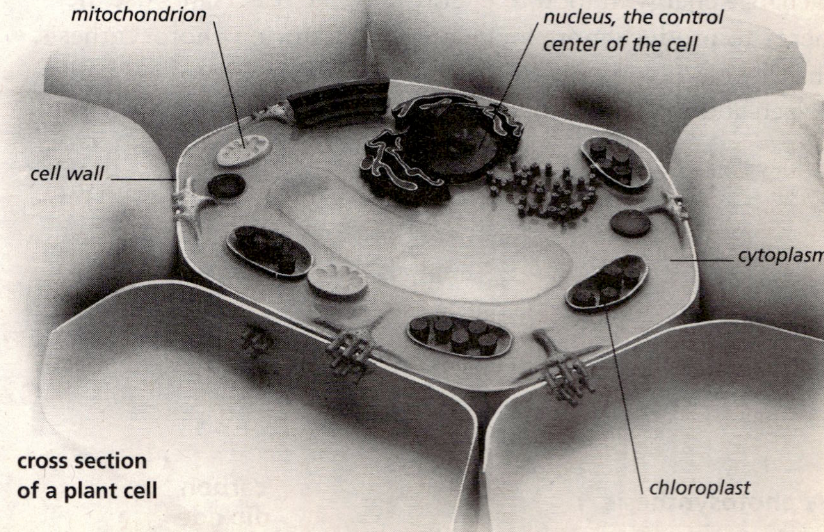

Energy from Food

When it is sunny outside, plants can make more glucose than they need. Extra glucose can be changed into other kinds of sugars and starches, which plants store.

When they need to use the stored foods, plants break down the sugars and starches to release the energy they contain. All organisms must break down food to release stored energy. This process is called **cellular respiration.**

Cellular respiration starts in the cytoplasm of cells. Cytoplasm is the jellylike fluid inside cells. Glucose in the cytoplasm is broken down into simpler substances. If cells contain oxygen, the simpler substances move into parts of the cell called mitochondria. In a mitochondrion, oxygen further breaks down the simpler substances. This entire process produces carbon dioxide and water. It also releases energy. Because mitochondria release energy, they are sometimes called the powerhouse of a cell. The process of cellular respiration is summarized in this equation.

$$glucose + oxygen \longrightarrow carbon\ dioxide + water + energy$$

cross section
of a plant cell

Life in the Biosphere

by Steve Miller

Genre	Comprehension Skill	Text Features	Science Content
Nonfiction	Main Idea and Details	• Captions • Diagrams • Glossary	Biomes

Scott Foresman Science 6.6

PEARSON
Scott Foresman

scottforesman.com

DK

ISBN 0-328-13986-6

90000

9 780328 139866

What did you learn?

1. How does a population differ from a community within an ecosystem?

2. Why are organisms in a biome similar even if they live many thousands of miles apart?

3. How does the canopy of a dense forest affect the plants on the floor of the forest?

4. **Writing** in Science One way that plants adapt to different conditions is their shape. Write to explain how climate can affect the shape of the main plants in a biome. Include details from the book to support your answer.

5. **Main Idea and Details** Make a graphic organizer. Complete the details that support this main idea: A population is a group of individuals of the same species that live in an area.

Vocabulary

abiotic factors
adaptation
biome
biotic factors
community
ecosystem
environment
population

Picture Credits
Every effort has been made to secure permission and provide appropriate credit for photographic material. The publisher deeply regrets any omission and pledges to correct errors called to its attention in subsequent editions.

Photo locators denoted as follows: Top (T), Center (C), Bottom (B), Left (L), Right (R), Background (Bkgd).

1 Digital Stock; 2 (B) Getty Images; 4 (B) Getty Images, (T) Getty Images; 6 (B) Getty Images; 8 (B) Getty Images, (TL) Digital Vision; 9 (BC) Digital Vision; 10 (B) Getty Images, (TL) Getty Images; 11 (T) Brand X Pictures; 12 (B) Getty Images; 13 (T) Getty Images, (BR) Digital Vision; 14 (B) Getty Images; 15 (R) Getty Images; 16 Getty Images.

Scott Foresman/Dorling Kindersley would also like to thank: Opener: (C) ©Jerry Young/DK Images; 12 (BC) ©Jerry Young/DK Images; 15 (BC) ©Jerry Young/DK Images.

Unless otherwise acknowledged, all photographs are the copyright © of Dorling Kindersley, a division of Pearson.

ISBN: 0-328-13986-6

Glossary

abiotic factors nonliving parts of an ecosystem, such as air, water, or minerals

adaptation a characteristic that helps an organism to survive in an environment

biome a large group of ecosystems that have similar climates and organisms

biotic factors the living parts of an ecosystem, such as plants, animals, and bacteria

community a group of populations of living organisms that live and interact in an area

ecosystem an entire community of organisms as well as the nonliving things with which they interact

environment the things that affect an organism

population the organisms of one species that live and interact in an area

Life in the Biosphere

by Steve Miller

PEARSON
Scott Foresman

DK

The biosphere includes all living things—even the people who live in this city.

How are organisms on Earth connected?

Connections in the Biosphere

The biosphere is the part of Earth where living things are found. The whole land surface of the planet is part of the biosphere. It also includes the atmosphere to about ten kilometers high and the oceans, from the surface to the deepest parts, eleven kilometers below the surface. No matter how cold or hot, wet or dry, there are living things in all these places.

All these organisms—plants, animals, and bacteria—share resources such as light, water, and air. As a result, life on the planet is connected. When something happens to one living thing, it affects those around it. The science called ecology studies how living things affect one another.

Tundra

The tundra is a biome that combines cold temperatures, a short growing season, and limited water. Most of Earth's organisms could not survive there. The tundra surrounds the Arctic, north of the taiga. Just below the surface is a permanently frozen soil layer called permafrost. When the top layer thaws in summer, water from the melted ice stays close to the surface. Although the growing season is short—two to four months— there are plants that grow in the tundra. Short bushes and shrubs, mosses, and grasses are the most common plants.

Animals that live in the tundra have adaptations that help them survive in cold, windy conditions. Most birds migrate when temperatures grow too cold for the insects that they eat. Many small mammals survive by eating the tundra plants. Larger herbivores such as caribou and reindeer move across large distances looking for food. Foxes and wolves prey on these animals, and polar bears catch seals and other marine animals for food.

Like the desert, the tundra has little water. Plants must also adapt to extremely cold winters.

Some tundra animals, such as this fox, have white winter coats that make them hard to see on the snowy tundra.

Desert

The key characteristic of the desert biome is that it is very dry. People often think of deserts as hot, but any area that gets little rain is a desert, even parts of Antarctica. Desert plants have adaptations that help them survive with little water. In general, they are small, compared to plants in other biomes, and they grow slowly. In the Americas, many desert plants are cactuses. Similar plants grow in other deserts.

In hot deserts, animals are usually active at night, when the temperature is much lower. Because there is a limited amount of shelter and food, there are not many large animals in deserts. Small mammals, snakes, lizards, and spiders are found in hot deserts. Many animals burrow under the ground where it is cooler during the day.

Because there is so little rain, deserts do not have a canopy. Leaves are small and thick to save moisture.

Many of the small mammals that live in the desert come out at night when it is cooler. This owl's excellent vision and hearing help it find the animals it hunts for food.

Organization of the Biosphere

What did you do before school today? Maybe you ate an apple, played with your baby sister, or drank a glass of water. Each of these activities is an interaction with something or someone else. Everything that you do, even breathing the air, affects things around you, and they affect you. The things around you make up your environment. An organism's **environment** is anything that can affect it. This includes living things, such as trees and plants, or any pet you might have. It also includes nonliving things, such as water and air.

Within an environment, there can be many different organisms of one species. A **population** is a group of individuals of the same species that live in one area. The frogs in the picture make up a population. The dragonflies are another population. If there were two kinds of frogs, they would make two different populations. That is because they are different species. There is also a population of each kind of plant and each species of fish in the pond.

How do the populations of frogs and dragonflies interact with one another?

The population of bison needs the prairie grasses for food.

In an environment, many different populations live together. A **community** is a group of populations that interact with each other in an area. A pond community includes frogs, dragonflies, other insects, and fish. It also includes all the plants that provide food and shelter for these animals. Some parts of the community are hidden, such as bacteria that are too small to see. These living things affect one another. Some are food for others. Some compete for the same resources. For example, frogs and lizards may both eat the same insects.

Communities of organisms also rely on nonliving parts of the environment for many of their needs. Each organism has needs for air, water, minerals, and shelter. The entire community of living things, along with the nonliving parts of the environment, is called an **ecosystem.** An ecosystem can be very small. The plants and animals in the terrarium are part of a tiny ecosystem. They interact with one another and with the air, water, and rocks. Other ecosystems are very large. These bison and the grasses they eat are part of a prairie ecosystem that once covered much of North America.

When there is little rain, the grass above ground dies, but the deep roots are ready for the next rainy season.

Grasslands

Grasslands are generally flat, open areas that get some rain, but not enough for large trees. There are grasslands on every continent except Antarctica. Grasses have deep roots, an adaptation that helps them survive the low amounts of rainfall in these areas. The height of the grass ranges from twenty centimeters to over two meters. Many roots extend more than two meters below the surface. During long dry periods or cold winters, the part of the grass plant above ground dies, but the deep roots are protected in the soil. When conditions are right, the grass begins to grow again.

The grasslands generally have good soil and produce a large amount of grasses and other flowering plants. Many animals graze in these open lands. Grasslands are home to many large animals, such as bison, elephants, rhinos, and antelope. Many smaller mammals tunnel in the ground among the grass roots. Predators, including lions, panthers, owls, and hawks, hunt in the grass.

Many animals, such as these meerkats, find shelter in underground burrows.

64

Rain Forests

The living things in tropical rain forests have adaptations for hot, wet weather. This biome is located all around the world near the equator. Plants grow all year in the rain forest and don't lose their leaves in winter.

The tropical rain forest grows in layers. Giant trees grow about seventy-five meters tall. Their leaves form a dense cover, called the canopy, which absorbs most of the light from the Sun. Thick vines climb up the trunks of the trees into the canopy and compete with the trees for sunlight. Below the canopy is a middle layer of vines, smaller trees, ferns, and palms. Many of these plants have huge leaves to capture as much light as possible.

An amazing number of plants and animals live in the rain forest. Some of them spend their whole lives in one tree. Because the climate is mild, there are many birds, reptiles, and amphibians. There are so many species in the rain forests around the world that scientists are constantly discovering new ones.

The rain forest grows in layers of plants competing for sunlight.

Many reptiles and amphibians have adaptations that suit the hot, wet climate of the rain forest.

The Needs of Organisms

The organisms that live in an ecosystem are called the **biotic factors.** In the prairie, the biotic factors include the bison and other animals. The grasses and wildflowers provide food for the bison, many of the birds, and small prairie animals, such as mice. Although you cannot see them in the picture, microorganisms, such as bacteria, live in all parts of the ecosystem. Some of the microorganisms live inside the bison's digestive system. They are also biotic factors of this ecosystem.

Living things provide for many of the needs of plants and animals. Other needs are provided for by the nonliving part of the environment, called the **abiotic factors.** These include water, air, sunlight, and even temperature. All these factors affect what types of organisms can survive in the ecosystem.

A terrarium is an ecosystem because it has a community of living things.

What are Earth's biomes?

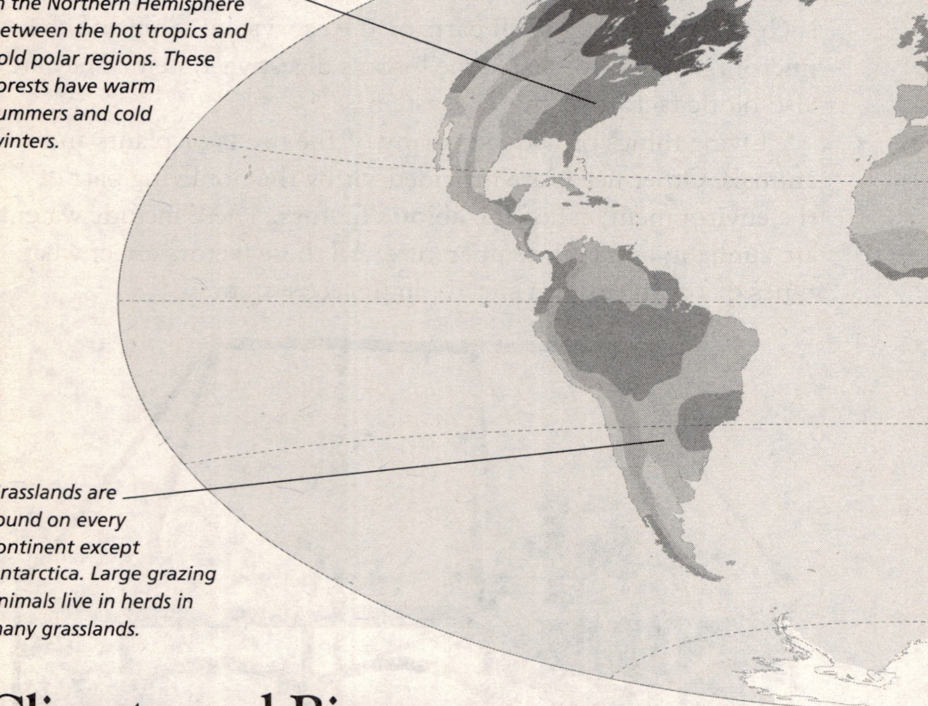

Climate and Biomes

Certain kinds of large ecosystems occur at different places around the world. The plants and animals of the Mohave Desert in the southwestern United States look a lot like those in the deserts of northern Africa and central China. This is because the climates of those regions are similar—very dry with hot days. All these desert ecosystems are similar. A **biome** is a large group of ecosystems with similar climates and organisms. The Mohave is part of the desert biome. This map shows the locations of some of the major biomes on Earth.

Taiga

Because of the shape of these trees, snow falls off them.

The taiga, or coniferous forest, covers areas of Alaska, Canada, northern Europe, and Russia. These forests have evergreen trees, such as pine, spruce, and fir, which stay green all year long. This is an adaptation for short growing seasons. Too much energy would be lost if the trees had to make new leaves every spring.

Most of the trees of the taiga produce nutlike seeds in cones. The seeds feed insects, birds, and small mammals, such as squirrels and mice. Because the climate is wet, there are plenty of places for insects to live. Many kinds of insect-eating birds live in this forest.

Many of the birds migrate to warmer areas in winter. Other animals are adapted to the cold winters. Some of the small mammals burrow underground to escape the cold. Others, such as brown bears and bats, hibernate through the winter, surviving by using fat stored in their bodies from the summer. Wolves, mink, and grizzly bears have thick winter coats, and they hunt other animals even in very cold weather.

The dormouse becomes fat in the summer and autumn, and hibernates in the winter.

Deciduous Forests

The living things in the deciduous forests have adaptations that suit cold winters and hot, rainy summers. The trees have wide leaves that gather lots of light during the growing season. The plants that grow on the forest floor must adapt to less sunlight because of the shade from the trees. As cold weather and shorter days approach, the trees stop producing food. The leaves change color and then fall. The floor of a deciduous forest is covered with rich soil produced by decaying leaves. The leaves and soil provide food and shelter for many species of plants and animals.

Many insects and caterpillars feed on the nutritious leaves of the trees. They become food for other animals, such as spiders, toads, moles, and birds. Larger animals that are common in this biome include skunks, raccoons, coyotes, deer, and bears. Because there is less food in the winter, some of the animals of the forest hibernate. Others, especially birds, migrate—that is, they move to places with a warmer climate—until spring.

If these trees did not lose their leaves in winter, the weight of the snow could break the branches.

The decaying leaves are home to many species of animals and plants.

slug

centipede

earthworm

The saguaro cactus has adapted to an environment with very little water.

Although they look similar, this euphorbia is not a close relative of the cactus.

Adaptation

Why are the plants and animals in a biome similar, even if they are on different continents? Organisms have features that suit the biotic and abiotic factors of an ecosystem. In places that have similar climates, the abiotic factors are often quite similar. The plants and animals also have similar adaptations. An **adaptation** is a characteristic that helps an organism live and reproduce in an environment.

The two plants on this page have adaptations to help them survive in similar environments. You may be familiar with cactus plants, such as the saguaro cactus shown here. Cactuses are found in many parts of North and South America. Adaptations help them survive in an environment that has high temperatures and very little water. The saguaro has soft, wet tissues full of water, and a thick skin to hold the water in the plant. There is very little rain in the desert, so the plants grow slowly. The spines on the cactus protect it from hungry animals. Now look at the picture of the euphorbia plant. It looks a lot like the saguaro cactus. It has soft, moist tissues, a thick skin, and protective spines. However, the euphorbia grows in Africa and is not a very close relative of the cactus plant. The two plants show similar adaptations to the hot, dry climate of their biomes.

Characteristics of Biomes

Climate is one factor that determines what types of organisms live in a particular place. In warm areas with a lot of rain, plants grow very quickly. Because there are a lot of leaves to provide food and shelter, there are usually a lot of animals as well. The tropical rain forests have many more species than other biomes. Most of these species would not be able to survive in cold climates. They might do well in a different rain forest, though. Their adaptations suit a particular biome.

Even though the ecosystems within a biome are similar, they are not exactly alike. These elephants live in the grasslands of Kenya in Africa. You can tell at a glance that they are different from the bison you saw before. The bison have long fur to protect them from the cold winters on the American plains. The elephants, on the other hand, have very little hair because the temperature rarely drops below freezing in the grasslands of Kenya.

Like bison, elephants live in a grassland biome.

69

Genre	Comprehension Skill	Text Features	Science Content
Nonfiction	Predict	• Captions • Charts • Diagrams • Glossary	Ecosystems

Scott Foresman Science 6.7

PEARSON
Scott Foresman

ISBN 0-328-13989-0
9 780328 139897 90000

scottforesman.com

Science

Science

Life Science

Earth's Ecosystems

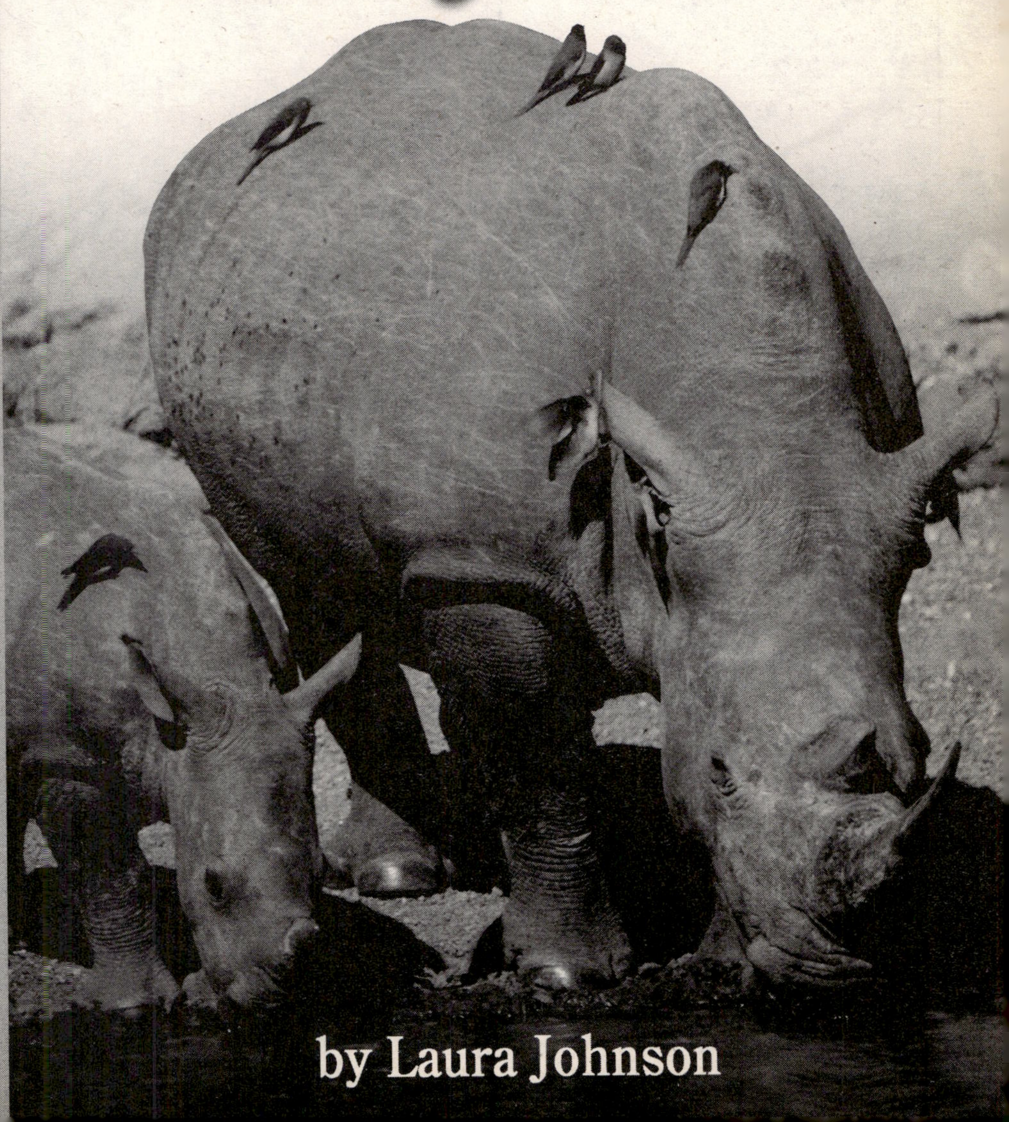

by Laura Johnson

What did you learn?

Vocabulary

competition
decomposer
energy pyramid
host
parasite
succession
symbiosis

1. What is the task of decomposers in an ecosystem?

2. What is the difference between a food chain and a food web?

3. What are two ways that carbon can enter an ecosystem?

4. **Writing** in Science Mutualism and commensalism are two different kinds of symbiosis. Explain the difference between them. Include an example of each.

5. **Predict** Based on what you read about structural adaptations, what kind of adaptation would you predict to find on animals that live in the deepest, darkest areas of the ocean?

Picture Credits
Every effort has been made to secure permission and provide appropriate credit for photographic material. The publisher deeply regrets any omission and pledges to correct errors called to its attention in subsequent editions.

Photo locators denoted as follows: Top (T), Center (C), Bottom (B), Left (L), Right (R), Background (Bkgd).

Opener: Mitch Reardon/Photo Researchers, Inc.; 2 (BL) Art Wolfe/Getty Images, (B) Digital Vision, (BR) Tim Fitzharris/Minden Pictures; 3 Jason Edwards/NGS Image Collection; 4 (C) Brand X Pictures, (B) Digital Vision; 6 (B) Digital Vision; 8 (B, TL, TCR, TR) Digital Vision, (C) ©Angus Beare/DK Images; 9 (BL) Brand X Pictures,(BCR) Getty Images, 9 (B, BC, BCL) Digital Vision; 10 (B) Digital Vision; 11 (R) Digital Vision; 12 (B) Digital Vision, (BC) Mitch Reardon/Photo Researchers, Inc.; 13 (CR) ©Ralph C. Eagle Jr./Photo Researchers, Inc., (BC) ©Eye of Science/Photo Researchers, Inc., (BR) ©Biophoto Associates/Photo Researchers, Inc.; 14 (B) Digital Vision, (CR) Getty Images; 16 (B) Digital Vision; 18 (B, BC) Digital Vision; 19 Shin Yoshino/Minden Pictures; 20 (B) Digital Vision, (C) Getty Images; 22 (B) Digital Vision, (BR, R) Getty Images; 23 (TR) Getty Images.

Unless otherwise acknowledged, all photographs are the copyright © of Dorling Kindersley, a division of Pearson.

ISBN: 0-328-13989-0

Glossary

competition — a struggle among organisms to survive in a habitat with limited resources

decomposers — organisms that get energy by breaking down the remains of dead organisms

energy pyramid — a triangle-shaped diagram that shows how much energy is present at each level of a food chain

host — an organism that is harmed by a symbiotic relationship which helps another organism

parasite — an organism that is helped by a symbiotic relationship which harms another organism

succession — a series of predictable changes that occur in an ecosystem

symbiosis — a close relationship between organisms of two different species that must be helpful to at least one of the organisms

Earth's Ecosystems

by Laura Johnson

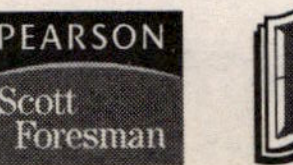

How do species adapt to their environment?

Surviving in the Environment

You know that different species of animals are found all over the world. Animals live in cold oceans, hot deserts, steamy rain forests, and on windblown mountaintops. Each one of them has a unique set of adaptations. You may be surprised to learn that animals of the same species have adaptations that allow them to survive in very different environments. Hares—animals closely related to rabbits—are a good example.

One kind of hare, the black-tailed jackrabbit, lives in deserts. These hares have enormous ears. When their body temperature rises, this adaptation allows body heat to escape from the large surface area of these ears.

Another hare, the arctic hare, has very small ears. This adaptation helps keep body heat from escaping into the extremely cold air that this hare lives in.

arctic hare

black-tailed
jackrabbit

Crews of workers tried to soak up the oil from the water's surface and the beaches. Ninety-seven volunteers spent hundreds of hours in an effort to seed new scallop beds. They carefully placed about eight thousand healthy scallops in the area to try to grow a new scallop population. Similar projects are underway to replace the oyster population. Unfortunately, even with the efforts of scientists and volunteers, much of the damage done to the animals and the ecosystem they live in cannot be undone.

Preventing Problems

Once we understand the effects that we have on the environment, we can find ways to reduce the harm we cause. One important way is to use resources wisely. Conserving resources decreases trash and reduces the need to build more landfills.

Explore ways that you as a citizen can make the environment healthy for all its organisms. Become a recycling "watchdog" at home and at school. More than four billion individual drink boxes are thrown away each year in the United States. These can sit in a landfill for more than three hundred years before they decompose! Setting up a program to recycle just these small items is a good way to begin!

Most products are thrown away. You can save bottles and wrapping paper to use again.

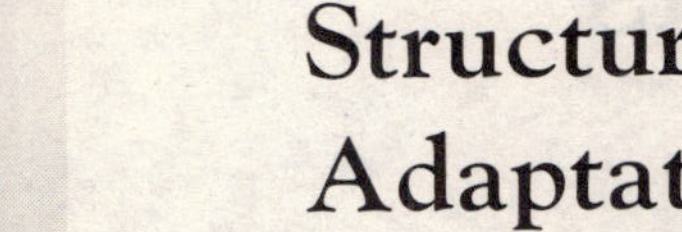

Saving Ecosystems

During a winter storm in 1996, an oil barge ran aground off the coast of Rhode Island. About 828,000 gallons of oil spilled into the ocean. The oil spill killed more than nine million lobsters, two thousand marine birds, and about one million pounds of clams, oysters, and scallops in the ecosystem. The oil also damaged the habitat of a bird called the piping plover, which was already on the list of endangered species.

Structural Adaptations

Adaptations do not develop during a single animal's lifetime, but over generations. When animals are born with a characteristic that helps them live in an environment, they are more likely to survive than animals without that characteristic. These animals pass on the improved characteristic to their offspring.

Structural adaptations have to do with an animal's body. A camel's head, for example, has adaptations that are important for survival in the desert. Its nostrils become narrow slits to keep out sand, and its eyelids let light through so it can walk in a sandstorm with its eyes closed.

Some frogs and toads bury themselves in mud during hot or dry periods. This is a behavioral adaptation.

Behaviors and Body Processes

Some adaptations are in the form of behaviors, not structures. Baby sea turtles know in which direction to crawl to reach the ocean after they are born, even though no one shows them. Desert lizards stand on tiptoe to keep from burning their feet on the hot sand. These behaviors are examples of behavioral adaptations that help animals survive.

How do organisms get energy?

Energy Flow in Ecosystems

All organisms need energy to grow, move, repair, and reproduce. How do living things get the energy they need? Most organisms get their energy from sunlight. This can happen either directly or indirectly. Lettuce, and most other plants, get energy directly from sunlight through photosynthesis. During photosynthesis, plant leaves produce glucose. The plants use the chemical energy in glucose to carry out life functions. In an ecosystem, plants are called producers because they use energy from sunlight to make, or produce, their own food.

People often harm the environment without even realizing it. When fossil fuels are burned, they create air pollution. Many of our everyday activities, such as driving cars and using electricity, depend on the use of fossil fuels. Think about how many times you rode in a car or a bus this week, and how many times you used electricity.

Another way people harm the environment without realizing it is by using too much water. Water is an important resource in every ecosystem. Do you turn off the water while you brush your teeth? Could you take a shorter shower? People in the United States use more water every year than people in any other country.

Most landfills can be used for about twenty years. Plants and animals are disturbed when each new landfill is started.

Human Impact on Ecosystems

People have an enormous impact on the ecosystems we live in. Our daily activities change ecosystems in ways that make it difficult, and sometimes even impossible, for other animals and plants to survive.

Landfills that we build to hold our trash change ecosystems. Each person in the United States creates about four pounds of trash every day! Together, we create about 600,000 tons per day! Some is recycled, some is burned, but most is taken to landfills. An advantage of landfills is that they reduce health hazards created by open-air dumps. However, hazardous materials, such as paint, acid from batteries, and chemicals, can leak out of landfills and harm ecosystems.

A rabbit, however, cannot get energy directly from sunlight. But as the rabbit eats the lettuce, it indirectly gets energy from the Sun that is stored in the leaves. Organisms that get energy by eating other organisms are called consumers.

Do you see the fungus growing in the picture on page 4? The fungus cannot make its own food from sunlight, but it doesn't eat other organisms either. So how does this organism get energy? It gets it by breaking down the remains of organisms that were once alive, such as trees that have fallen down. Organisms such as the fungus are called **decomposers.** They release materials from dead plants and animals back into the environment, where other consumers can use them. Without decomposers, nothing would decay.

Food Chains

As you know, organisms either use energy from sunlight to produce their own food or they eat other organisms that have energy. A food chain shows one possible path of how organisms within an ecosystem get their food. Because the original source of energy is sunlight, a food chain begins with plant life and ends with an animal. Notice that the arrows in a food chain always point toward the organism that receives the energy. In the diagram below, find the food chain that connects the path of energy from wheat, to the mouse, to the snake, and on to the owl.

Succession is a series of changes that occur in an ecosystem. This is how succession worked in Yellowstone after the fires. Plants called pioneer species began to grow on the damaged land. Pioneer plants can grow under difficult conditions. The following spring, about two dozen different kinds of plants began to grow out of the ashes. Many of these plants had existed before the fires, but only as roots. The forest floor had been so thick that they could not compete for the resources necessary to grow stems and leaves. As the pioneer plants died each season, their bodies decomposed and built up the soil.

After enough soil formed, other organisms were able to live in the ecosystem. Seeds took root and formed new plants in the rich soil. Some of these seeds may have survived the fire because they were buried deep in the ground. Others blew in from unburned areas. For the most part, park rangers did not replant Yellowstone. Yellowstone's forests replanted themselves.

How do ecosystems change?

All ecosystems sustain natural changes over time. People also cause changes to ecosystems.

Natural Changes

In the summer of 1988, raging forest fires burned throughout Yellowstone National Park. The fires, which were started by lightning, charred one-third of this national park. The park follows a "natural burn" rule. This means that fires started accidentally by humans are put out, but fires started by a natural event, such as lightning, are allowed to burn unless they threaten people's lives and property. Park managers know that natural disasters, such as forest fires, volcanic eruptions, and floods, are an important part of ecology. They change ecosystems by killing old plants and allowing new ones to grow.

Food Webs

Every chain has a producer that makes its own food and consumers that eat other organisms. Most organisms are part of more than one food chain and eat more than one kind of food. Because organisms in an ecosystem often belong to more than one food chain, the food chains become interconnected, or mixed. These interconnected food chains form a food web. Study the food web shown here. Wheat, clover, and dandelions are the producers at the bottom of this food web. The owl and the hawk are the consumers at the top because no animals in this ecosystem eat them. How many food chains is the mouse part of?

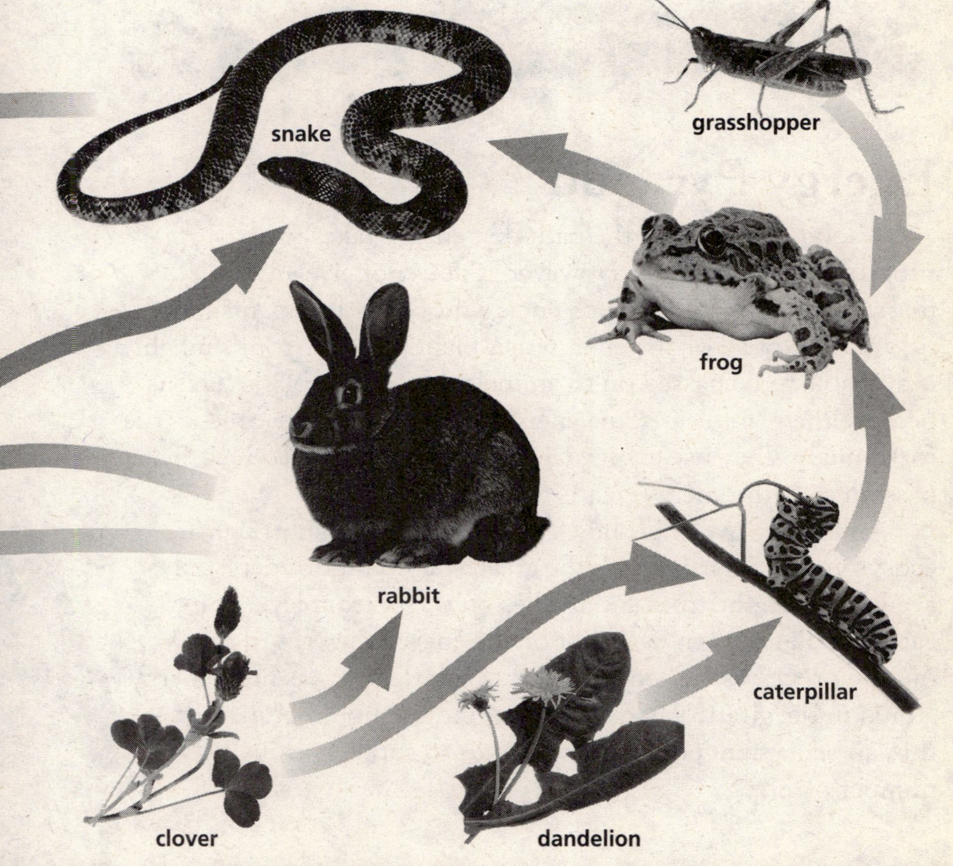

Energy Pyramid

A food chain shows the path that energy takes from producers to consumers. However, it does not give any information about how much energy moves from organism to organism. Not all of the energy that plants receive from sunlight is available to be passed on to animals that eat the plant. This is because the plant uses some energy to stay alive. The same is true for animals. They use energy to grow, move, and reproduce. They pass on only the energy that is left over.

An **energy pyramid** shows how energy moves through an ecosystem. In this pyramid, the greatest amount of energy is available from the trees and bushes on the bottom level. Giraffes eat these plants, then use most of the energy they get to carry out life processes. When a lion eats a giraffe, there is little energy stored in the giraffe's body to pass on to the lion. Because of this, an ecosystem needs many giraffes to support a small number of lions.

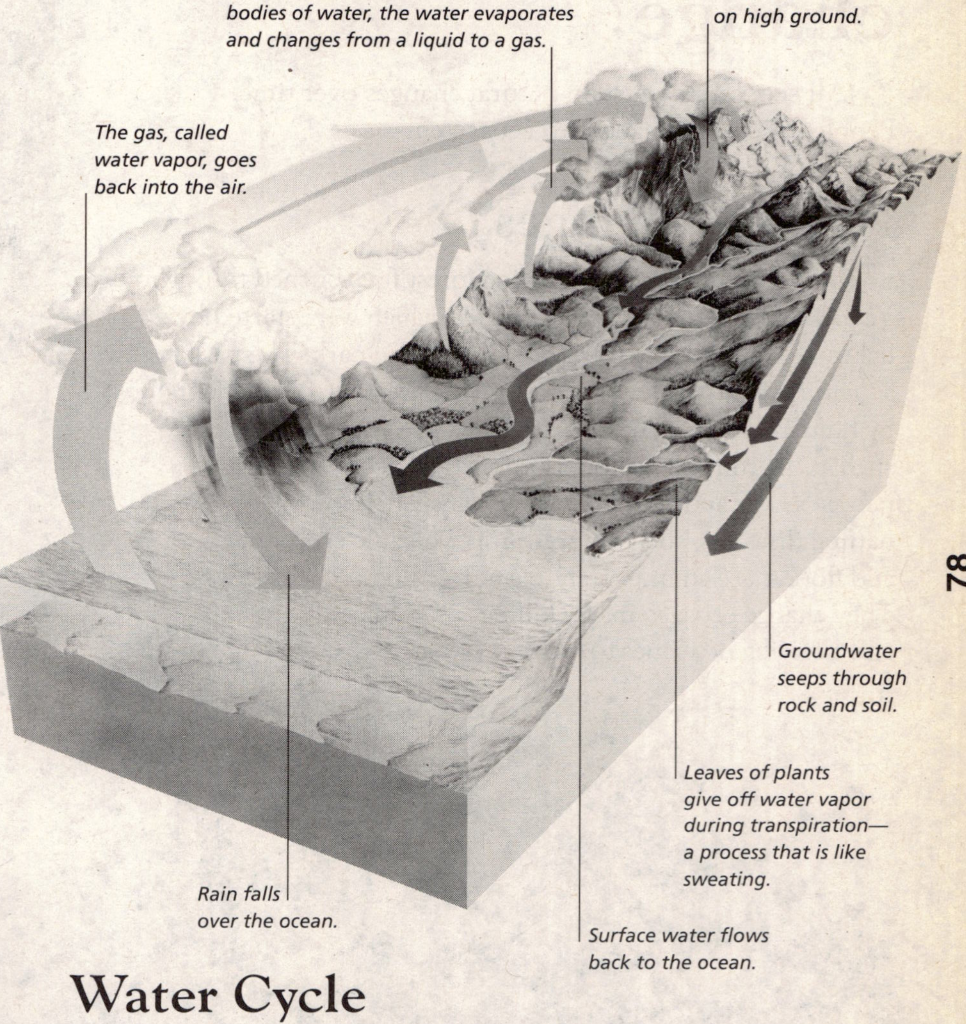

Water Cycle

You may not have known about the importance of nitrogen and carbon, but you certainly know that all living things need water. This diagram shows how water cycles through an ecosystem.

Carbon Cycle

All living things contain an element called carbon. It is also found in nonliving materials such as air, rocks, and soil. Like nitrogen, carbon cycles through ecosystems. This occurs in several ways, as shown in this diagram.

How do organisms compete for resources?

Competition for Resources

All plants and animals need food, water, and space. Within an ecosystem, these resources are limited, so there is always a **competition** for them. Animals with different needs can live side by side with little competition. Look at the bills on the birds in the illustration. Do you see how each kind of bird has a differently shaped bill? This is because the birds eat different foods. These birds do not need to compete for food in this ecosystem.

Competition occurs only when organisms of an ecosystem have the same needs. Sometimes competition is between members of the same species, such as two herons. If there is a drought and the marsh becomes dry, the herons that can survive with less food and water have a better chance of survival than those who need more.

Sometimes competition is between different species. Suppose a stork came to this marsh to find food. Since storks and herons eat the same kind of fish and frogs, the two species would compete for the same resources.

Cycle of Predators and Prey

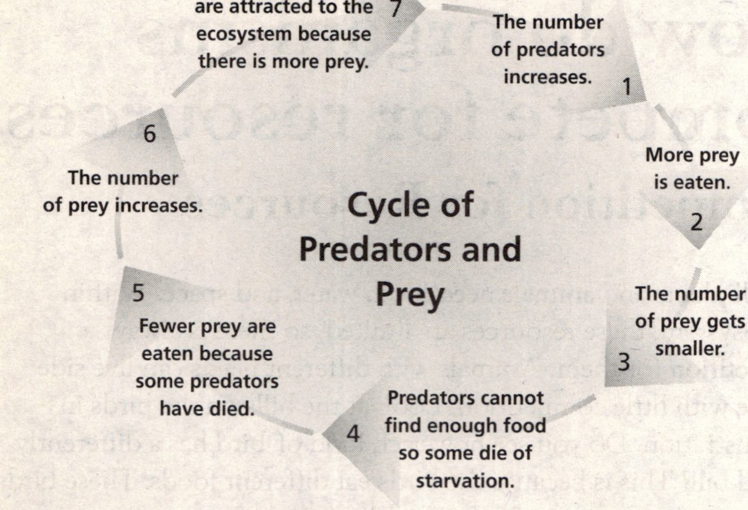

Predators and Prey

An animal that hunts and eats other animals is called a predator. The animal that is eaten by a predator is called a prey animal. In a healthy ecosystem, the populations of predators and prey have a natural cycle that works like this.

Adaptations Of Predators And Prey

Many predators have structural and behavioral adaptations that help them catch their prey. An alligator snapping turtle, for example, has a tongue that looks like a worm. It sits on the river bottom with its mouth wide open. When a fish arrives to eat what appears to be a worm, the turtle's mouth snaps shut and it eats the fish.

The eyes and nostrils of the sidewinding viper are on top of its head. This allows the snake to bury itself almost completely in the sand and snatch unsuspecting prey.

A small amount of free nitrogen in the air is fixed by lightning. During a storm, rain carries the fixed nitrogen to the ground. Do you remember how decomposers break down the remains of dead plants and animals? When this happens, the fixed nitrogen in these organisms is released into the soil.

How does nitrogen become part of a cycle? How does nitrogen return to the air? Not all bacteria live on plant roots. Some bacteria live freely in the soil. These bacteria can break down fixed nitrogen and turn it back into free nitrogen. The free nitrogen passes into the air. This movement of nitrogen is called the nitrogen cycle.

The nitrogen cycle

Free nitrogen in the air is fixed by lightning.

Decomposers break down dead plants, and fixed nitrogen is released into the soil.

Bacteria break down fixed nitrogen and turn it into free nitrogen that passes into the air.

How do materials cycle in ecosystems?

Nature depends on a recycling system so resources can be used over and over. The nitrogen cycle, the carbon cycle, and the water cycle are very important in nature.

Recycling Matter

When you hear the word *recycling* you probably think of materials such as paper and glass. People recycle these materials to conserve resources. For the same reason, nature has its own recycling system. Organisms need nitrogen, carbon, and water. If these were not recycled, they would be used up. Because of Earth's cycles, organisms are able to use these same materials over and over again.

Nitrogen Cycle

About 78 percent of the air we breathe is nitrogen. The nitrogen in air is free nitrogen, which means it is not combined with other elements. Most plants and animals cannot use nitrogen in this form. They can use it only in a fixed form when it is combined with other elements.

Bacteria that live on the roots of plants fix free nitrogen. The plants and the bacteria have a mutualistic relationship—the bacteria gets food from the plant, and the plant takes nitrogen from the bacteria. Animals get nitrogen indirectly by eating plants or by eating prey that have eaten plants.

As you probably guessed, many prey also have adaptations that help them avoid—and even trick—their predators. The frilled lizard is an example. This lizard cannot defend itself from predators, but it can scare them away. When it senses danger, the lizard opens its mouth wide and a frill, or collar of skin, stands out around its head. This makes the lizard look so large that predators usually run away.

Katydids look amazingly like leaves. By keeping still, the katydid can fool many predators.

frilled lizard

12

Symbiosis

Symbiosis is a close relationship between organisms of two different species. A symbiotic relationship must be helpful to at least one of the organisms. There are three types of symbiosis: parasitism, mutualism, and commensalism.

Parasitism is a type of symbiosis in which one of the organisms is helped and the other organism is harmed. The organism that is helped is called a **parasite.** The organism that is harmed is called a **host.** Tapeworms are parasites that can live in the digestive systems of humans and animals. They absorb the host's digested food.

Mutualism is a symbiotic relationship in which both organisms are helped. A bird called the cattle egret and the rhinoceros have this kind of relationship. The bird eats parasites that live in the rhino's hide. This helps the rhino by removing the harmful parasites and helps the bird by providing food.

A bird called the cattle egret and the rhinoceros have a helpful relationship. The bird eats parasites that live in the rhino's hide and the rhino provides food for the bird.

Commensalism is a type of symbiosis that helps one organism, but doesn't help or harm the other. There is a worm that lives inside shells used by hermit crabs. When the crab catches food, the worm comes out of the shell to eat some of the prey. The worm does not do anything to harm or help the crab.

Symbiosis in the Human Body

Symbiotic relationships exist in your own body. Most are harmless, but some are parasitic relationships that can be harmful. Can you recognize which type of symbiosis each of these organisms share with humans?

Mites that cover your skin and live at the base of your eyelashes get food by eating dead skin cells.

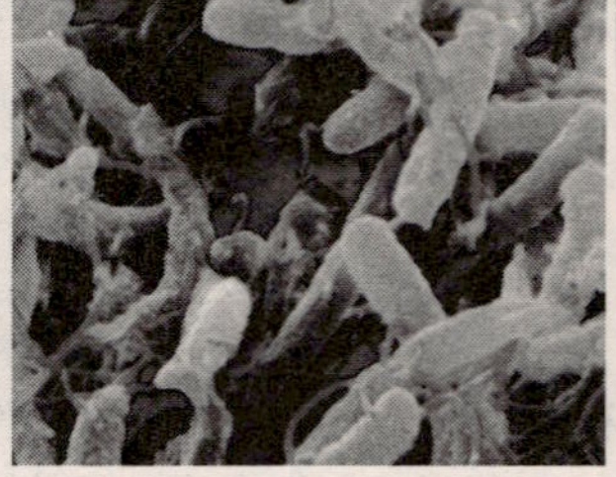

Fleas and ticks get food by piercing the skin and sucking out blood.

E. coli bacteria live in the intestine and feed on digested food. They make vitamin K, which helps your blood clot.

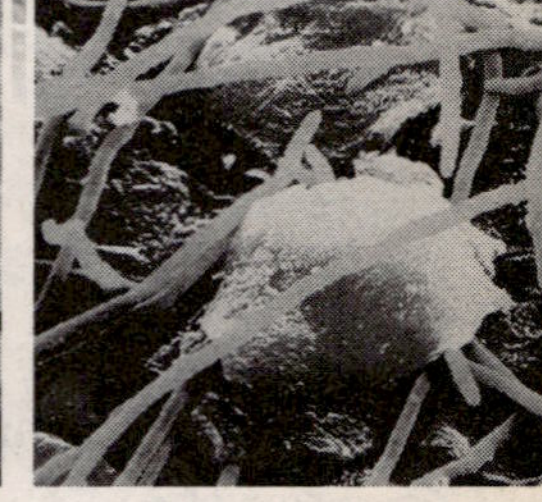

Athlete's foot is caused by a fungus. A foot infected with athlete's foot looks dry and cracked, and it itches.

13

Earth's LAYERS

by Emily Gray

Genre	Comprehension Skill	Text Features	Science Content
Nonfiction	Draw Conclusions	• Captions • Charts • Diagrams • Glossary	Plate Tectonics

Scott Foresman Science 6.8

PEARSON
Scott Foresman

DK

ISBN 0-328-13992-0

90000

9 780328 139927

scottforesman.com

What did you learn?

1. What layer of Earth do we live on?

2. Describe the makeup of Earth's core.

3. Where are most volcanoes found, and at what type of plate boundary?

4. **Writing** in Science Provide the names of the two types of waves that occur during an earthquake and describe how they are different.

5. **Draw Conclusions** List three pieces of evidence to support new findings of seafloor spreading and continental drift. Give details from the book to support your answer.

Picture Credits
Every effort has been made to secure permission and provide appropriate credit for photographic material.
The publisher deeply regrets any omission and pledges to correct errors called to its attention in subsequent editions.

Photo locators denoted as follows: Top (T), Center (C), Bottom (B), Left (L), Right (R), Background (Bkgd).

6 Getty Images; 20 (BL) Getty Images; 22 (CR) Science Museum, London/DK Images;
23 (TR) Science Museum, London/DK Images.

Unless otherwise acknowledged, all photographs are the copyright © of Dorling Kindersley, a division of Pearson.

ISBN: 0-328-13992-0

Earth's LAYERS

by Emily Gray

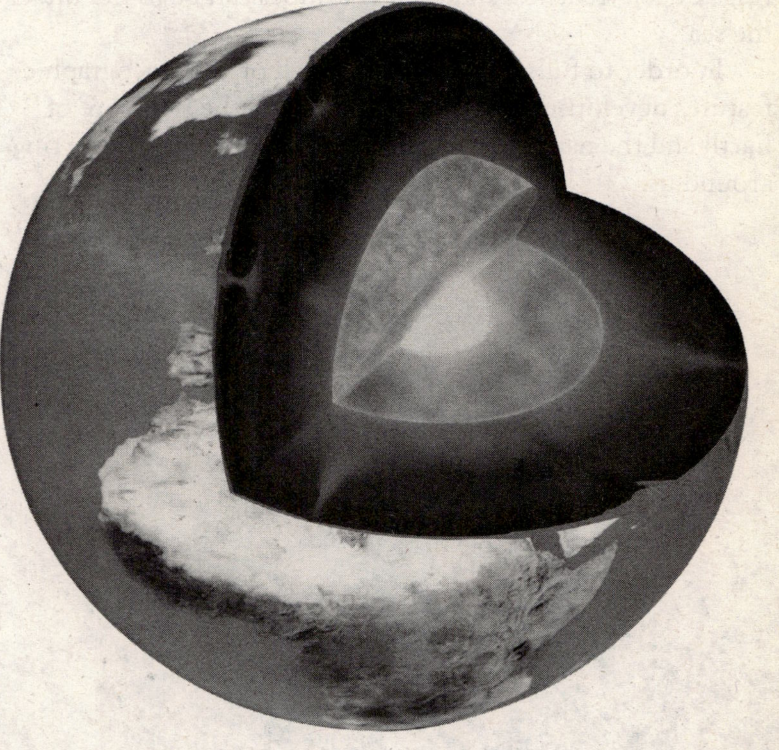

Glossary

continental drift — movement of continents as described by the theory of plate tectonics

core — innermost layer of Earth, composed of the inner core (solid) and outer core (liquid)

crust — outermost solid layer of Earth; the outermost part of the lithosphere

fault — a crack in Earth's crust where there has been rock movement on either side

lithosphere — Earth's crust and the outermost solid layer of the mantle

mantle — layer below the crust that consists of solid and liquid layers of matter

plate boundary — area where two plates meet

plate tectonics — theory that explains geographic features and events based on the movement of Earth's plates

What are Earth's layers made of?

Earth has many dramatic physical features. Landforms such as plateaus, mountains, plains, and valleys are all over the world, but these features did not develop immediately. Small changes over millions of years have eventually produced landscapes, such as the Grand Canyon, the Himalaya Mountains, and the Hawaiian Islands as we know them.

Earth also has important features under its oceans. Mountain ridges, deep trenches, and even volcanoes can be found under the sea.

In order to fully understand how all of these geographic features developed we need to understand the structure of Earth and the natural processes that are constantly occurring around us.

Small shifts in ground level would cause a ball in a dragon's mouth to fall into a frog's mouth. The frog that contained the ball would indicate the direction from which the earthquake occurred.

The first instrument used to predict earthquakes was invented in China in A.D. 132.

The shaking of an earthquake and eruptions of magma from a volcano may cause immediate damage, but other damaging effects can follow. Mudslides can occur after earthquakes, and tsunamis, or giant waves, can develop after an undersea earthquake or volcanic eruption. Damage from these events can be minimized if proper precautions are taken.

Predicting Earthquakes And Volcano's Eruptions

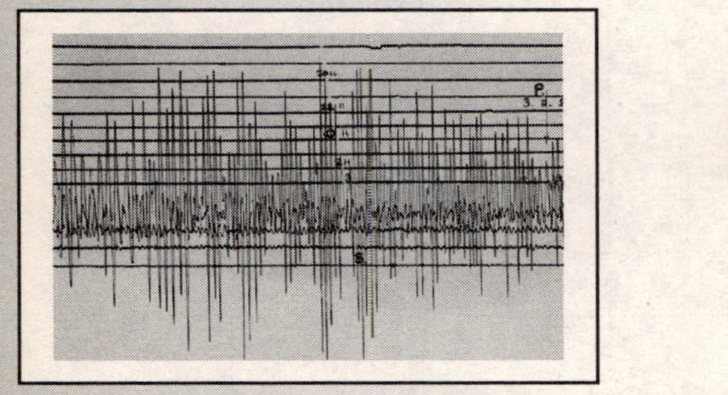

This seismograph recording of a 1923 earthquake in Japan shows P and S waves.

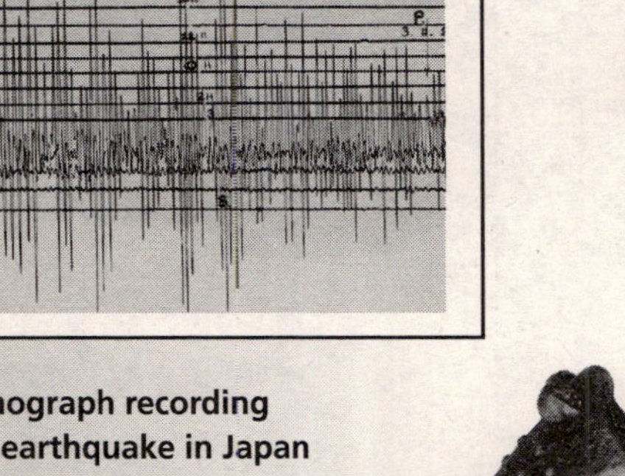

A modern seismograph

Many people live in areas that are threatened by earthquakes, volcanoes, or their side effects. Scientists use several methods to help them make predictions about when or where future earthquakes or volcanoes may occur.

Seismometers are used to detect tremors in Earth's crust that may indicate that there is volcanic or earthquake activity. A tiltmeter is an instrument that scientists use to detect changes in the angle of the land. These changes may indicate that magma is rising within a volcano, preceding an eruption.

Earth's Layers

Earth is composed of several layers. Not all of these layers are solid. The atmosphere is above the surface of Earth and is a thin gaseous layer that permits the existence of living things.

The layer of Earth that we live on is the **crust.** This is the outermost solid layer of Earth. The crust is about five kilometers thick in places covered by the ocean, and about thirty kilometers thick in places that are land. Although the crust seems thick to us, it is only a thin shell covering Earth.

The layer below the crust is the **mantle,** and this layer is much thicker than the crust. The mantle is composed of several solid and liquid parts, and makes up more than 80 percent of Earth's mass. The mantle extends to a depth of about 2,900 kilometers below the crust.

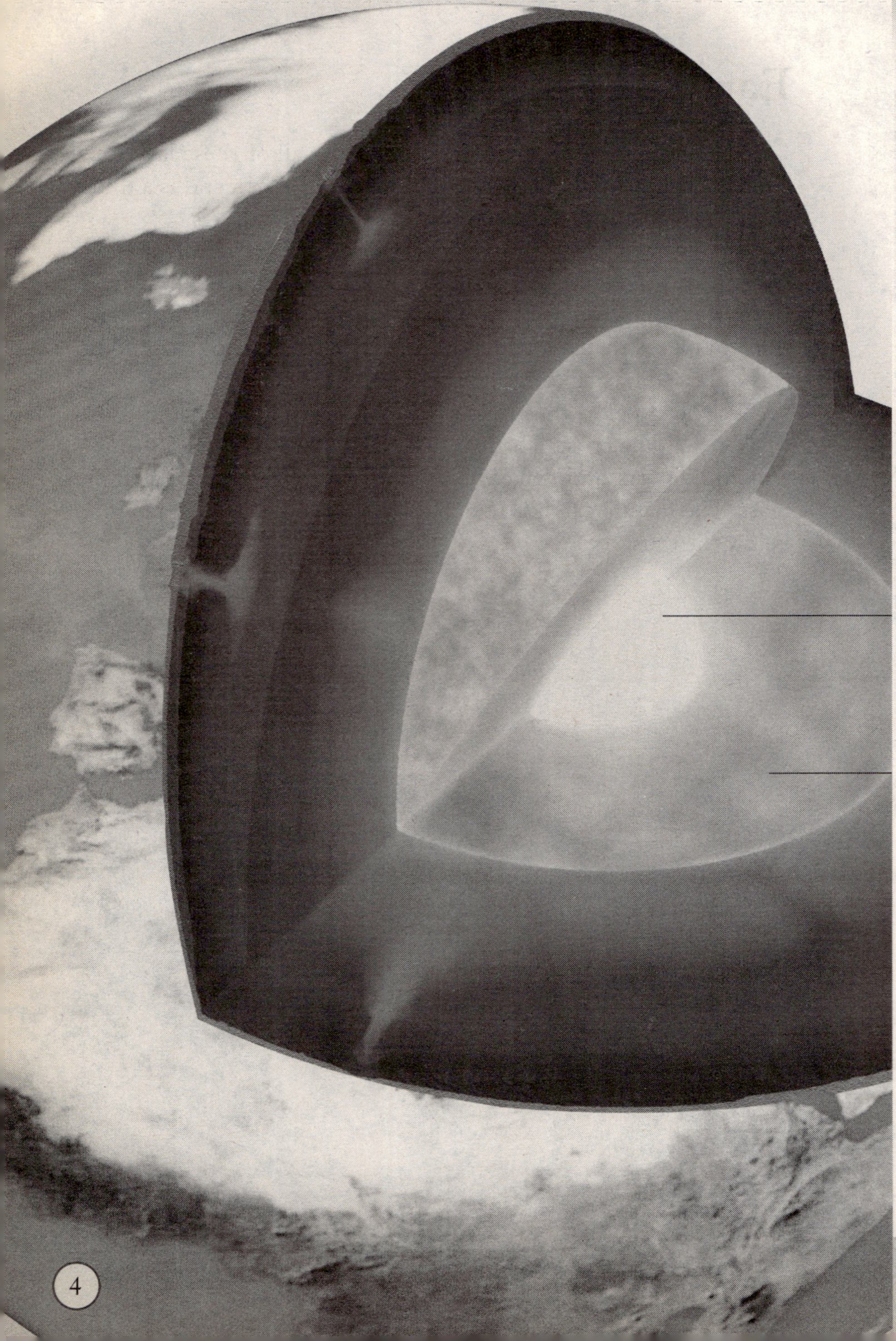

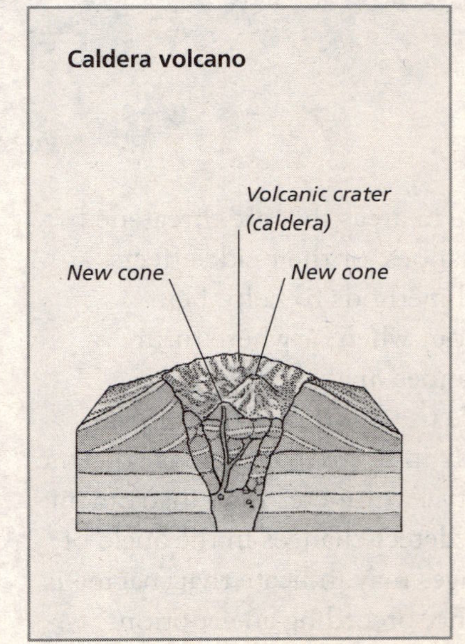

Ash cinder volcano
Slightly concave sides
Vent
Cinder
Fine ash

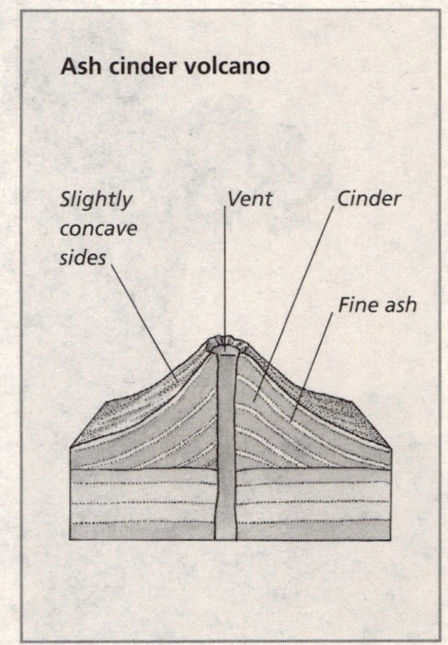

Shield volcano
Gentle slope built up by basaltic lava flows
Vent

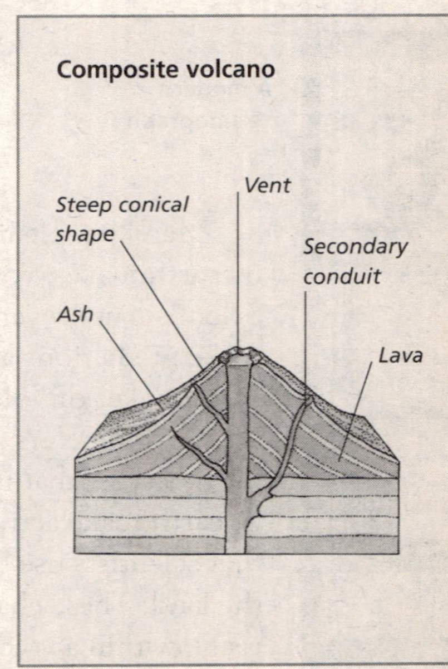

Caldera volcano
Volcanic crater (caldera)
New cone
New cone

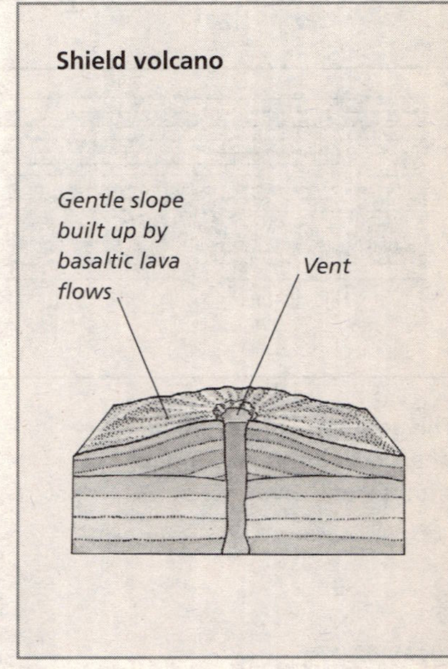

Composite volcano
Steep conical shape
Vent
Secondary conduit
Ash
Lava

Types of Volcanoes

When we think of volcanoes, most of us have a picture in our mind of a cone-shaped mountain that spews lava. However, volcanoes that have formed on land have many different shapes and sizes. This is mainly based on the way the volcano erupts, the frequency of the eruptions, and the makeup of the magma.

Composite volcanoes, such as Mount Fuji in Japan, shown below, repeatedly erupt from the same vent over long periods of time. Cinder cone volcanoes usually only erupt once. Shield volcanoes have gently sloping sides because they do not erupt with force. Lava flows out of shield volcanoes slowly and across large areas. Two examples of this type of volcano are the Hawaiian volcanoes Mauna Loa and Haleakala.

A caldera is a crater that forms after the ground collapses because of explosive eruptions. To be considered a caldera, the volcanic crater must be at least a kilometer wide, but some are over thirty-kilometers wide. Yellowstone National Park in Wyoming has several examples of calderas.

Volcanic plateaus may also form on land where lava flows out of a fissure vent. These plateaus can cover thousands of square kilometers.

Mount Fuji, Japan

Haleakala crater, Hawaii

Earth's **core** is made up of the inner core and the outer core. The core is the densest layer of Earth and is mainly composed of iron with smaller amounts of nickel, sulfur, and radioactive material. A combination of heat and pressure make the outer core a liquid mass. The inner core is a solid because the pressure is so great that the iron cannot melt. The temperature of the core is about 5,000°C.

Humans have never seen Earth below the crust layer, and scientists have theorized about Earth's composition by studying waves generated by earthquakes.

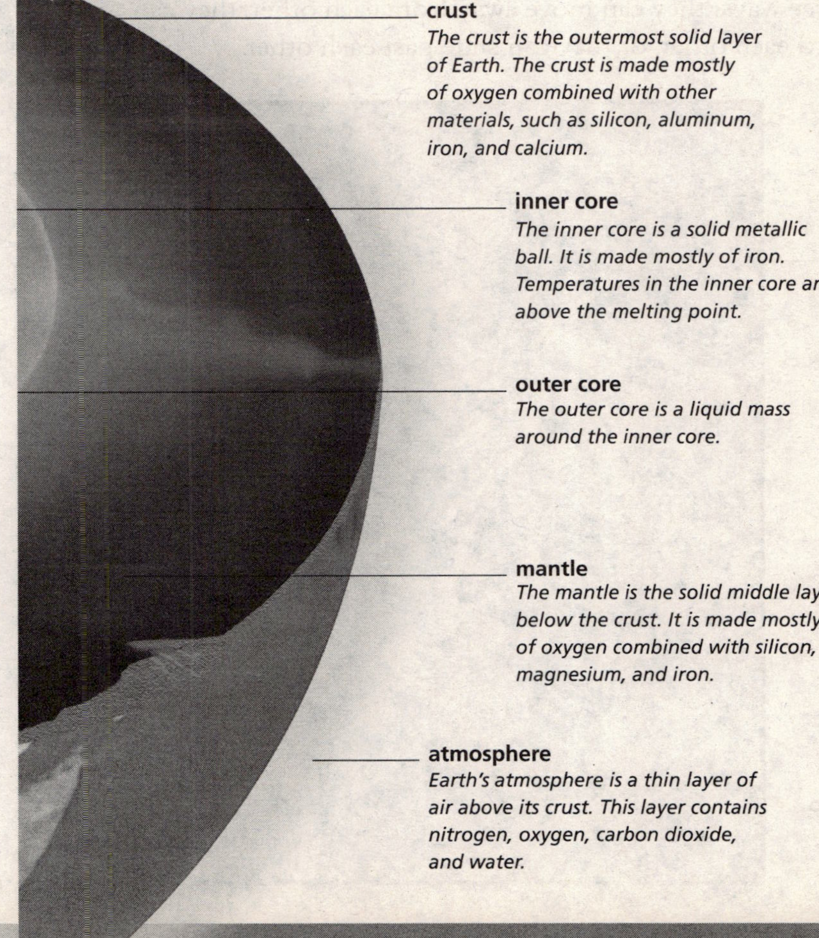

crust
The crust is the outermost solid layer of Earth. The crust is made mostly of oxygen combined with other materials, such as silicon, aluminum, iron, and calcium.

inner core
The inner core is a solid metallic ball. It is made mostly of iron. Temperatures in the inner core are above the melting point.

outer core
The outer core is a liquid mass around the inner core.

mantle
The mantle is the solid middle layer below the crust. It is made mostly of oxygen combined with silicon, magnesium, and iron.

atmosphere
Earth's atmosphere is a thin layer of air above its crust. This layer contains nitrogen, oxygen, carbon dioxide, and water.

Earth's Plates

The crust and the outermost solid part of the mantle are called the **lithosphere.**

Earth's lithosphere layer is broken up into pieces known as tectonic plates. Tectonic comes from the Greek word *tektonikos*, which means "builder." Earth has about twelve large plates and many smaller plates of different shapes and sizes. Most of Earth's plates are covered by water and are not visible when viewed from outer space.

Tectonic plates fit together like jigsaw puzzle pieces, and move around on Earth's surface over long periods of time. Plates can move in three ways: they can move away from each other, they can move toward each other, or they can slide past each other.

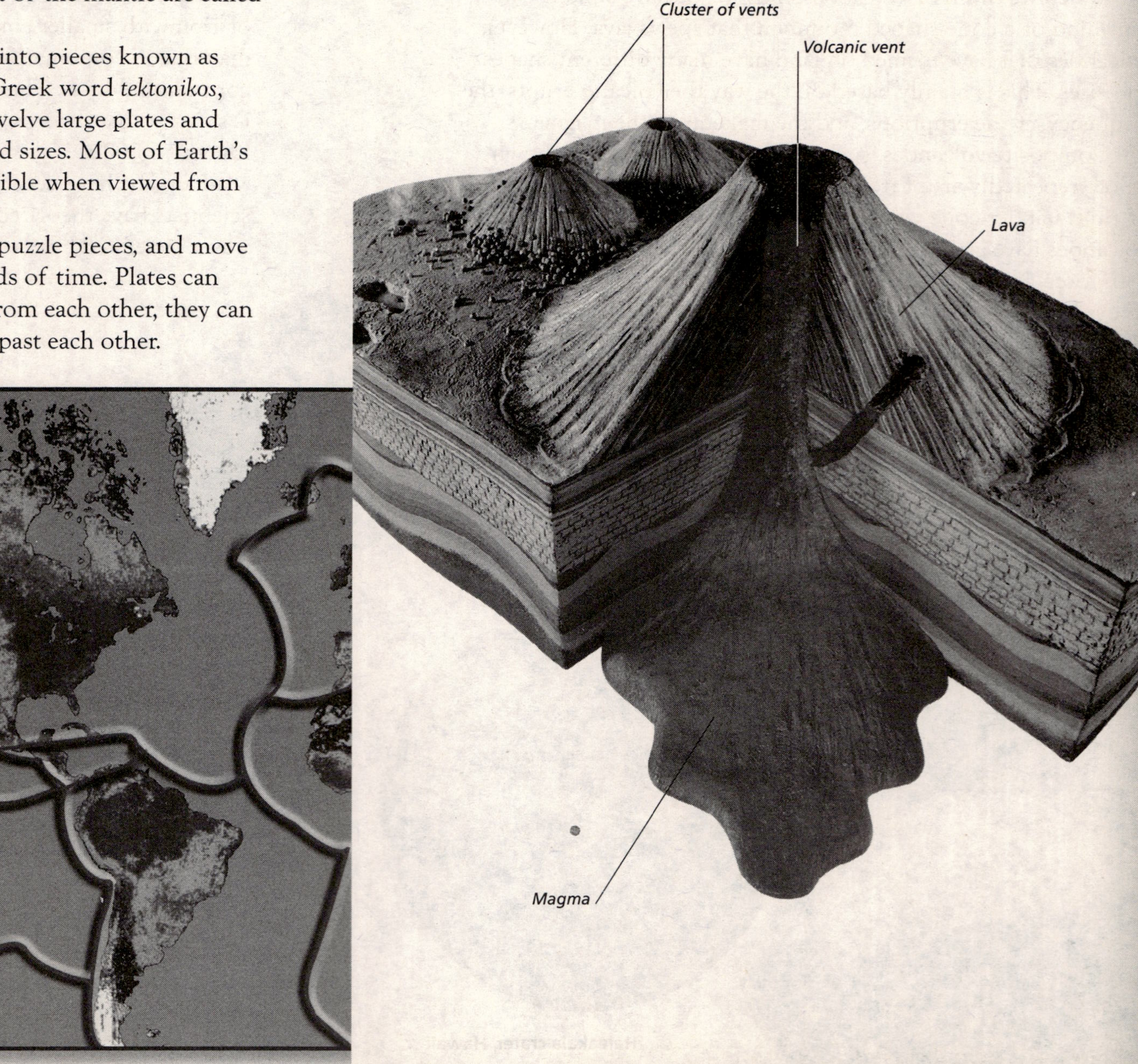

Earth's lithosphere is broken up into pieces like a jigsaw puzzle.

Volcanoes

Volcanoes form deep within Earth, usually in the upper part of the mantle. Magma, or molten rock, accumulates under high temperatures and pressures, and eventually rises to the surface of Earth. The theory of plate tectonics can help explain why most volcanoes occur near plate boundaries.

At locations where there are convergent plates boundaries, one plate may sink beneath another. This crust may eventually sink far enough to melt and become magma. Gases trapped in the magma cause pressure to build up, and the pressure can increase to such an extent that the crust cannot hold it. This pushes magma toward the surface through volcanoes. Magma that reaches the surface is known as lava.

Magma can erupt from a single vent known as a volcanic vent, from a cluster of vents, or along one long crack, or fissure, in Earth's crust. Most volcanoes are found on divergent plate boundaries under the ocean and have grown to form mid-ocean ridges. As plates move away from each other, magma rises to the surface and cools. The lava forms new crust and the ridges become larger.

Some plates are made up of continental crust, which is the land that makes up the continents. This accounts for about 40 percent of Earth's surface. Continental crust is older, thicker, and less dense than oceanic crust.

Oceanic crust covers about 60 percent of Earth's surface. This type of crust makes up the floor of the ocean and is thinner and denser than continental crust. Oceanic crust is constantly produced in some places on the ocean floor. Magma rises through cracks and cools, forming new crust.

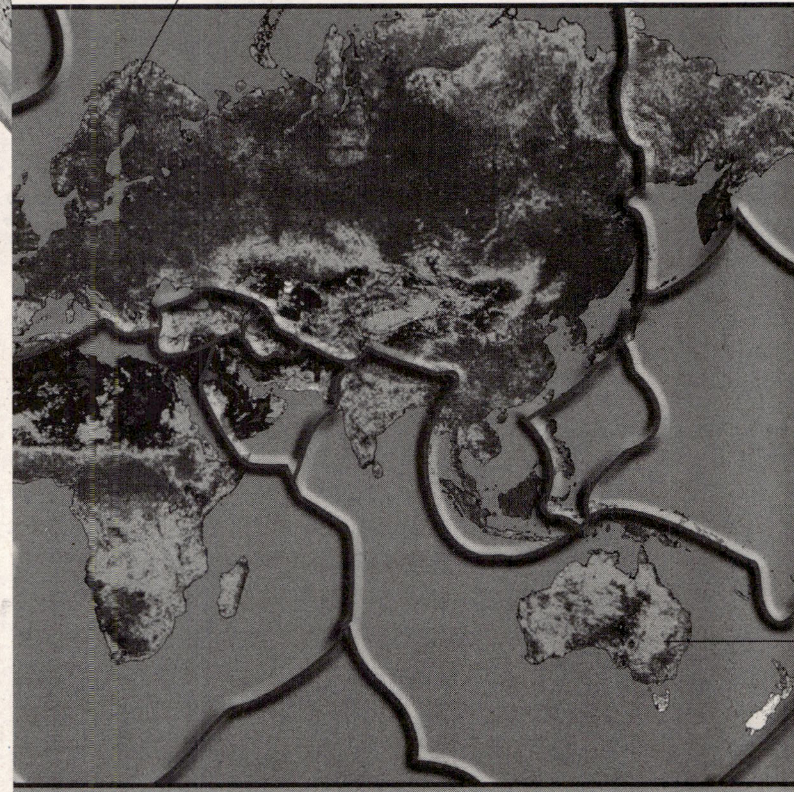

Earth's Landforms

Continents drift apart continuously, in slow motion. One of its effects may be the creation of landforms.

Continental Drift

In the past, most people thought that Earth's continents remained in the same place and did not move, but in the early 1500s explorers started to notice that the continents of Africa and South America looked like they might fit together. It wasn't until the 1900s that a comprehensive explanation was developed.

In 1912, a German scientist named Alfred Wegener proposed that about 200 million to 225 million years ago the continents were joined together as one continent he named Pangaea. Wegener theorized that Pangaea broke apart and shifted to form the continents as we know them today. This theory is known as **continental drift.**

Wegener did not have any firm proof that continental drift had occurred, but several other pieces of evidence supported his theory. Rocks of the same age and type were found on the coastlines of South America and Africa. Fossils of similar animals and plants were also found along those areas.

Ultimately, Wegener could not explain what kind of forces could move such large land masses across Earth, and many scientists rejected the theory of continental drift.

the earthquake originates. The epicenter is the point on Earth's surface right above the focus.

The study of earthquakes is known as seismology, from the Greek word *seismos*, "to shake." About one thousand instruments known as seismographs are used around the world to detect earthquakes. About one million mild earthquakes are recorded each year. About twenty moderate earthquakes occur each year. Major earthquakes happen once every few years.

Seismologists compare measurements taken at several different locations to determine an earthquake's epicenter and magnitude. The strength of an earthquake is measured using the Richter scale, which measures the height of seismic surface waves. It uses a series of numbers from zero to nine, and each whole number on the scale represents a tenfold increase in strength.

The Causes Of Earthquakes And Volcanoes

Earthquakes

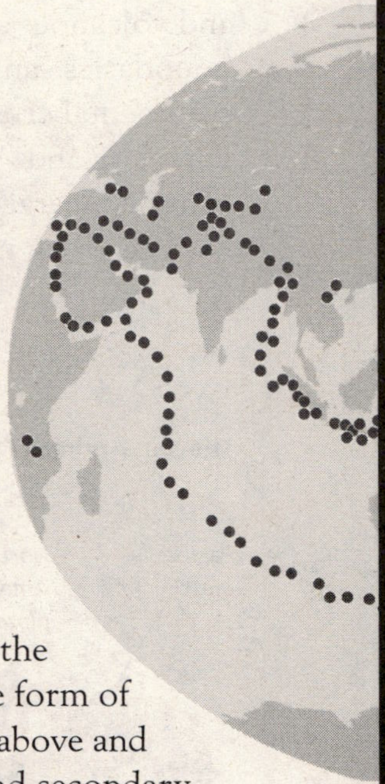

Tectonic plates move so slowly that you cannot feel or see the movement. Some plates may also stop moving if the edges of the lithosphere get caught against each other. An earthquake happens when this energy and pressure build up and eventually release suddenly, shaking Earth.

During an earthquake, the rapid movement of the rocks transmits energy through Earth's crust in the form of waves. There are several types of waves that travel above and below the surface of Earth. Primary, or P waves, and secondary, or S waves, are body waves that travel below Earth's surface.

How an earthquake happens

P waves move the ground back and forth and are the fastest type of wave. S waves may move the ground up and down, or in a circular motion.

Waves lose energy as they spread out from the epicenter, so the damage caused by earthquakes is greatest at their point of origin. Aftershocks, or smaller earthquakes that happen after the initial earthquake, are caused by strain on the rocks after the original earthquake.

The focus of the earthquake is the point within Earth along the fault where

Scientists believe that 200 million years ago Earth had only one continent called Pangaea. This continent broke apart to form the continents as they are today.

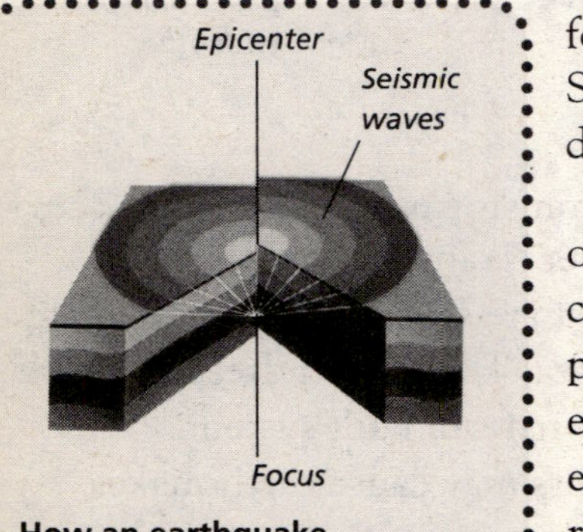

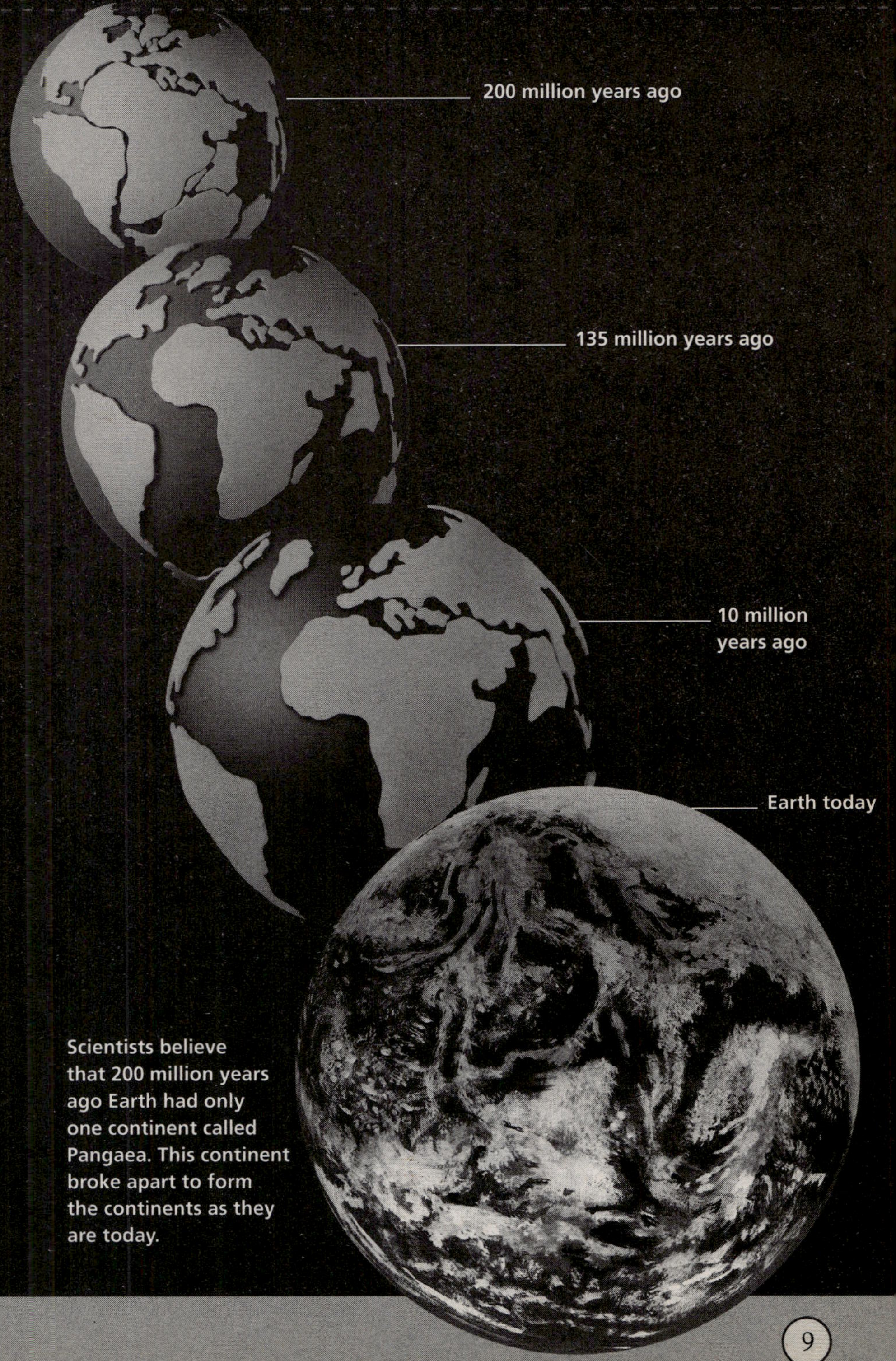

The Spreading Ocean Bottom

In the 1950s technology was developed that allowed scientists to map the ocean's floor. Long, deep trenches and mid-ocean ridges, or mountains, were discovered. These discoveries supported Wegener's theory of continental drift.

American geologist Harry Hess proposed that these ridges form when magma, or molten rock, pushes up through Earth's crust. The magma cools and forms a new crust that creates a ridge. Another scientist, Robert Dietz, named this process seafloor spreading. Hess also proposed that since the size of Earth remains the same, the crust must be recycled under mountains and along trenches on the ocean floor.

Proof of Continental Drift

As Earth's plates move, magma rises to fill the space. When a liquid is heated, particles that make up the liquid move faster and spread apart. Hot liquids are less dense than cooler liquids and float to the top. As the liquid cools, however, it becomes denser and sinks, moving in a circular pattern. The process responsible for this is known as convection.

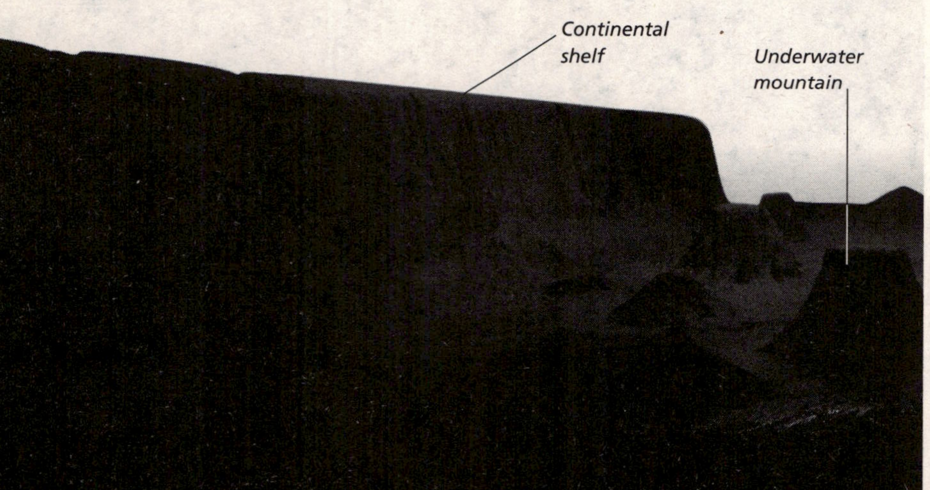

Convergent plate boundaries occur when plates are recycled back into Earth's mantle. Rock layers in these areas can fold, and volcanoes and earthquakes may occur. Convergent plate boundaries can also double the normal thickness of the continental crust, creating mountain ranges and plateaus. The Himalaya and Andes mountain ranges were both formed when plates converged. A **fault** is a crack in Earth's crust where there has been rock movement on either side.

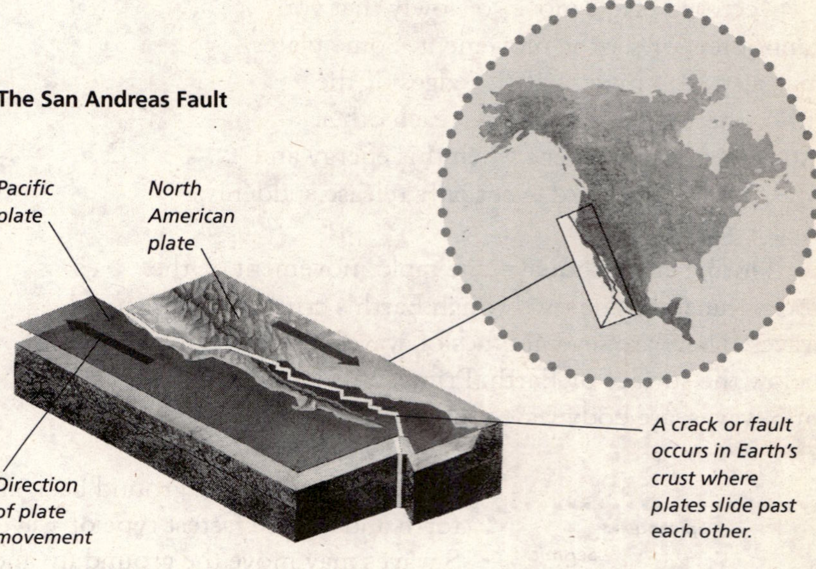

Transform plate boundaries, or transform fault systems, occur when two plates slide past one another. Transform faults may divide the centers of ocean ridges that are spreading or may create steep cliffs on mountains under the sea. The San Andreas Fault in California is another example of a transform fault system.

All three types of plate movements may cause earthquakes, although the frequency and magnitude are not the same in all areas. Volcanic activity usually occurs along convergent or divergent plate boundaries.

Plate Boundaries

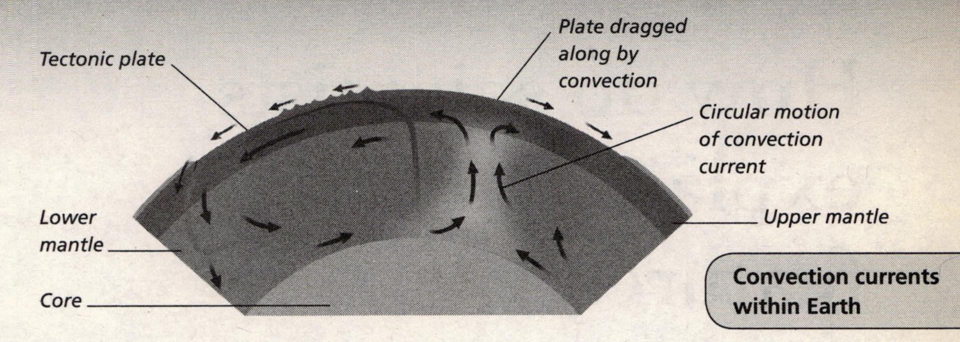

A **plate boundary** is the area where two plates meet. As you previously learned, the theory of plate tectonics states that plates can move in three ways: they can move away from each other, they can move toward each other, or they can slide past each other.

Divergent plate boundaries occur when plates move away from each other. When this occurs, magma rises to the surface, forming rift valleys on dry land and seafloor spreading in the ocean's crust. The Mid-Atlantic Ridge, found near the middle of the Atlantic Ocean, was created at a divergent plate boundary and is still spreading. The Great Rift Valley, found in the Middle East and Africa, was created after land shifted upward.

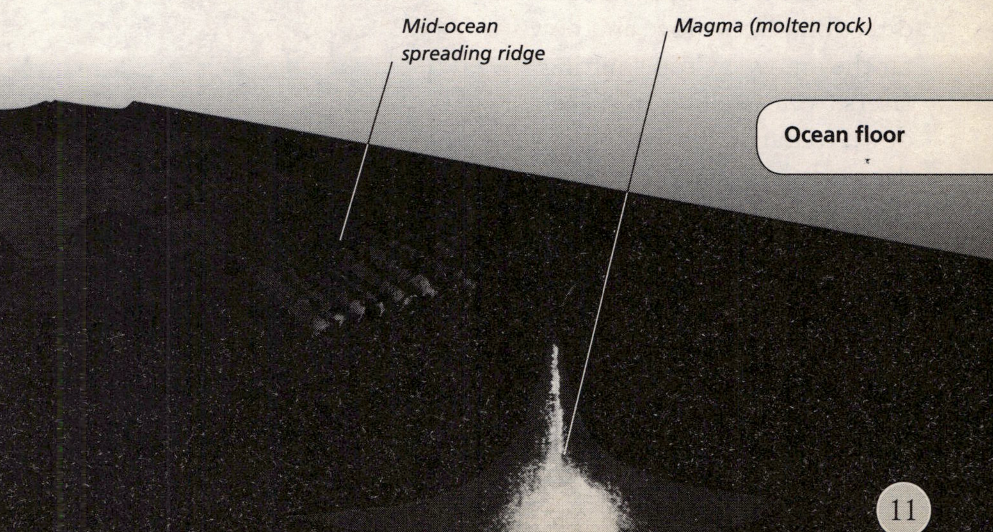

Convection is only one of the processes involved in plate movement. Scientists also believe that gravity plays a major role in the movement of tectonic plates. Since the plates are slightly cooler and denser than the layer of the mantle below them, they tend to slide down toward trenches and penetrate the mantle.

In the 1960s scientists found more evidence to support the concept of seafloor spreading. Scientists studying the rocks near the Mid-Atlantic Ridge noticed a strange pattern. In some areas the magnetism of the rocks pointed north. In other areas the magnetism pointed south. These areas form patterns that run parallel to the mid-ocean ridge and are the same on both sides of it. Earth's magnetism flips about once every half-million years. When magma cools to form new crust it keeps the magnetic pattern of the time it was formed. This caused the alternating bands of positive and negative rock to form. This showed that the crust is spreading and supports the theory of continental drift.

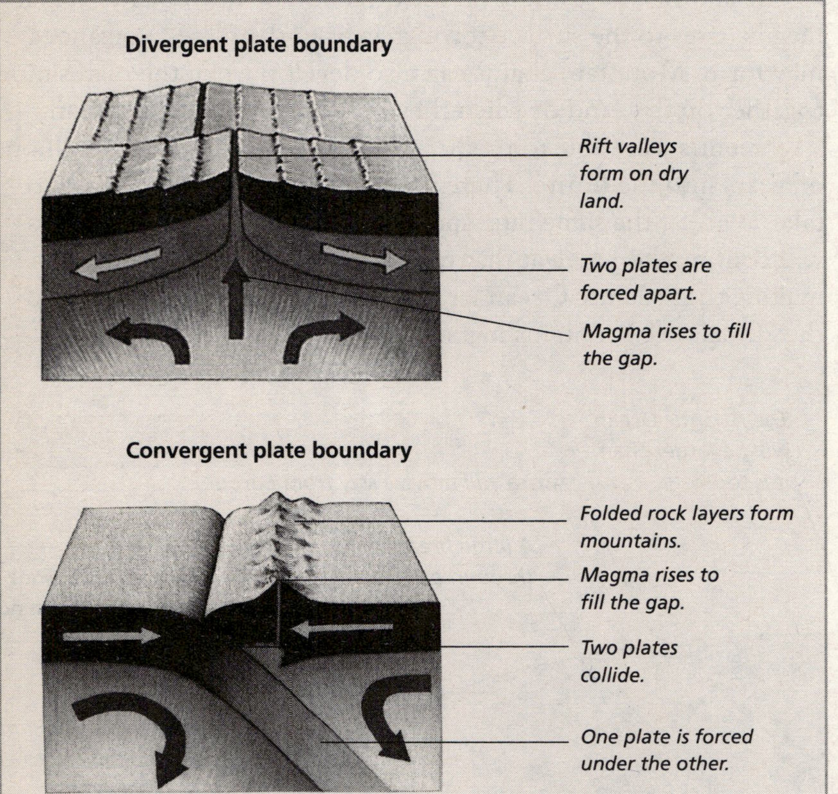

How do scientists explain Earth's features?

The theory of continental drift was integral to understanding how and why the ocean floor spreads, but it cannot explain other features of Earth's crust.

Plate Tectonics Explanation

Scientists use the theory of **plate tectonics** to explain why the features of Earth look the way they do and why certain geological events happen.

Earth's lithosphere is made up of about twenty moving plates. Some, such as the North American plate, are the size of continents. Others, such as the Caribbean plate, are much smaller. These plates float on a layer of partly melted rock. They move in a continuous motion in different directions. The surfaces of these plates form the continents and the ocean floor. Scientists can determine the direction plates move and how far they move by transmitting lasers from satellites in space down to Earth. For example, data indicates that the North American plate and the Eurasian plate are moving about 2.5 centimeters apart each year.

As the plates shift, continents may separate or move closer to one another, depending on the direction of movement. When magma rises to the surface through gaps in the plates, volcanoes may form. Mountain chains can also develop when the plates move together on dry land or when they move together in the ocean.

Scientists are able to predict what Earth may look like millions of years into the future. There is evidence that continental drift takes place at the same rate, and scientists predict that the plates will continue to move at that rate. Currently, plate movement is making the Atlantic Ocean larger, the Pacific Ocean smaller, and the Himalaya Mountains higher.

MINERALS AND ROCKS

by Lucy Ann Sibson

Genre	Comprehension Skill	Text Features	Science Content
Nonfiction	Compare and Contrast	• Captions • Charts • Diagrams • Glossary	Rocks and Minerals

Scott Foresman Science 6.9

PEARSON

Scott Foresman

scottforesman.com

ISBN 0-328-13995-5

90000

9 780328 139958

What did you learn?

Vocabulary

crystals
humus
igneous rock
metamorphic rock
mineral
organic matter
rock
sedimentary rock

1. What are the three main types of rocks?

2. What are the three main layers of soil?

3. Use the vocabulary words to write a short newspaper article that urges students to look carefully at the geology around them.

4. **Writing** in Science Igneous rocks form when molten earth hardens. Write to explain where igneous rocks are formed. Discuss how igneous rocks form in ways that are dangerous to human and animal habitats. Include details from the book as well as your own opinions about how human and animal needs intersect with how rocks are formed.

5. **Compare and Contrast** Compare and contrast how desert and valley soils form. List the similarities and differences in chart form and then write a few sentences that sum up what you know.

Picture Credits
Every effort has been made to secure permission and provide appropriate credit for photographic material.
The publisher deeply regrets any omission and pledges to correct errors called to its attention in subsequent editions.

Photo locators denoted as follows: Top (T), Center (C), Bottom (B), Left (L), Right (R), Background (Bkgd).

6 (T) Digital Stock; 7 Getty Images; 9 Getty Images; 15 ©David Muench/Corbis.

Unless otherwise acknowledged, all photographs are the copyright © of Dorling Kindersley, a division of Pearson.

ISBN: 0-328-13995-5

Copyright © Pearson Education, Inc.

MINERALS AND ROCKS

by Lucy Ann Sibson

Glossary

crystals	materials with a repeating angles and flat surfaces
humus	a brown or black organic substance consisting of decaying plant or animal matter
igneous rock	a rock that was formed from a molten state
metamorphic rock	a sedimentary or igneous rock that changes due to heat, pressure, and chemical reactions
mineral	a natural inorganic substance having a definite chemical composition
organic matter	a material that is derived from living organisms
rock	a natural, solid material formed when one or more minerals come together
sedimentary rock	pieces of rocks and minerals that form in layers and are good depositories for fossils.

What are minerals and rocks?

Minerals

Whether you realize it or not, you are already familiar with many **minerals.** Iron, aluminum, copper, gold, silver, and diamonds are just a few you probably know off the top of your head. Other materials you might think are "minerals" are actually a combination of minerals, such as steel and brass. What makes up a mineral? How do some minerals form together to become rocks?

A mineral is a nonliving solid with a definite chemical structure. Each kind of mineral is made up of particles that are arranged in a different way. These differences result in more than four thousand kinds of minerals. About two hundred of these are recognized as common minerals; thirty occur frequently enough to be considered rock-forming minerals. But only around twenty-five minerals are commonly found on Earth's surface. Some you see every day, such as nickel, copper, and graphite—the material used to make the center of the pencils on your desk!

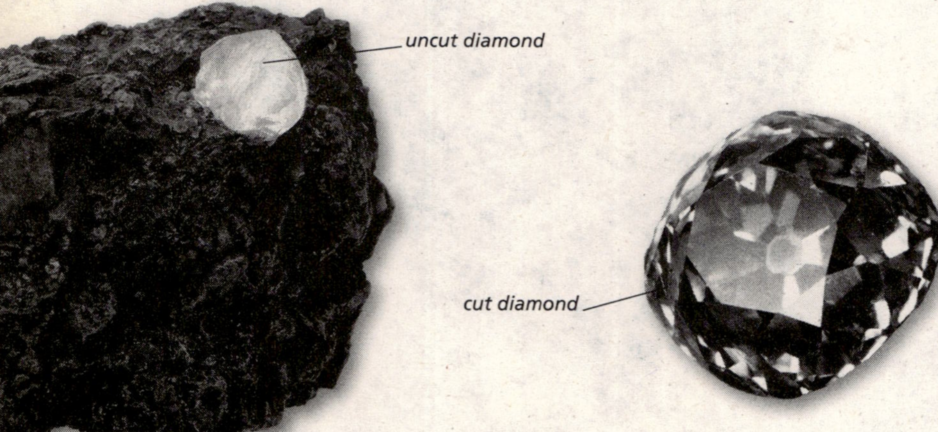

uncut diamond

cut diamond

Factors that Affect Soil

An area's climate is probably the most important factor in how soil forms. Topsoil in a tropical region is thin and weak. Where there is a lot of rain and high temperatures, minerals are more quickly washed from topsoil down into the subsoil. Desert areas don't get much rain; the weathering process there occurs much more slowly. Rain, when it falls, evaporates fast. The minerals that are deposited by the rain tend to collect on the soil's surface.

The kinds of rocks and minerals in a soil contribute to what the soil looks like. For example, if you see a soil that is red, you know that it was made from minerals rich in iron, which has a distinctive red color to it. Regions with humus-filled soil, such as the eastern forest regions of the United States, are known for their dark soils.

Still another factor that affects how soils form is geography. In mountainous regions, there is usually only a thin layer of topsoil. This is because soil erodes easily down the slopes of the mountains. In valleys or other flatlands, there is usually a thick, plentiful layer of topsoil.

Kinds of Soils

Because there are so many different kinds of rocks and minerals, it makes sense that there are many different kinds of soils. One type is clay. This kind of soil is fine grained and holds water very well. When a lot of rain falls, clay soils become full of water and can resemble modeling clay. Clay soils are full of nutrients and support many different types of living organisms, but can be too hard for plant roots to push through. Silt soils have medium sized grains. They drain fairly well. Sandy soils have the largest grains. They do not hold water well. Still, they do contain nutrients, and some plants thrive in sandy soils. Most soils are actually mixtures of clay, silt, and sand. Loam is soil that contains roughly equal parts of all three kinds of soils. It is useful in planting and farming.

Desert plants can survive in dry, sandy soil.

How to Tell Minerals Apart

Minerals can be distinguished from one another by their particular characteristics. Minerals are made up of crystals that have distinct shapes. **Crystals** are materials with repeating angles and flat surfaces into which many substances solidify. They vary in size due to how they form.

A mineral's hardness is an important property. Talc is the softest mineral on the Mohs hardness scale, which ranks ten common minerals. On the other end of the scale is a diamond, the hardest mineral known.

The materials that form a mineral's crystals determine its color. A mineral's true color can best be seen in its streak, the mark it makes when it is rubbed against tile. For example, galena and hematite are minerals that both appear similar in color. However, the streak of galena is a steely gray and that of hematite is a deep red. Both color and streak help us to identify minerals.

Another property that distinguishes minerals is the shape of the crystal. Certain minerals form distinct shapes. For example, the mineral siderite forms in a rhombohedron shape, resembling a slightly crushed box. A diamond in nature is always an octagonal shape. Diamonds crystallize in the isometric (cubic) system, and form cubes and octahedra—eight-sided crystals.

talc

hematite

siderite

Cleavage is also a characteristic used to distinguish minerals. Some minerals tend to split, or cleave, along flat planes. They split in patterns that scientists can recognize. Other minerals do not split. Instead they break into uneven bits, in a process called fracture.

Luster is a another property of minerals. This describes how a mineral looks. It may be metallic, or nonmetallic, greasy, or waxy. Still other minerals are known for their odor; sulfur may be the best example. Some minerals appear to have different colors when exposed to ultraviolet light. And several minerals, including platinum and tantalite, are magnetic.

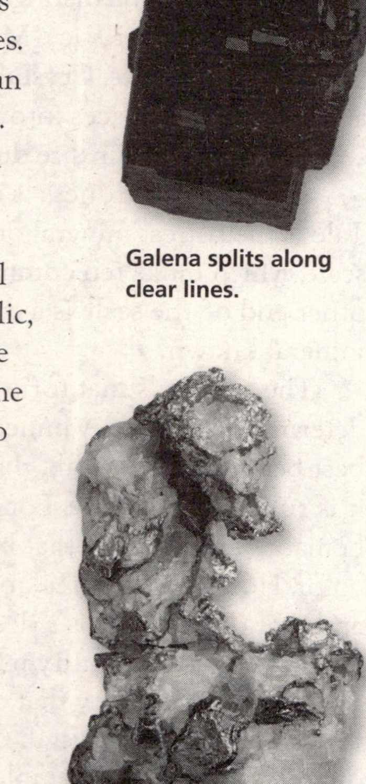

Galena splits along clear lines.

The veins of gold on this quartz have a metallic luster.

Sulfur has a very strong odor.

Platinum is a magnetic mineral.

The outermost layer is called topsoil, which contains small rocks, humus, and other matter. Most things that live in soil, from tulips planted as bulbs to worms, live in topsoil. Loose matter, such as acorns, twigs, leaves, and branches, covers topsoil and protects it from the harshest weather conditions. Rainwater, though, can penetrate the covering and will carry minerals through the topsoil and into the second layer of soil.

This second layer of soil is called subsoil. It is lighter in color. That is because it has less organic matter in it; organic matter, you will remember, is what gives soil its rich, dark color. Minerals carried from topsoil are stored in the subsoil. So scientists can study the subsoil and find good sources of minerals as well as information about what the minerals are composed of.

The bottom layer of soil is actually made up of the parent rock. There is very little organic material in this layer. The rocks themselves are of interest to scientists, who study them to find out about their properties.

Recall that sedimentary rock forms in layers. Soil also forms in several layers. The three main soil layers are topsoil, subsoil, and parent rock, which is also called bedrock. A soil profile, which is a cross section of the soil and rock that lies beneath it, can show you what is inside any sample of soil. Each soil layer is different, both in color and composition.

Rocks

Most minerals are not usually found in their pure forms in nature. Instead, they are mixed with other minerals into **rocks.** There are three types of rocks: sedimentary, igneous, and metamorphic.

Pieces of rocks and minerals that form in layers are examples of **sedimentary rock.** In a sedimentary rock formation, the oldest layers are at the bottom. Sedimentary rocks are good depositories for fossils, the remaining evidence of plants or animals that lived in the past. One sedimentary rock is limestone. It is made up of sea animal shells and minerals from seawater.

When molten rock, or magma, inside Earth cools and then hardens, it forms **igneous rock.** This type of rock is found in volcanic eruptions. It is also found below Earth's surface and is exposed when layers of rock above it are worn away.

Sedimentary rock forms in layers made from pieces of rocks or rocks and minerals. This shelly limestone contains many fossils.

Volcanoes push new rock onto Earth's surface.

Metamorphic rock forms when heat, pressure, or chemical reactions change rocks from one type to another. Both sedimentary and igneous rocks form metamorphic rock. The sedimentary rock limestone can be changed to become marble, while sandstone can become quartzite.

Though solid, rocks can continually change. The minerals that make them up change over time in a process called the rock cycle. These changes take place over millions of years. Rocks break down and the minerals in them are recycled.

The living parts of soil are very important, as well. Bacteria, fungi, and plants can grow in this mixture of air, water, and rock. These organisms will eventually die as the process known as decay begins. What is left after the organism dies is known as **organic matter,** meaning that it is made of things that live or once lived. One type of organic matter is **humus,** which is dark in color and is formed from plant and animal remains. It is an important part of the soil because it contains nutrients plants need to grow.

Why is soil so important to living things?

Forming Soil

The rock cycle is one important cycle of which rocks are a part. Another cycle is that which produces soil. This happens as rock begins to break down. This process, called weathering, can be due to frost, drought (lack of moisture), or temperature changes. Water and materials dissolved in it can also break down rocks. Over time, the rock that forms mountains is weathered and broken into smaller and smaller pieces. Air and water fill in the spaces between the little pieces of rock. Air, water, and rock make up the inorganic, or nonliving, part of soil.

Clues to the Past

Each and every rock you see can tell a different story about what happened as far back as millions and millions of years ago or as little as a year or two ago. You may have been to a lake and seen pebble-sized rocks in a lakebed that look small, rounded, and well polished. A year or two earlier, they would not have looked exactly the same. A century earlier, they would have been larger still. These rocks tell a little bit of the story of life in a lake.

The best place to look for clues to Earth's history is in sedimentary rock. Remember that sedimentary rock forms in layers. Geologists know that the bottom layers of sedimentary rock are the oldest. Using a method called relative dating, scientists find out the relative age of each layer and the materials found within it. This helps scientists to sequence, or order, the events in Earth's history. Many places in the southwestern United States have sedimentary rock formations that tell Earth's story dramatically. These locations include Arches, Bryce Canyon, and Capitol Reef national parks in Utah.

Arches National Park, Utah

The wind has created this unusual rock formation.

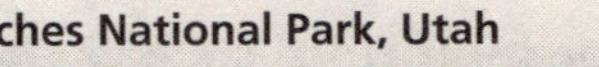
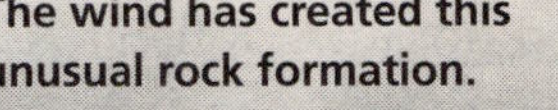

cephalopod

trilobite

Fossils

An animal or plant whose remains are buried in mud becomes a fossil. Fossils are usually the hard parts—the bones, wood, or shells—of living things. They do not lose their shape or disappear. Other types of fossils can be footprints, such as those of dinosaurs. When fossils form underwater minerals can harden to replace parts of the buried plants or animals.

Fossils can be made of recently deceased organisms, or they can be made of organisms that are now extinct. Scientists study how and where these fossils are found to help determine the age of the organism. Scientists who find a fossil from a creature called a paleoparadoxia know that the rock that surrounds it must be from around the same time the creature lived. Since paleoparadoxia lived between eight million and twelve million years ago, the rock, and things buried in it, must also be that old.

Space Rocks

Did you know that rocks have been found on the Moon and other places in outer space? The largest of these kinds of rocks, meteors, can travel through space, and some have even struck Earth. When they have done so, they have created large dents, known as craters, in Earth's surface. Throughout the world, there are many examples of meteor craters. Recently the Silverpit crater was discovered in the North Sea. It is nearly twenty kilometers wide. It is believed that the crater was created when a meteor fell from the sky sixty to sixty-five million years ago. Meteor Crater, in Arizona, is nearly twelve hundred meters in diameter and 180 meters deep. It was formed by a large meteorite between five thousand and fifty thousand years ago.

Meteor Crater, Arizona

The Ever-Changing Surface of Earth

by L. L. Owens

Genre	Comprehension Skill	Text Features	Science Content
Nonfiction	Draw Conclusions	• Captions • Diagrams • Glossary	Earth's Surface

Scott Foresman Science 6.10

PEARSON

Scott Foresman

DK

ISBN 0-328-13998-X

9 780328 139989

90000

scottforesman.com

What did you learn?

1. What are some examples of landforms?

2. What is one of the primary causes of erosion?

3. What are sediments?

4. **Writing** in Science The weathering process breaks down rock into smaller pieces. Write to explain the difference between mechanical weathering and chemical weathering. Include details from the book to support your answer.

5. **Draw Conclusions** Soil erosion is part of the weathering process, which is caused by wind, water, ice, and gravity. What happens to soil without plants?

Vocabulary

chemical weathering
deposition
erosion
mechanical weathering
sediments
weathering

Picture Credits
Every effort has been made to secure permission and provide appropriate credit for photographic material.
The publisher deeply regrets any omission and pledges to correct errors called to its attention in subsequent editions.

Photo locators denoted as follows: Top (T), Center (C), Bottom (B), Left (L), Right (R), Background (Bkgd).

4 ©Vince Streano/Corbis; 7 (CL) ©Jeremy Horner/Corbis, (T) ©James L. Amos/Corbis; 12 Digital Vision;
14 ©Richard Cooke/Alamy Images; 15 Digital Vision.

Unless otherwise acknowledged, all photographs are the copyright © of Dorling Kindersley, a division of Pearson.

ISBN: 0-328-13998-X

Glossary

chemical weathering	the process by which the minerals that make up rock are changed
deposition	the process of adding sediments that began in one place to another place
erosion	the process by which soil and sediments are moved from one place to another
mechanical weathering	the process by which forces such as wind, water, and ice break down rock without changing its makeup
sediments	particles of rock and soil that are moved from place to place by wind, water or glaciers, or gravity
weathering	the process of breaking down rock into smaller pieces

The Ever-Changing Surface of Earth

by L. L. Owens

PEARSON
Scott Foresman

DK

How Earth's Surface Changes over Time

Landforms

Take a look outside. What do you see when you look at the ground? Is it flat in every direction? Do you see any hills— or any holes? One thing is certain: you will see something different on Earth's surface wherever you look.

Earth's surface is made up of many different natural features, or landforms. Examples of landforms include mountains, canyons, plateaus, caves, beaches, and valleys. The landforms change over time. The changes happen both suddenly and slowly.

glaciers in Mount Rainier National Park, Washington State

Beaches: Dynamic Systems

Beaches are another part of Earth's surface affected by the constant influences of wind and moving water. They contain such varied coastal landforms as dunes, sandbars, bluffs, and cliffs.

Wind can blow large amounts of loose sand into huge piles, or dunes, along a beach's edge. Its force can also slowly wear away at landforms. Wind can shape interesting rock formations and imposing cliffs that seem to hang in midair.

Large ocean waves can be powerful enough to cause cracks in rocks. Even large rocks can break into smaller pieces due to constant exposure to high-energy waves. Of course, this process usually takes a long time, but it shows you just how strong waves can be.

Beaches are also changed over time by the sediments carried in waves. The stones and sand that make up the sediments act like a file, wearing away the solid surfaces they pass over.

Beaches change over time.

Earth's surface is constantly changing. Some changes take place instantly, such as when a sudden heavy rain causes mud to slide down a steep hill. Other changes take place slowly, over hundreds and thousands of years. River waters rushing over land slowly carry and deposit **sediments,** solid particles that are moved from one place to another. Rivers shift their course or cut deep into the land, forming canyons.

Glaciers that moved through the east-central region shared by the United States and Canada formed the Great Lakes in North America. As the huge masses of ice made their way across the area, they slowly carved out what is now one of the largest sources of fresh water in the world. The Great Lakes include Lakes Superior, Michigan, Huron, Erie, and Ontario.

These waves carry a lot of energy.

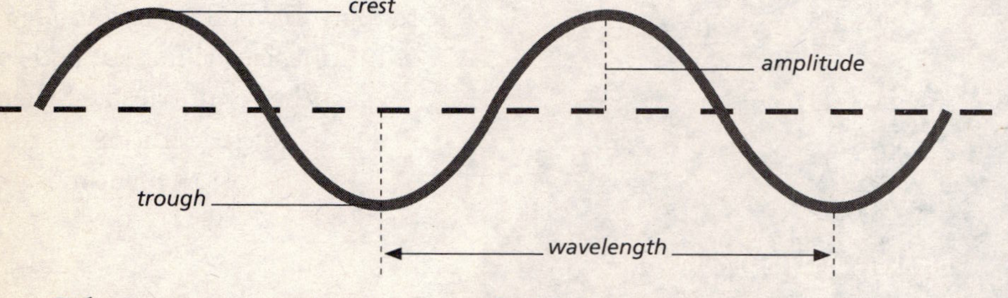

Characteristics of Waves

The diagram above illustrates characteristics shared by all waves, including water waves.

In any wave, the crest is the highest part, and the trough is the lowest part. The heavy dotted line on the diagram shows the position of the water before a wave passes through it. A wave's amplitude is the distance between this line and either the crest or the trough. As waves gain energy from the wind, their amplitude increases.

Wavelength is the distance between a given point on a wave to the corresponding point on the next wave. To measure wavelength, all you need to do is find the distance from one crest to the next. You can also measure wavelength by determining the distance from trough to trough.

Weathering

Many changes to Earth's surface happen over long periods of time. Sometimes significant changes—such as the formation of the Grand Canyon over many millions of years—cannot be easily measured. **Weathering** is the physical process that causes such dramatic, long-range alterations to Earth's surface. This happens when rock breaks down into smaller pieces. It can occur as either a mechanical process or a chemical process.

During **mechanical weathering,** rock breaks down due to the physical movement of wind, water, and ice over the rock. Although the rock breaks down into smaller pieces, the minerals that make up the rock do not change. In regions that experience cold winters and warm summers, such as the Yukon Territory in Canada, water repeatedly freezes and thaws within the tiny cracks naturally found in rock. The force of the water expanding in a crack as it freezes causes the crack to deepen and widen. Eventually the rock can be broken.

What Causes Waves

Most waves you see at the beach are usually caused by the wind. They form out on the open ocean, when wind touches the water and causes an energy transfer. This transfer results in waves. The faster the wind is blowing, the bigger the waves.

Tectonic activity in Earth's crust also causes waves. Examples include underwater landslides, earthquakes, and volcanic eruptions. Tectonic activity can result in dangerously high and fast-moving waves called tsunamis. A tsunami that reaches shore can cause severe damage. Two of the largest tsunamis in U.S. history hit Alaska in 1964 and Hawaii in 1960. One of the most destructive tsunamis of all time occurred in the Indian Ocean in December 2004. More than 170,000 people in Indonesia, Sri Lanka, and other countries lost their lives. Millions more lost their homes.

breakers in Natal, South Africa

Wave energy

How Waves Affect Coastal Landforms

Ocean waves hit the coast with great force. They steadily wear down landforms along the coast. But they also build up new ones.

Do you know what it feels like to have an ocean wave hit you? A weak or slow-moving wave can splash onto your toes and barely cause you to move. A strong, fast-moving wave, however, can cover your head and knock you over. Now think about how ocean waves—of all speeds and sizes—might affect coastal landforms. Through erosion, waves wear down and build up coastal landforms, causing their surfaces to change over time.

Wave Energy

If you watch ocean waves, you might think that the water moves along with the waves. But this isn't so. Only the energy moves. The water stays in the same spot. It rises and falls in a circular motion. You can see how this works by studying the diagram. As a wave nears shore, the water moves slightly forward and then downward and then back. The water rises and falls in a circular motion, making a loop. Each time a wave passes, the water ends up just about where it began.

As waves move toward the shore, the ocean bottom gets in the way. It interferes with the pattern of the waves' movements. The ocean floor makes the bottom parts of waves slow down. But the tops of the waves keep moving quickly. This causes the tops to tumble forward. Finally the waves crash at the shore in the form of breakers. This is the part of the wave you can see.

Rock also breaks down as a result of **chemical weathering,** but during this process the minerals that make up the rock change. Chemical weathering occurs more frequently in warmer climates. For example, rock formations in Nevada's Valley of Fire State Park were broken down and turned red due to the effects of chemical weathering. This happened when oxygen in the air reacted with iron in the rock.

Erosion

Erosion occurs when wind, water, ice, and gravity carry soil and sediments from one place to another. Eroded materials can travel long distances down mountainsides and across valleys, changing the surface of Earth. These changes can take decades, centuries, and even millions of years!

Erosion can also happen quickly. Soil without plants can be washed away by wind and water. This can damage an ecosystem or ruin farmland. To prevent this, farmers plant cover crops in fields that are not in use.

Valley of Fire State Park, Nevada

How Water Affects Earth's Features

The force of moving water is one of the primary causes of erosion. Erosion results in major changes to Earth's features. Water running downhill carries and deposits sediment. Gravity pulls these small pieces of sediment through Earth's complex systems of streams and rivers. As rock and soil move, they change the face of Earth. Sediment in the moving water can act like a file, wearing down the rocks and the riverbed as it passes. Some changes take place so slowly that they can't be measured by the human eye—or even within a human's lifetime.

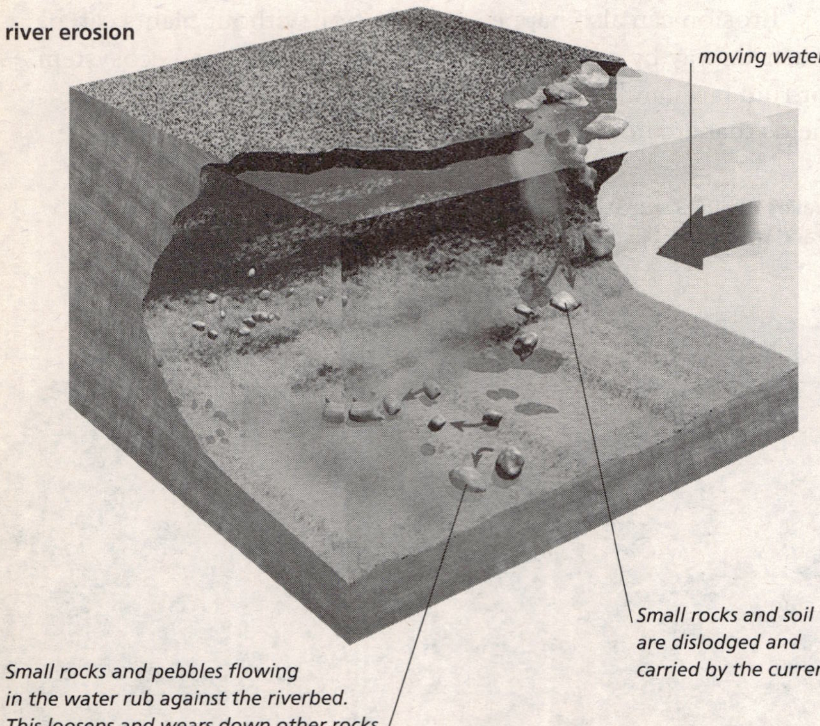

The Ganges River divides into thousands of smaller channels that spread into a delta about 400 km wide. The river channels empty into the Indian Ocean.

River Systems

Like Earth's surface, Earth's systems of rivers and streams are dynamic. That means they are constantly changing.

A stream begins on land that is above sea level. Gravity causes its water to flow downward toward sea level. Multiple streams can flow together to form a river. A river carries sediments through its waters as it breaks down rock and soil into smaller particles.

Sediments are left behind in different spots along a river's path. This deposition process happens as the water slows down. Waters often slow down at low areas, such as the mouth of a river. As water movement slows, the water contains less energy, and its ability to carry sediment decreases. Heavy sediments such as boulders and rocks are deposited first. Lighter sediments such as tiny pebbles and fine grains of soil travel greater distances.

Landforms called deltas form when large amounts of sediment accumulate at the mouth of a river. The Mississippi Delta, for example, extends beyond the coastline where the Mississippi River flows into the Gulf of Mexico.

Floodplains

Sometimes excess rain adds too much water to rivers and streams, and this results in flooding. Because there's so much energy in floodwaters, they can move large amounts of sediments along rivers and streams.

The part of the landscape most likely to hold overflow and sediment from a flooded river is a floodplain. A floodplain is an area of flat land adjacent to a stream or a river. Living in a floodplain includes both benefits and risks. Some farmers rely on the nutrients deposited in the soil by floodwaters. The extra nutrients help them grow healthy crops. But dangerous flood levels can sometimes cause loss of homes and other property, injury, and even death.

braided river sections

The garbage and small rocks in this picture were deposited by the moving water.

Deposition

Moving water carries and drops sediment as it flows downhill. The process of dropping sediment in a new place is called **deposition.** Deposition can change the shape and direction of flow. Sediment includes rocks—from small pebbles and stones to huge boulders—soil, such as silt or mud, and almost anything else moving water picks up, from plant material to garbage. The sediment gets deposited when the force of a river slows down and the water can no longer carry it.

When you see a large boulder in the middle of a river or a soda can that has washed up on a riverbank, you're seeing the effects of deposition.

Minerals in Lakes and Oceans

Streams and river systems flow into lakes and, eventually, into Earth's oceans. The water carries sediments and dissolved minerals. Some dissolved minerals are deposited in lakes, along coastlines, and on ocean floors. Others travel through ocean waters and help support plant and animal life in the ocean.

Have you heard the term *salt water* in connection with oceans? Salt is one of the minerals that water carries. In fact, each year Earth's rivers carry about four billion tons of dissolved salt to the oceans. Because salt is one of the minerals left behind as ocean water evaporates, the salt content of Earth's oceans continually increases. Ocean water is made up of about 3.5 percent dissolved salt. If you've ever accidentally swallowed ocean water while swimming, you know just how salty it tastes!

Great Salt Lake

The Great Salt Lake is located in northern Utah near Salt Lake City. Its water has one of the highest salt contents of all Earth's water bodies. It has even greater salinity than ocean water.

Water travels to the Great Salt Lake from the Bear, Weber, and Jordan Rivers. It doesn't continue on to the ocean, however; the Great Salt Lake has no outlet. The rivers transport about 1.1 million tons of salt into the lake each year. In the warm climate of Utah, the lake's water evaporates quickly and this results in even more salt deposits. Because this salt doesn't move on to the ocean, it builds up in the Great Salt Lake.

Great Salt Lake, Utah

frozen surface of the Great Salt Lake

Resources on Earth

Genre	Comprehension Skill	Text Features	Science Content
Nonfiction	Main Idea and Details	• Glossary	Natural Resources

Scott Foresman Science 6.11

PEARSON
Scott
Foresman

DK

ISBN 0-328-14001-5

9 780328 140015   90000

scottforesman.com

What did you learn?

1. What is the difference between renewable and nonrenewable resources? Give examples of each in your explanation.

2. What are some ways in which air, land, and water provide resources?

3. What is an advantage and disadvantage of nuclear power?

4. **Writing** in Science By carefully managing the resources that are available to us, we can make sure that they remain available. Write about the ways in which we can use resources responsibly. Include examples and details from the book to support your answer.

5. **Main Idea and Details** Which details expand on the main idea that as the world became more industrialized, its demand for energy increased?

Picture Credits
Every effort has been made to secure permission and provide appropriate credit for photographic material.
The publisher deeply regrets any omission and pledges to correct errors called to its attention in subsequent editions.

Photo locators denoted as follows: Top (T), Center (C), Bottom (B), Left (L), Right (R), Background (Bkgd).

Illustrations
20, 21 Peter Bollinger.

Photographs
Opener: ©Joe Sohm/Alamy Images; 1 ©Jeff Greenberg/Index Stock Imagery; 2 ©Buddy Mays/Corbis;
4 (B) ©Jeff Greenberg/Index Stock Imagery, (CR) ©EPA; 7 (B) ©Robert Brook /Photo Researchers, Inc.;
8 (B) Getty Images; 9 (TR) ©Eric Sanderson/Wildlife Conservation Society and Center for International Earth Science
Information; 12 (B) Data courtesy Marc Imhoff of NASA GSFC and Christopher Elvidge of NOAA NGDC.
Image by Craig Mayhew and Robert Simmon, NASA GSFC/NASA; 13 Getty Images; 14 (T) Getty Images, (CR) Science
Museum, London/DK Images; 15 (TR) Getty Images; 16 (B) Getty Images; 17 (BR) ©Sylvain Grandadam/Alamy Images,
(TR) Getty Images; 18 Robert Harding Picture Library Ltd/Alamy Images; 22 (TR, CR) ©Airphoto, (BR) Getty Images;
23 ©W. Perry Conway/Corbis.

Scott Foresman/Dorling Kindersley would also like to thank: 7 (TR) Natural History Museum, London/DK Images;
10 NASA/DK Images.

Unless otherwise acknowledged, all photographs are the copyright © of Dorling Kindersley, a division of Pearson.

ISBN: 0-328-14001-5

Resources on Earth

by Donna Latham

Glossary

acid precipitation rain or snow that carries acid

coal a solid fossil fuel formed by swamp plants

fossil fuels energy sources from the remains of living organisms

geothermal energy heat energy found deep inside Earth

natural gas a fossil fuel that is a mixture of gases

nonrenewable resources resources that cannot be replaced as quickly as they are used

petroleum a liquid fossil fuel; also called oil or crude oil

renewable resources resources that can be replaced through natural processes almost as quickly as they are used

24

Earth's Natural Resources

You are on a swamp boat in the Everglades National Park in Florida. You feel the Sun's warmth on your arms. You hear the gentle swooshing sound as the wind rustles through the tall saw grass.

You gesture toward a tear-shaped island, where cypress trees, with their wide trunks and long roots, stand tall on the waterlogged land. You point out a pelican that has scooped up its lunch in the expandable pouch of its bill. Your eyes scan the surface of the water, searching for dozing alligators, which everyone is hoping to see. As you look over the water, you notice that the Everglades seem to go on forever. The air, water, and land around you in the Everglades are only a few of many resources that can be found on Earth.

Swamp boats in the Everglades are surrounded by air, water, and land—some of Earth's precious resources.

Coal Mining and Reclamation

Coal is removed from the ground in different ways than natural gas and petroleum. One way is by digging tunnels under Earth's surface. Another way is strip mining. Soil and rock are stripped away to get to the coal. Strip mining is usually used when the coal is less than 30 meters from Earth's surface. Deeper coal deposits require underground tunnels.

Both of these methods of coal mining affect our environment in harmful ways. Plants can't grow and animals don't have shelter when soil is taken away. Soil can wear away to the point that the land can't be used at all. Coal mining can also cause water pollution. The huge caves left behind by coal mining can cause the ground above them to collapse.

When land is reclaimed, it is returned to productive use. Laws have been enacted to reclaim the land that has been harmfully affected by coal mining.

Before: Land that has been damaged by coal mining.

After: Land that has been reclaimed and restored.

Processing and Delivering Petroleum

The oil that is removed from the ground is called crude oil. Crude oil is extracted by drilling into an oil reservoir. This is the starting point in the production of gas, oil, and other petroleum products. Crude oil is then transported to refineries through pipelines or by ocean tankers. Crude oil is a mixture of other substances, which are separated during processing.

At the oil refinery, crude oil is processed to obtain different products. The main process used is distillation. After each product is separated, it is refined to remove unwanted materials, such as water, salts, and oxygen.

After the petroleum has been processed, it gets stored in tanks where it will eventually be shipped and sold to places such as airports, gas stations, and factories. The petroleum can then be used for fuel.

Renewable and Nonrenewable Resources

The air, water, and land around you are just a few of the many resources on Earth. Some resources can be replaced just about as quickly as they are used. These are called **renewable resources.** The sunlight and wind are renewable resources. In contrast, **nonrenewable resources** cannot be quickly replaced. Some of them, such as minerals and fossil fuels, take millions of years to develop.

Since all living things share Earth's resources, the way we use them is extremely important. The way we use one resource can affect another. For instance, when we cut trees for lumber, many organisms lose their habitats. We could plant new trees to replace those that were cut, but it would take many years for them to fully grow. In the meantime, the displaced organisms might not survive.

Trees, such as these cypress trees, take a long time to grow.

Atmosphere

Did you know that the gases that make up Earth's atmosphere make life possible? The renewable gases nitrogen, oxygen, and carbon dioxide are necessary for living things. They cycle in the environment. That means they are constantly used and reused.

But when harmful materials enter the atmosphere, air pollution results. Burning fuels, such as coal, oil, and natural gas, releases these materials into the air we breathe. When the air is polluted, all living things are affected.

Every day, the Environmental Protection Agency (EPA) lets us know how clean our air is with its air quality index (AQI), which uses a color-coded system as shown below. Colors range from green to maroon—green being the most healthful, and maroon, the least.

The AQI lets people know how clean air is.

The wind that ripples through these trees and the sunlight that helps them grow are examples of renewable resources.

Now take a look at the stages in the formation of oil and natural gas. They also formed from the remains of living organisms—but those organisms lived in oceans, not swamps. Lighter than oil, natural gas is often found on top of oil. When the areas of trapped oil and natural gas are drilled, the deposits can be gathered for energy use.

When ocean organisms die, they sink. They become buried under layers of sediment.

Heat and pressure act on the decaying material to form oil and natural gas.

Oil and natural gas travel up toward the surface of Earth.

Unable to pass through rocks, oil and natural gas become trapped.

Oil and Natural Gas

This map can be found at the Energy Information Administration of the Department of Energy's Web site. It shows you the locations of oil and natural gas deposits in the United States.

United States: Oil and Gas Fields

Formation of Fossil Fuels

Fossil fuels began to form about 340 million years ago. For many millions of years, the remains of plants and animals were buried in Earth's crust. Coal, petroleum, and natural gas formed from these buried remains. But each formed in a different way.

The diagram below shows how coal formed from swamp plants. Notice that coal changes form at each stage. This is due to heat and pressure. Each type of coal contains more carbon than the coal at the previous stage. The more carbon that coal has, the more cleanly it burns.

Dead swamp plants drop to the bottom of the swamp water. There, they form peat.

Peat changes to lignite from the heat and pressure of the sediment layers. Lignite contains a lot of water.

Through more heat and pressure changes, lignite becomes bituminous coal.

The last stage of coal formation is anthracite. This is the hardest form of coal.

Land

Land is an important resource. We rely on it in many ways. Land resources include farmlands, grazing lands, and forests. Soil and minerals are resources that come from land. Most plants need land to survive. Land is home to deer, herons, snakes, and other animals.

Soil has great value in our lives. People use it to grow crops and other plants. Soil can take hundreds of years to form. Wind and water cause it to quickly erode, or wear down. When farmers rotate crops, or vary the types of crops they grow, they allow soil to regain lost nutrients.

Minerals also come from land, and take thousands of years to form. Many objects we use every day are made of minerals, such as copper, iron, and quartz.

heron

soil

Forests

Forests are not only habitats for wildlife; they also supply us with many useful materials. Some nuts, fruits, and medicines come from forests. So does the wood we use to build homes and furniture, and the paper we write on.

Through photosynthesis, trees take in carbon dioxide and release oxygen. So forests play a key role in controlling the amount of carbon dioxide in Earth's atmosphere.

Too much carbon dioxide in the atmosphere traps heat, causing temperatures to rise. Higher temperatures can harm Earth's organisms, since not all of them can adjust.

The clearing and burning of forests causes more carbon dioxide to be trapped in the atmosphere.

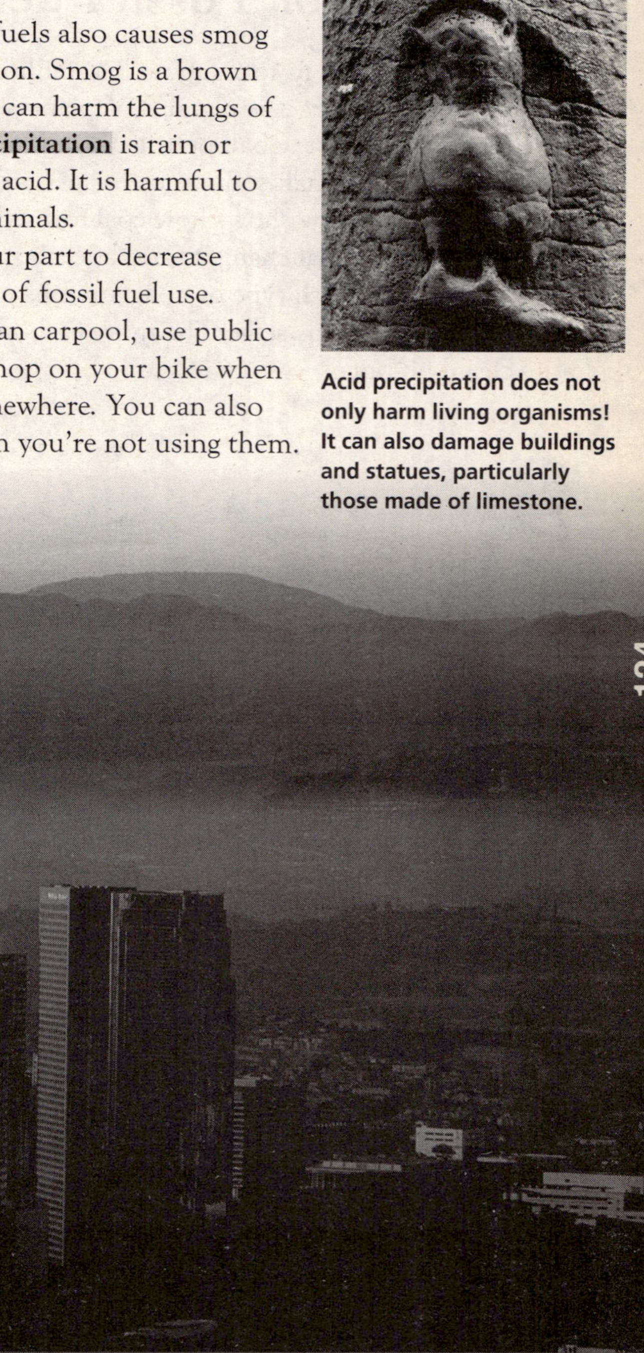

The forests of Minnesota provide homes for bears, wolves, muskrats, beavers, and minks.

Burning fossil fuels also causes smog and acid precipitation. Smog is a brown or yellow haze that can harm the lungs of humans. **Acid precipitation** is rain or snow that contains acid. It is harmful to many plants and animals.

You can do your part to decrease the harmful effects of fossil fuel use. For example, you can carpool, use public transportation, or hop on your bike when you need to go somewhere. You can also turn off lights when you're not using them.

Acid precipitation does not only harm living organisms! It can also damage buildings and statues, particularly those made of limestone.

Water

Animals such as this lobster live in water ecosystems.

Water is a renewable resource. It is recycled through the water cycle. It is hard to imagine how different our lives would be without this resource! We depend on water for drinking, bathing, and growing crops. But beyond these daily needs is another need you might not be aware of. The cells of all living things need water to carry out their life processes. Without it, cells stop working and die.

When water is polluted, it can no longer be used. As water flows across land, it can pick up pesticides and fertilizers. The chemicals from industry are another source of pollution. Some industries take water from lakes and rivers to cool off machinery that becomes hot when it is used. As the water flows through the warm machines, it heats up. When it is returned to the lake or river, it has a higher temperature than it did when it was first removed. As a result, changes can occur in ecosystems and affect organisms.

The way we use one resource can affect another. Even a small increase in water temperature can cause changes in a river or lake ecosystem.

Using Fossil Fuels

Most of the energy that we use in the United States comes from fossil fuels. Remember, these are nonrenewable resources, so they won't last forever. For this reason, scientists are working to locate other sources of energy. Gathering, processing, and using fossil fuels can also cause problems. When they are burned, they produce gases, called greenhouse gases. These gases can trap heat in our atmosphere. This is known as the greenhouse effect. Some scientists worry that as more gases are produced, more heat will be trapped. The additional heat will cause Earth to grow warmer—causing some living organisms to die.

Burning fossils fuels can cause smog. Have you seen this haze in your area?

Oceans

Like land, oceans supply us with many minerals. Seawater is an important source of salt. Other minerals, such as tin, magnesium, iron, and copper, are found in large amounts on the ocean floor.

The ocean floor also contains deposits of oil and natural gas. When wells are drilled deep into the ocean floor, these resources can be removed.

The energy released by moving water can be used to generate electricity. This energy source is renewable and causes little pollution. Unfortunately, few areas have the tides or the coastline needed to produce tidal energy.

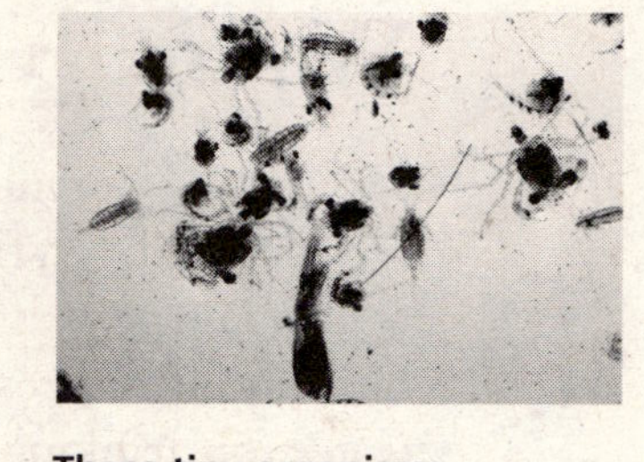

These tiny organisms make up plankton, which are important because they carry on photosynthesis.

The main source of about 50 percent of the world's energy production is **petroleum,** also known as crude oil, or oil. Unlike coal, it is a liquid fossil fuel. The oil under the ocean floor can be gathered through offshore drilling. Offshore drilling provides nearly 25 percent of the United States' natural gas and nearly 24 percent of its oil.

Natural gas provides heat for many homes. In addition, it supplies electricity. This fossil fuel is a mixture of gases, primarily methane and ethane. After being removed from underground sources, natural gas gets stored inside huge tanks.

Crude oil, or petroleum, can seep through surface rocks. But most of it is located in sedimentary rocks deep under Earth's surface. It is also found under the ocean floor.

Large drills can be lowered from platforms like this to remove oil and natural gas from beneath the ocean floor.

This hair dryer is powered by electricity, which was generated from natural gas.

The first offshore oil well was drilled in 1897, off the coast of Summerland, California.

What are fossil fuels?

Types of Fossil Fuels

When you enjoy the cool air of an air-conditioned room or ride in a plane, you are actually using energy from the Sun. How does this work? **Fossil fuels** form from organisms that lived long ago. They might have been plants that captured the Sun's energy, or animals that took in that energy when they ate plants. Either way, when the organisms died some of the energy inside their bodies changed. It became the energy of fossil fuels. When we use fossil fuels now, we are freeing the energy that was stored millions of years ago. Fossil fuels are a nonrenewable energy source.

Coal is a solid fossil fuel. At one time coal was the primary fuel used in the United States. It powered factories, fueled homes, and propelled trains and ships. Today it is mostly burned in power plants to produce electricity.

Coal, a sedimentary rock that is usually black or brown in color, is a solid fuel.

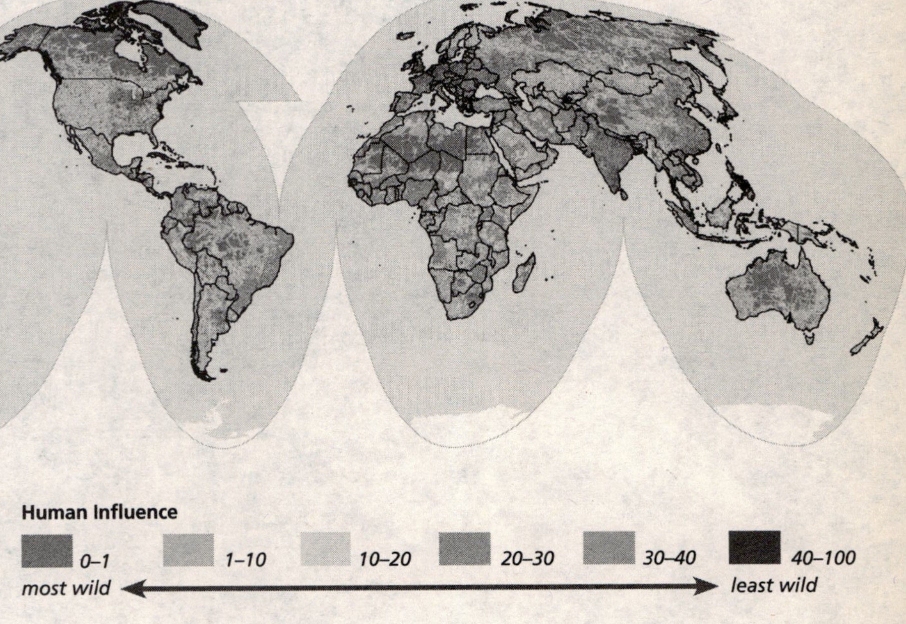

Coal can be removed through surface and underground mining.

Human Impact on Resources

Human Footprint Map

A group of scientists, some from NASA, teamed up to learn how much of Earth has been affected by human activities. This map, the Human Footprint, is the outcome of their study. A scale of zero to one hundred shows the level of human impact on an area, with zero showing the least impact. Find your region on the map. What level of impact does it reflect?

In studying their data, the scientists learned that human activity has affected 83 percent of Earth's land. The world's three main crops are rice, wheat, and maize. Scientists found that 98 percent of land where these crops can be grown is completely affected by human activity. Scientists conducted this study to help people understand their impact on the environment.

Reducing the Impact

Did you know that humans have had such a major impact on Earth's environment? Now that you've learned about it, think about actions you can take to avoid causing further harm to the environment.

All the parts of Earth—its land, water, air, and living organisms—are interconnected. That means they are closely related and linked. Realizing that this interconnection exists can help people make good choices about how they live. Read the chain of causes and effects on page 11 to discover what can happen when humans change an environment.

Energy from Sunlight and Wind

Energy from the Sun is called solar energy. Solar energy can heat both homes and buildings. It can also be converted into electricity without the use of turbines. Although solar energy does not cause pollution and is renewable, it can't be effectively used everywhere. Perhaps future technology will make its use more widespread.

Wind energy is clean and efficient. It is a renewable resource that does not cause pollution. But in areas of the world that do not experience regular, continuous winds, it is not an effective energy choice.

These solar panels capture the Sun's heat.

Some areas in the United States are good spots for wind turbines.

Energy from Water

Moving water, such as flowing rivers, can be used as an energy source to generate electricity. Hydroelectric power is made when water, held back by dams, flows through turbines, turning their blades. The water's kinetic energy is changed to electrical energy. Hydroelectric power is a renewable source that does not pollute. Building dams across rivers, however, changes the habitats in front and behind the dam.

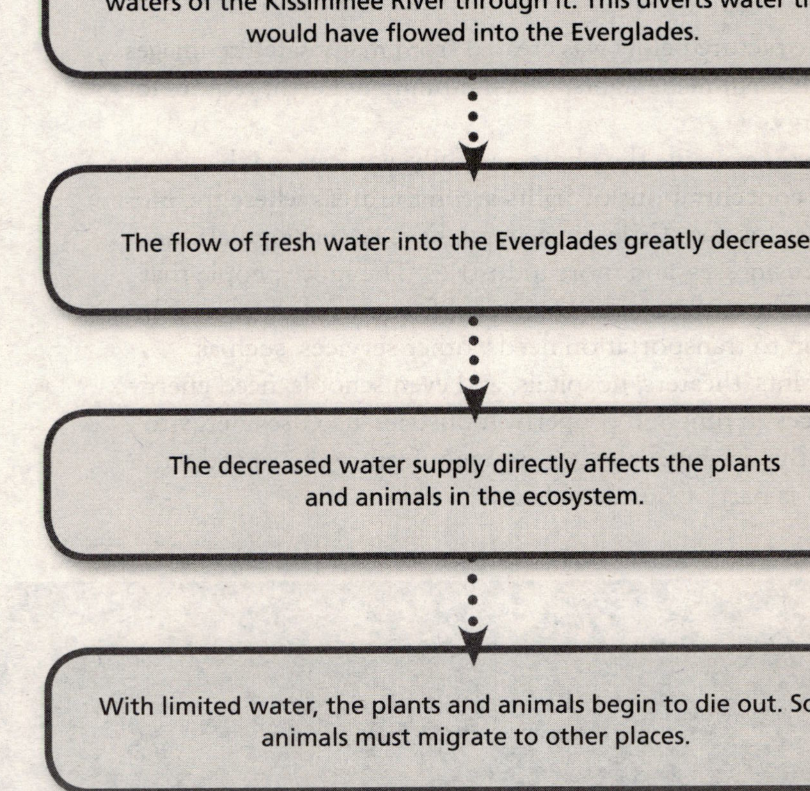

Energy from Earth's Heat and Atoms

When atoms of uranium split, heat is produced and nuclear energy results. Uranium is a mineral, so nuclear energy is a nonrenewable resource. Although nuclear energy doesn't cause air pollution, waste materials from nuclear power plants can harm living organisms. It must be disposed of safely.

uranium

Deep inside Earth, it is extremely hot. The energy of this heat is called **geothermal energy.** In some places, geothermal energy heats water below Earth's surface. By drilling into certain parts of Earth's crust, water is released in the form of steam. This steam can then be used to turn turbines, which can produce electricity. Geothermal energy is a renewable resource.

Engineers create a concrete canal and force the naturally flowing waters of the Kissimmee River through it. This diverts water that would have flowed into the Everglades.

The flow of fresh water into the Everglades greatly decreases.

The decreased water supply directly affects the plants and animals in the ecosystem.

With limited water, the plants and animals begin to die out. Some animals must migrate to other places.

As you can see, one change to the environment had many effects. Remember, not all resources are renewable! If humans don't manage nonrenewable resources such as minerals, oil, coal, and natural gas, they will run out one day. Practice conservation to help manage resources wisely. Follow the three R's—Reduce, Recycle, and Reuse—to conserve.

Sources of Energy

Energy Needs

The picture below was created from many satellite images. These human-made lights, which illuminate Earth, require lots of energy.

If you examine the photo carefully, you can see that the largest concentrations of lights are in the areas where the most cities are located. Cities, in general, have larger populations, more businesses, and more industries. The more people that live in an area the greater their need for sources of energy. In addition to transportation needs, other services, such as restaurants, theaters, hospitals, and even schools, need energy resources to function properly. Industries also use energy to power the machines they use to manufacture their products. Energy is part of our daily lives.

Human-made lights illuminate Earth. Can you find your region?

Energy Needs over Time

Over time, the need for energy resources has grown. People of the past used few sources of energy. They burned wood to provide light and heat, while their animals pulled plows and provided transportation. But late in the 1700s, people in the United States turned to industry, with machines and factories replacing jobs that were previously done by hand. This required more and new energy sources. Later, as the automobile industry grew, the demand for cars caused a dramatic increase in the need for energy.

Today factories are used to produce many different things.

As the population of the United States increased, so did its need for energy. Inventions such as the electric light, also increased this demand. Today, in a world that has grown increasingly industrialized, energy use continues to soar.

Except for lightning, electricity is a resource that is not found in nature. We use energy sources such as fossil fuels, hydropower, and nuclear energy to generate electricity.

Electricity generation in the United States

years	billions of kilowatt hours
1950	334.1
1960	759.2
1970	1535.1
1980	2289.6
1990	3038
2000	3802.1

Earth's Climate and Weather

by Colin Kong

Genre	Comprehension Skill	Text Features	Science Content
Nonfiction	Cause and Effect	• Captions • Charts • Diagrams • Glossary	Climate and Weather

Scott Foresman Science 6.12

ISBN 0-328-14004-X

PEARSON
Scott Foresman

scottforesman.com

What did you learn?

1. How does air pressure affect you if you were driving up and then down a mountain road?

2. What is the difference between sleet and freezing rain or glaze?

3. What are three tools that meteorologists use to help gather weather information?

4. **Writing** in Science Climate differs from one area to another, and there are many factors that affect climate. Write to explain how some factors cause the climate to be cool and how other factors cause the climate to be warm. Include details from the book to support your answer.

5. **Cause and Effect** What causes precipitation to form and fall to the ground?

132

Picture Credits
Every effort has been made to secure permission and provide appropriate credit for photographic material.
The publisher deeply regrets any omission and pledges to correct errors called to its attention in subsequent editions.

Photo locators denoted as follows: Top (T), Center (C), Bottom (B), Left (L), Right (R), Background (Bkgd).

Illustration
4, 14, 20 Peter Bollinger.

Photographs
Opener: NASA/Photo Researchers, Inc.; 1 Getty Images; 3 Aguilar Patrice/Alamy Images; 5 (BL) Jim Schwabel/Alamy Images, (BR) Michael S. Lewis/Corbis; 7 (BR) Getty Images; 9 Digital Vision; 11 Getty Images; 13 Gene Moore/Alamy Images; 17 Digital Vision; 18 Roland Seitre/Peter Arnold, Inc.; 21 NOAA; 22 (TR) Galen Rowell/Corbis, (BC) Simon Fraser/Acey Harper Photography; 23 (BL) A. T. Willett/Alamy Images, (BC, BR) Getty Images, (TR) Brand X Pictures.

Unless otherwise acknowledged, all photographs are the copyright © of Dorling Kindersley, a division of Pearson.

ISBN: 0-328-14004-X

Copyright © Pearson Education, Inc.

All Rights Reserved. Printed in the United States of America. The blackline masters in this publication are designed for use with appropriate equipment to reproduce copies for classroom use only. Scott Foresman grants permission to classroom teachers to reproduce from these masters.

2 3 4 5 6 7 8 9 10 V004 13 12 11 10 09 08 07 06 05

Glossary

air mass	a very large body of air with similar properties distributed through it
air pressure	the measure of force with which air particles push on matter
atmosphere	the blanket of air that surrounds a planet
climate	the average condition of the weather at a place over a long period of time
front	a boundary that forms between air masses
humidity	the amount of water vapor in the air
meteorologists	scientists who study the weather
relative humidity	the ratio of the amount of water vapor actually present in the air as compared to the greatest amount possible at the same temperature
weather	the day-to-day condition of the atmosphere at a particular time and place

Earth's Climate and Weather

by Colin Kong

Earth's Atmosphere

The different layers in Earth's atmosphere are made up of gases. Each layer has different ranges of air pressure and temperature. Winds are created when there are differences in air pressure.

Gases in the Atmosphere

Air surrounds you all the time. You cannot see it or smell it, but it is there. Some planets are surrounded by a blanket of air called an **atmosphere.** Earth's atmosphere is made up of many different gases, but it is mostly nitrogen and oxygen. There are different layers to Earth's atmosphere, each with its own characteristics. Compared to Earth's total size, its atmosphere is very thin.

Many of the gases from Earth's atmosphere came from the molten rock within Earth. When molten rock cools, gases such as nitrogen, water vapor, and carbon dioxide are released. Some of the gases are trapped within Earth, while others escape as volcanoes erupt. This process has been going on for more than four billion years.

Earth's atmosphere did not always have the same level of oxygen that it has today. As more plants and trees grew on Earth, they took in carbon dioxide from the atmosphere. Then through photosynthesis, they released oxygen. The current level of oxygen in our atmosphere has accumulated over millions of years.

78% nitrogen

21% oxygen

1% other gases

gases in Earth's atmosphere

Because our planet is a sphere, different areas of the world receive different amounts of sunlight. Earth's polar regions do not receive much sunlight.

134

Volcanic eruptions release large amounts of ash and smoke into the atmosphere. This can block sunlight.

Pollution can affect climate. When fossil fuels burn, the amount of carbon dioxide increases in the atmosphere.

Climate

Weather in an area is constantly changing. However, **climate** is a pattern of weather that occurs in an area over a long period of time. This weather pattern is analyzed over at least thirty years. Climate is usually described in terms of average temperatures and precipitation throughout different seasons.

The climate is different from one area of Earth to another. Many factors affect climate. They include ocean currents, the amount of sunlight an area receives, and the amount of water vapor and carbon dioxide in the air. Study the pictures on these pages to see the many different factors that affect the climate of an area.

Forest fires release carbon dioxide into the atmosphere. As fewer trees remain, carbon dioxide traps heat, which makes areas warmer.

When volcanoes erupt they release gases such as nitrogen, water vapor, and carbon dioxide into Earth's atmosphere.

As air rises over mountains, it cools and water vapor condenses. This causes rain to fall on one side of the mountain, while the other side stays dry.

Low clouds reflect sunlight. So clouds such as stratocumulus clouds cause areas to be cooler.

Air Pressure and Temperature

Gases are made of very small particles that are constantly moving. They move around and bump into other matter. **Air pressure** is the measure of force with which air particles push on matter. As you pump air into your bicycle tires, the air particles start to fill in and push on the walls inside the tires. The tires get firmer because of the air pressure inside.

Air does not only push down on you. It pushes on all sides. Luckily, the air inside your body is pushing out with the same force as air outside is pushing in. Because of this you do not feel the pressure of the air. Cool air particles are packed together more closely than warm air particles. The result is greater air pressure in cool air.

Air Pressure and Altitude

Air pressure changes with altitude. It is greatest at Earth's surface because there are more air particles above you that push down. At higher altitudes, air pressure decreases because there are fewer air particles from above pushing down. Air pressure is measured in metric units called millibars (mb).

When flying in an airplane, you feel the effects of the change in air pressure. Your ears pop as you are moving from one altitude to another. You feel the popping because the pressure inside your ears is adapting to the change in outside air pressure. The pressure inside your ears is becoming equal to the pressure outside.

Cayman Island beach: air pressure of 1,000 mb at sea level.

Mt. Everest: air pressure of 330 mb at about 8,900 meters of altitude.

Far above Earth's surface, satellites are recording images of the planet. From these images, scientists can track weather fronts, hurricanes, and other conditions to help make forecasts. Satellites also track other data, such as solar particles moving toward Earth.

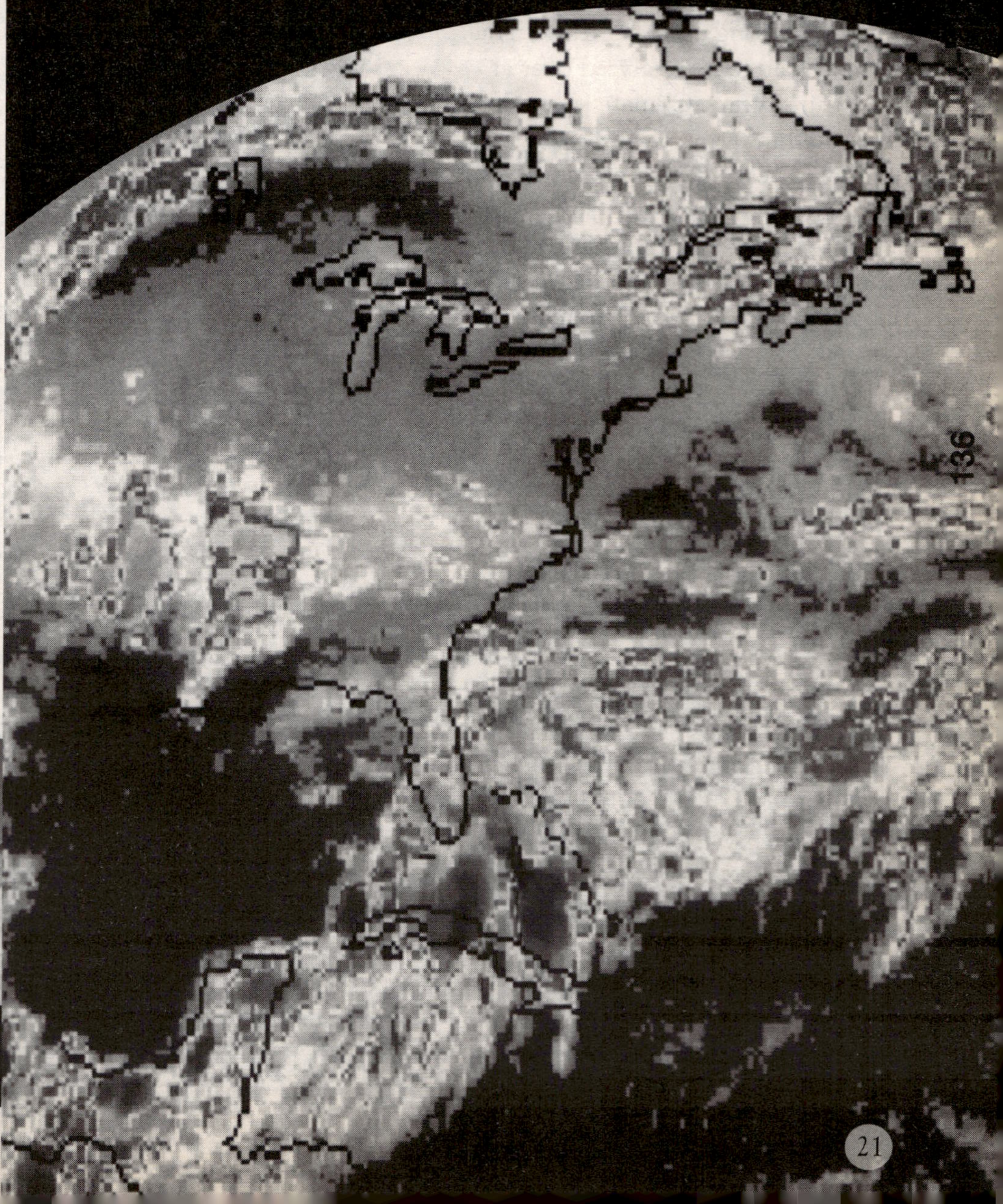

Weather Satellites

With advances in technology, such as Doppler radar and satellites, weather forecasts have improved in accuracy. Doppler radar uses radio waves to measure wind speed, wind direction, and precipitation. It can also help scientists determine the direction in which a storm is headed. With this tool, scientists can watch the movement of a storm and study the winds within it. As a result, meteorologists are better able to predict severe weather.

GOES-10 Satellite
Many satellites orbit Earth. The GOES-10 satellite orbits Earth about 35,720 kilometers above the equator and sends back information that helps meteorologists make weather forecasts.

Layers of the Atmosphere

Earth's atmosphere is made up of different layers. It is not the same from top to bottom. Each layer has its own characteristics.

Global Winds

Wind is moving air. It is caused by differences in air pressure. Usually winds move from high-pressure areas to low-pressure areas. Releasing air from a balloon is a good example of this. Air rushes out from inside the balloon because air pressure is higher inside than outside the balloon.

Differences in air temperature cause differences in air pressure. When air is heated, its particles move faster and expand. This warm air is less dense than cooler air, so it rises above cooler air. A hot air balloon floats in this way.

The Sun does not warm all places on Earth equally. The air near the equator is much warmer than the air near the poles. As the air near the equator warms, expands, and rises, cooler air blows in to take its place. In this way, the warm air is pushed away from the equator. As it rises higher it begins to cool and sinks back to Earth's surface. This forms the cycles of air movement illustrated on the left side of this globe. Earth's rotation bends these winds as shown by the arrows.

Warm air rises over the equator and cools. At about 30° north of the equator the air cools enough and the pressure rises enough to create winds that blow from east to west back toward the equator. They are called trade winds.

Gathering Data

Weather forecasting is a very complicated process, but meteorologists have many tools they use to gather weather information. They take measurements all over the world many times each day. They have thermometers to measure temperature, barometers to measure air pressure, hygrometers to measure humidity in the air, and anemometers to measure wind speed. Rain gauges measure the amount of precipitation that falls to the ground.

Meteorologists also need to gather data from Earth's atmosphere. For this reason, scientists release weather balloons at hundreds of stations around the world. These balloons are released several times a day to collect data about Earth's weather from the troposphere.

Weather balloons are released all around the world to collect data for meteorologists.

Barometers measure air pressure.

Forecasting Weather

Weather can change very quickly. One minute it can be sunny, and the next minute clouds can roll in for a storm. A weather forecast can help you prepare for the day's conditions. You can find these forecasts on television, in newspapers, on the radio, and on the Internet. If severe weather develops, these sources will provide warnings and safety instructions.

Weather forecasting involves looking at weather conditions all over the world. Meteorologists have to gather data on temperature, wind speed, humidity, and air pressure. Then they put all the data into computers to analyze the information and make predictions. The National Weather Service operates these computers in the United States. Forecasters use the information they gather to predict both local and national weather.

Differences in air pressure and air temperature can also create local winds. You probably experienced these local winds if you have spent time by any large body of water, such as an ocean. When the Sun is shining during the day, heat builds up on land. The temperature of water does not rise as quickly as the temperature on land, so the Sun does not affect the water's temperature as much. As the air above the land becomes warmer, it rises. The cool air that comes in from over the water replaces this air. As a result, winds move from the water to the land. At night, the airflow is reversed.

Winds and Local Weather

Different regions in the world sometimes have very different weather patterns. Local weather is affected by jet streams. They are high-speed bands of winds that blow in the upper troposphere and lower stratosphere. These winds move from west to east. Jet streams affect day-to-day weather and seasons.

Sailboats need local winds in order to maneuver in the water.

Clouds and Precipitation

When surface water—from puddles to oceans—evaporates, it enters the atmosphere. When air that contains water vapor rises and cools, clouds form. Clouds can form precipitation, such as sleet, snow, or hail.

Humidity

Have you ever walked outside and just started sweating because it was so hot and muggy? It was probably a result of humidity. **Humidity** is the amount of water vapor in the air.

Water enters the atmosphere as water vapor. This is part of the water cycle. Air can hold different amounts of water vapor. Warm air can hold more water vapor than cool air. Then, as air gets cooler, the water vapor condenses. It changes from a gas to a liquid, forming dew, fog, or clouds.

Air can hold only a certain amount of water. **Relative humidity** is the amount of water vapor *actually* in the air as compared to the amount of water vapor the air *can* hold at that temperature. If the relative humidity is 50 percent at 34°C, the air has half the amount of water vapor it can hold at that temperature. On very hot and humid days, the relative humidity can reach almost 100 percent.

Severe Weather Safety Tips

Thunderstorm
- Find shelter in a building or car. Keep windows closed.
- If in the woods, take shelter under the shorter trees. If swimming or boating, find shelter on land.
- If in an open area, squat low to the ground. Put your hands on your knees and lower your head.

Tornado
- Take shelter in a basement or storm shelter.
- If there is no basement or shelter, take cover inside a small room, bathroom, hallway, or closet on the first floor. Stay away from windows.
- If outside, lie face down. Cover your head with your hands.

Hurricane
- Prepare a disaster plan and a disaster supply kit ahead of time.
- Evacuate if told to do so. If you do not need to evacuate, stay indoors away from windows. Take cover in a bathtub or hallway.
- Avoid using the phone.

Severe Weather

At some point you will probably experience some severe weather. Knowing what to do when such weather hits is very important.

Thunderstorms

A thunderstorm is a small, intense storm. It produces strong winds, heavy rain, lightning, and thunder. These storms can occur at any time. But they happen more often in the spring and summer months.

Thunderstorms are dangerous because they bring lightning and heavy rains. Every year, lightning kills more people than tornadoes do. The heavy rains can cause flash flooding.

Tornadoes

A tornado is a rapidly spinning column of air with extremely strong winds. These winds have reached speeds of 419 kilometers per hour. It is difficult to predict tornadoes because they form very quickly from thunderstorms. Tornadoes are dangerous because they can destroy everything in their path.

Tornadoes can happen in any part of the United States, but they are most common in the Midwest. Most tornadoes develop in spring and summer.

Hurricanes

A hurricane is a large, spiraling storm that is fueled by warm water. A hurricane's wind speeds reach at least 120 kilometers per hour. Their strong winds and heavy rains can cause a lot of damage.

A hurricane is made up of many groups of thunderstorms. Hurricanes release a lot of energy. They usually form over warm ocean waters. The warm, moist air keeps a hurricane moving.

Clouds

Clouds form when air containing water vapor rises and cools. Since cooler air cannot hold as much water vapor, the water in the rising air condenses. It forms tiny droplets around small particles in the air, such as dust, smoke, and salt. These droplets float in the air. Clouds are made up of millions of these water droplets. If the temperature in the clouds is cold enough, the droplets freeze to form ice crystals. As more water droplets or ice crystals form, the cloud grows larger in size.

Clouds vary in their shape and their height above Earth's surface. Based on these qualities, there are three main classifications of clouds: cirrus, cumulus, and stratus. All other clouds are modifications or a combination of these.

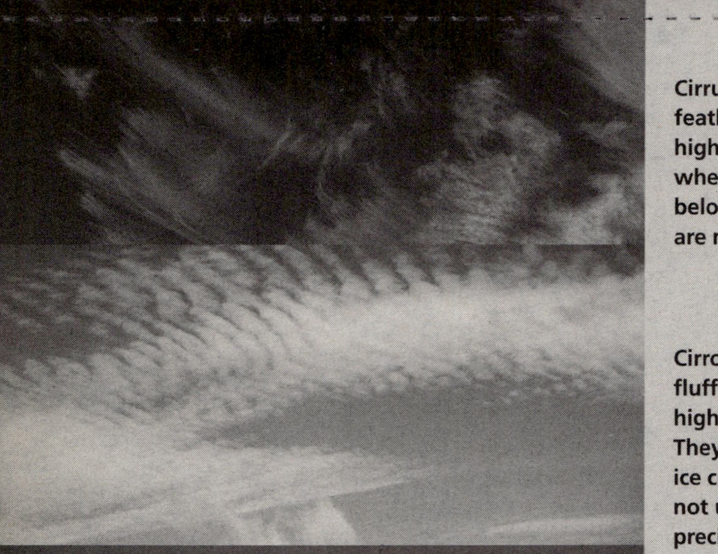

Cirrus clouds look thin and feathery. Because they form high in the atmosphere where temperatures are below 0°C. Cirrus clouds are made of ice crystals.

Cirrocumulus clouds are fluffy clouds that form high in the atmosphere. They are made of ice crystals. They do not usually produce precipitation.

Cumulonimbus clouds are dark and heavy. They can reach high into the atmosphere. They are called thunderheads because they usually result in a short, heavy rainfall or a thunderstorm.

Cumulus clouds are close to Earth's surface. These puffy clouds stack up on top of one another. Cumulus clouds are made up of air warmed by the land that rises into the atmosphere.

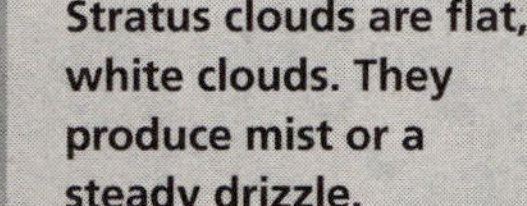

Stratus clouds are flat, white clouds. They produce mist or a steady drizzle.

Fronts Moving Across Land

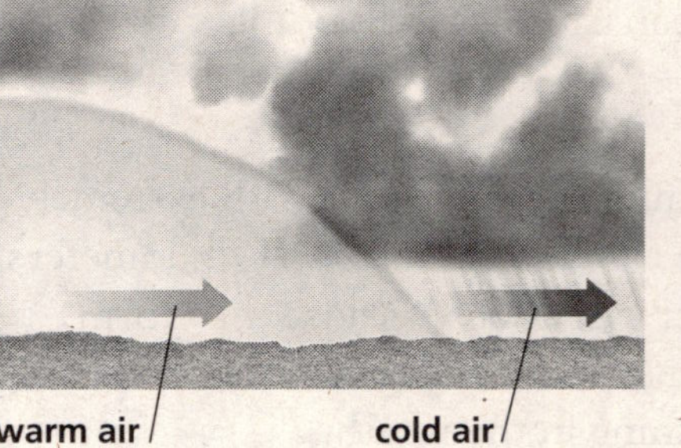

Warm Front
A mass of warm air runs into a mass of cooler air. The warm air moves above the cooler air. The warm air cools and condenses to form clouds. A warm front produces periods of steady rain or drizzle.

Cold Front
A mass of cold air runs into a mass of warm air. The warm air moves above the cold air. As the warm air rises, it cools and condenses to form clouds. Heavy rains or snow may come. Cold fronts move quicker than warm fronts.

Stationary Front
A warm air mass and a cold air mass meet. But they do not move toward one another. A stationary front does not move quickly. It can stay over an area for days. The weather produced is similar to that produced by a warm front.

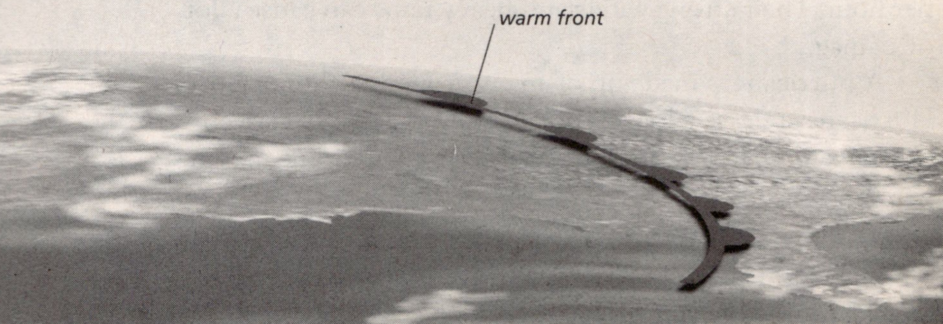

Weather and Climate

Air Masses and Fronts

Weather is the condition of the atmosphere at a specific time and place. It is always changing due to the different air masses and fronts. You may have seen a weather forecaster on the news speaking about these air masses and fronts.

An **air mass** is a very large body of air. The temperature and humidity is similar throughout. An air mass forms when the same air stays over an area for a period of time. This may be for days, a week, or even longer. The temperature and moisture of the air mass come from the area of Earth's surface over which it forms. For example, an air mass forming over the desert would be dry.

When air masses of different temperatures come together, they usually do not mix. A boundary called a **front** forms between these two air masses. The weather at these fronts is often cloudy or stormy. Scientists called **meteorologists** study the weather. They track the movement of air masses very carefully in order to predict weather conditions.

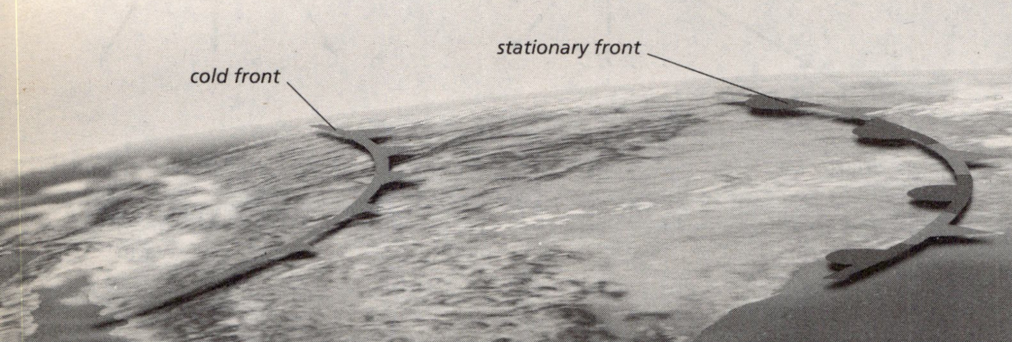

Types of Precipitation

Precipitation is any form of moisture that falls from the atmosphere to Earth's surface. It can be rain, sleet, snow, or hail. Before a cloud can produce precipitation, it must accumulate a lot of moisture. The form that falls depends on the temperature and other weather conditions.

Rain and Snow

Both water droplets and ice crystals can form rain. If water droplets fall through temperatures above freezing, rain falls from the clouds. If ice crystals fall through temperatures above freezing, it melts to form rain.

If the temperature below the cloud is below freezing, the ice crystals join together to form snowflakes. These crystals can either be feathery and six-sided or flat hexagons. The temperature and amount of moisture in a cloud determine the shape of the snowflakes. The temperature of the ground is also important. Dry snow, which is light and powdery, forms if the ground is cold. Wet snow, which is denser, accumulates if ground temperatures are warm.

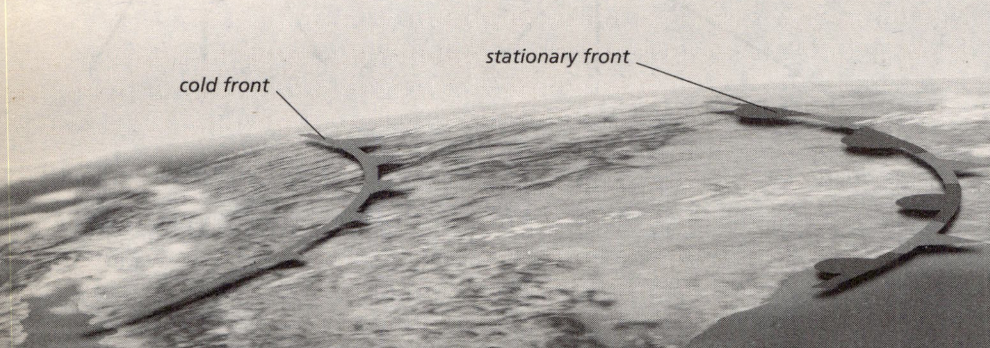

Wet snow accumulates on these cows because it is heavier, causing it to stick together.

Sleet and Hail

Sleet forms when water droplets fall through a layer of freezing air. The droplets freeze and reach the ground as small particles of ice. Freezing rain, or glaze, occurs when water droplets pass through cold air that is not cold enough to freeze the drops. The raindrops freeze only after hitting a frozen surface.

Hail falls in the form of hard, round particles of ice. This precipitation usually occurs in warm summer months. Hail forms when winds toss ice crystals up and down. As they move around, droplets of water attach to the ice crystals and freeze. Soon the hailstones grow to be too heavy to stay in the clouds. They fall to the ground. A hailstone can be as large as a baseball when it falls from the sky!

How Precipitation Forms

Water droplets and ice crystals in clouds may start out as being very small. But they get larger as more water clings to them. Precipitation forms when these droplets and ice crystals become too heavy to remain in the atmosphere. The form of precipitation that falls depends on the temperature and weather conditions the precipitation falls through.

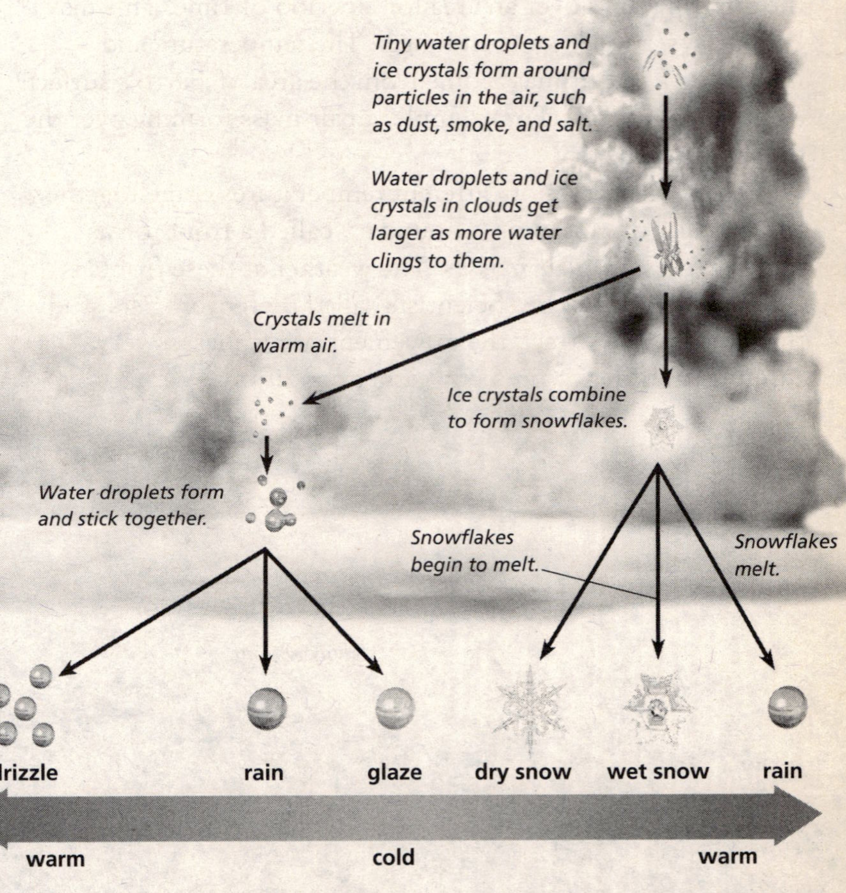

Properties of Matter

by Lillian Duggan

Genre	Comprehension Skill	Text Features	Science Content
Nonfiction	Sequence	• Captions • Charts • Diagrams • Glossary	Matter

Scott Foresman Science 6.13

PEARSON

Scott Foresman

scottforesman.com

ISBN 0-328-14007-4

9 780328 140077

90000

What did you learn?

Vocabulary

chemical change
chemical properties
condensation
density
mass
physical change
physical properties
volume
weight

1. Suppose you have a substance with a mass of 26 grams and a volume of 10 cm^3. Figure out its density and use the density table on page 5 to identify the substance.

2. Potassium burns when it comes in contact with water. Is this a chemical property or a physical property?

3. Write about a physical change that you observed or made happen recently.

4. **Writing** in Science Mass and weight are two different properties of matter. Write to explain the differences between the two. Use information from the book to support your answer.

5. **Sequence** Use sequence words—*first, next, after,* and *finally*—to describe how condensation forms on a pan of boiled water.

Picture Credits
Every effort has been made to secure permission and provide appropriate credit for photographic material. The publisher deeply regrets any omission and pledges to correct errors called to its attention in subsequent editions.

Photo locators denoted as follows: Top (T), Center (C), Bottom (B), Left (L), Right (R), Background (Bkgd).

4 (B) NASA; 9 ©Comstock Inc.; 13 (C) Syracuse Newspapers/C.W. McKeen /The Image Works, Inc., (BL) Dan Lim/Masterfile Corporation; 14 Alamy Images.

Scott Foresman/Dorling Kindersley would also like to thank: 1, 5 (TR), 10 (TR) Natural History Museum, London/DK Images.

Unless otherwise acknowledged, all photographs are the copyright © of Dorling Kindersley, a division of Pearson.

ISBN: 0-328-14007-4

Glossary

chemical change — a change in which a substance changes into a new substance with different properties

chemical properties — qualities of a substance that tells how the substance forms new substances when it mixes with something else

condensation — the change of state from a gas to a liquid

density — a measure of the amount of matter in a given space

mass — a measure of the amount of matter in an object

physical change — a change in which the appearance of a substance changes but its properties stay the same

physical properties — qualities of a substance that can be seen or measured without changing the substance into something else

volume — the amount of space that something takes up

weight — a measure of the pull of gravity on an object

Properties of Matter

by Lillian Duggan

PEARSON
Scott Foresman

DK

Matter

All matter has physical properties such as volume, mass, density, and boiling point. Matter also has chemical properties that explain how it reacts with other types of matter. Matter can change both physically and chemically.

Measuring Matter

Everything around you, even the air that fills the room, is matter. Matter is anything that has mass and takes up space.

Two properties of matter that can be measured are mass and volume. An object's **mass** is the amount of matter that makes up that object. Mass is measured in grams. **Volume** is the amount of space that something takes up. The volume of a liquid is measured in milliliters. The volume of a solid is measured in cubic units, such as cubic centimeters (cm^3). To find the volume of a solid, multiply its height by its width by its depth.

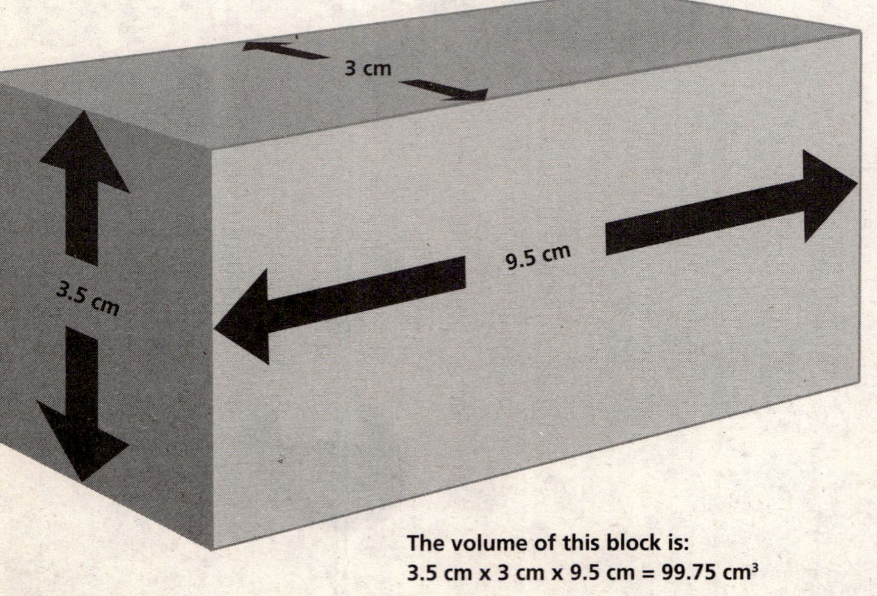

The volume of this block is:
3.5 cm x 3 cm x 9.5 cm = 99.75 cm³

Chemical Changes

A loaf of bread rises because of a chemical change. During a **chemical change,** substances change into new substances with different properties.

One of the most important ingredients in bread is yeast. Yeast is a living organism that needs moisture, air, and food to grow. First, the yeast is mixed with sugar and water. It eats the sugar and gives off bubbles of carbon dioxide. Then the yeast mixture is added to flour and water to make dough. The carbon dioxide bubbles cause the dough to expand. When the bread is baked in the oven, the heat kills the yeast.

Baking bread involves a chemical change caused by the yeast. The yeast uses up sugar and gives off a new substance—carbon dioxide.

The bubbles produced by the yeast are a clue that a chemical change is taking place. These bubbles give the bread its fluffy texture.

Everything we know in nature is made up of matter. Matter is anything in the universe that has mass and occupies space. Matter changes all the time. The changes can be physical changes or chemical changes. Matter has properties that can be measured, such as mass, volume, and density. Think about all the different kinds of matter you see every day, and how it changes!

Although the feathers take up more space, they still weigh less than the rocks.

Physical Changes

Melting, freezing, and boiling points are all physical properties. When a substance melts, freezes, or boils it changes its state, but it is still the same substance. A change of state, such as from a liquid to a gas, is a physical change. During a **physical change,** the appearance of a substance changes but it does not change into a different substance.

A physical change involves changing the size, shape, or state of a substance. Slicing bread is a physical change—the bread is still bread, but it's in a different shape. Melting butter or carving wood are also physical changes.

Some physical changes cause substances to change their appearance completely. You can't see the salt dissolved in seawater. But when the water is left to evaporate in the Sun, salt crystals are left behind.

Evaporating water to get salt from it causes a physical change.

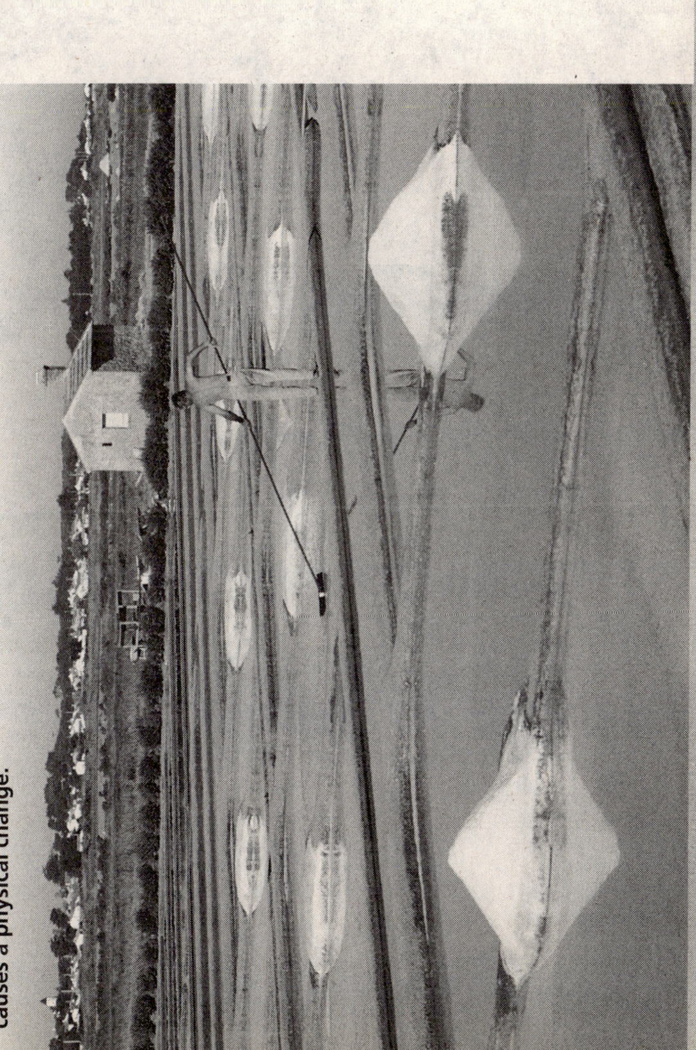

Density Differences

Suppose you had two piles the same size—one of feathers and the other of rocks. Would both piles have the same amount of mass? The answer is no. The rocks have more mass. The matter that makes up the rocks is more tightly packed than the matter that makes up the feathers.

Density is a measure of the amount of matter in a given space. Density is also described as mass per unit volume. The rocks have a much higher density than the feathers.

To calculate the density of a substance, all you need to know are its mass and its volume. Use this formula:

$$\text{density} = \text{mass/volume or m/v}$$

If an object has a mass of 30 grams and a volume of 10 cubic centimeters, what is its density?

$$\text{density} = \text{m/v} = 30 \text{ g}/10 \text{ cm}^3 = 3 \text{ g/cm}^3$$

Mass and Weight

Mass and weight are two different properties of matter. Mass is a measure of the amount of matter in an object. No matter where an object is in the universe, its mass is always the same. Mass can be measured with a balance. Weight is a measure of the pull of gravity on an object. The force of gravity is different on each of the large bodies in the universe. The larger the body, the greater the pull of its gravity, and the more an object weighs there. You can find the weight of an object by using a spring scale. A spring scale measures weight in units called newtons. On Earth, one newton equals about a quarter of a pound.

The Moon is much smaller than Earth and has only one-sixth the gravity of Earth. A person's weight would be only one-sixth of their weight on Earth.

Melting and Boiling Points

Substance	Melting/Freezing Point (°C)	Boiling Point (°C)
Hydrogen peroxide	-2	158
Water	0	100
Lead	328	1740
Silver	962	2212

Hydrogen peroxide will gradually evaporate if left in an open container.

Ice melts quickly at room temperature.

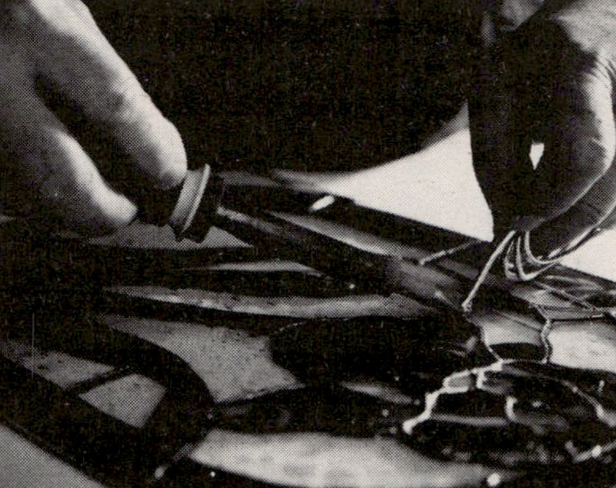

The relatively low melting point of lead makes it useful for welding together pieces of metal.

Silver has a very high melting point.

Water boils at 100°C.

Boiling

When a liquid is heated, its particles speed up. With enough added heat, the particles will move fast enough to escape their attraction to each other. A substance reaches its boiling point when it gains enough energy to change from a liquid to a gas.

When water is boiled on the stove, the air surrounding the pan becomes moist. This happens because water is slowly turning to water vapor and escaping from the pan. Later, if the water vapor in the air cools, it loses energy. The particles slow down again and move closer together, returning to a liquid state. The change of state from a gas to a liquid is called **condensation.**

Adding and removing heat are not the only ways to cause a substance to change its state. Changing the air pressure around the substance has similar effects. Normally water does not freeze at room temperatures. But if the air pressure was ten thousand times higher than normal, water would turn to solid ice. Under very low air pressure, water could change to a gas without being heated.

Densities of Common Materials

Material	Density (g/cm³)
Gold	19.32
Copper	8.96
Aluminum	2.64
Glass	2.60
Water	1.00
Plastic	0.96
Paper	0.93

The density of gold is 19.32 grams per cubic centimeter.

Using Density

Every substance has a particular density, and that density never changes. For example, the density of copper is 8.96 grams per cubic centimeter, whether the copper is formed into a pipe or a wire. Also, the density of a substance is unique. Rarely do two or more substances have the same density.

Because the density of each substance is different, you can use density to identify an unknown substance. Suppose you have a piece of metal, but you don't know what kind of metal it is. If you measure its mass and its volume, you can use these measurements to calculate its density. Then you can identify the metal by finding its density on a table, such as the one above.

The density of aluminum is 2.64 grams per cubic centimeter.

The density of paper is 0.93 grams per cubic centimeter.

Physical Properties

Physical properties of matter are those that can be seen or measured without changing the substance into something else. Density is one physical property of matter.

Gold has several physical properties that make it unique. Of all the metals, gold is the most malleable, meaning it can be spread or shaped with a hammer or by being pressed through rollers. Gold is also ductile, or easily shaped into wire or thread.

Another physical property of gold is its ability to conduct electricity. It can be used in making electronic equipment.

Other physical properties of matter include whether it can conduct heat, whether it can be dissolved in other substances, whether it is magnetic, and the temperature at which it freezes and boils.

Because of its ability to be reshaped, gold is highly prized for making jewelry.

Melting and Freezing

Melting is the process by which a solid becomes a liquid. A solid substance becomes a liquid when it is heated to its melting point. Every substance has a unique melting point. The melting point of mercury is −39°C. The melting point of water is 0°C.

Before iron can be shaped into items such as tools, it must be heated to its melting point of 1,535°C.

Mercury has a melting point of −39°C.

When a substance loses heat, it freezes. Freezing happens because the particles that make up a substance slow down and hold their attractions to each other. The temperature at which a substance freezes is called its freezing point. The freezing point and melting point of a substance are the same.

152

Properties of Aluminum

Physical Properties	Chemical Properties
• Lightweight silvery-white metal	• Does not corrode
• Reflects light and heat	• Combines with oxygen to form protective coating
• Malleable and ductile	

Some substances are useful to people because they don't form new substances easily. Aluminum doesn't corrode, which is one reason it's used for building airplanes.

Chemical Properties

The chemical properties of a substance are those that tell how the substance forms new substances when it mixes with something else. Different materials react in different ways when they are combined with other materials. For example, when iron is exposed to oxygen, it forms rust.

A substance's chemical properties can make it useful to people. Wood, for example, is flammable. It burns in the presence of oxygen. The burning of wood produces heat for fireplaces and bonfires.

Changes of State

If you look around you, you'll see solids, liquids, and gases all existing at the same temperature.

Some types of matter have particles that are more strongly attracted to each other than the particles of other types. The particles that make up a drinking glass have a stronger attraction than the particles that make up the orange juice inside.

The temperature of a substance affects the force of attraction between the particles that make it up. Adding heat to a substance gives its particles energy, causing them to move faster and break the forces of attraction. If you heat a solid to a high enough temperature, it will become a liquid. Heat it even more, and it will become a gas.

Why is water a liquid and wood a solid?
The attraction between the particles that make up wood is stronger than the attraction between the particles that make up water.

How Matter Changes

The four states of matter are solid, liquid, gas, and plasma. Matter can change from one state to another. When the state of matter changes, the energy of the particles that make it up changes too.

States of Matter

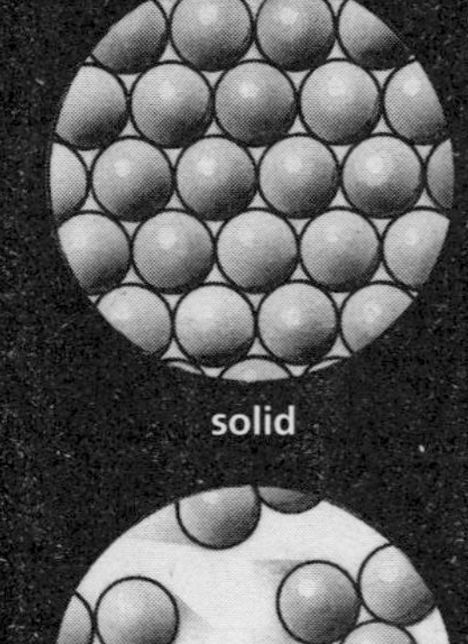

The diagrams show the movement of particles in a solid, a liquid, and a gas.

All matter is made up of tiny particles. These particles are constantly in motion. How fast they move and how strongly they are attracted to each other determine whether the matter they make up is a solid, liquid, gas, or plasma.

A solid has a definite shape and volume. The particles that make up a solid move slowly and have a strong attraction to each other.

A liquid has a definite volume, but not a definite shape. Its particles move quickly enough to resist some of the attraction between them. The particles slide past each other, allowing the liquid to take the shape of the container that holds it.

A gas has no particular shape or volume. The particles that make up a gas move quickly and in many directions. A gas fills up and takes the shape of the container that holds it.

Similar to a gas, plasma does not have a definite shape or volume. The particles that make up plasma can conduct electricity.

The Sun is made of plasma. Plasmas are rare on Earth, but scientists think that most of the known matter in the universe is made up of plasma.

Structure of MATTER

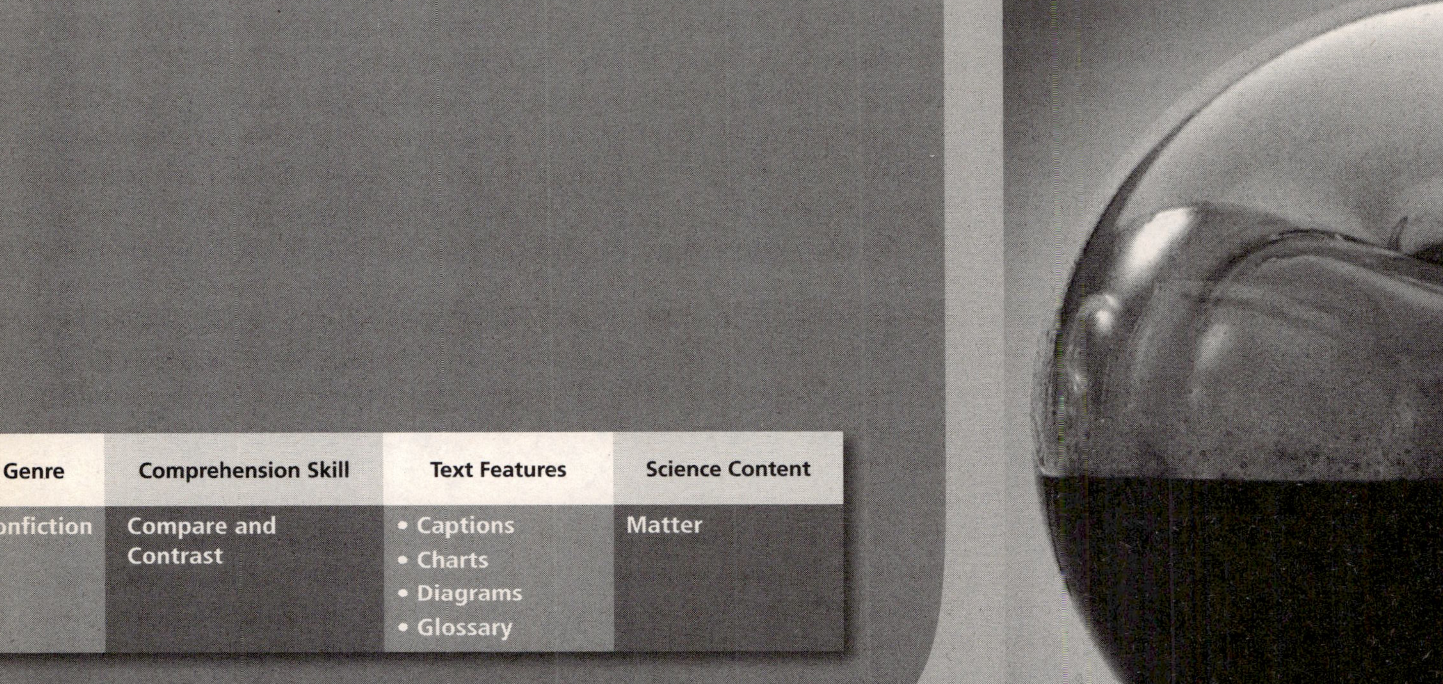

by Colin Kong

Genre	Comprehension Skill	Text Features	Science Content
Nonfiction	Compare and Contrast	• Captions • Charts • Diagrams • Glossary	Matter

Scott Foresman Science 6.14

PEARSON
Scott Foresman

scottforesman.com

DK

ISBN 0-328-14010-4

9 780328 140107

90000

What did you learn?

1. What are the two regions of an atom from the electron cloud model?

2. What do helium, neon, and argon have in common?

3. How do you separate sugar from a sugar-sand mixture?

4. **Writing** in Science All matter found in nature can be classified as elements, compounds, or mixtures. Make a table listing the properties for each to help identify them.

5. **Compare and Contrast** What are the similarities and differences between acids and bases?

Vocabulary

compound
concentration
element
mixture
periodic table
solubility
solute
solution
solvent

Picture Credits
Every effort has been made to secure permission and provide appropriate credit for photographic material.
The publisher deeply regrets any omission and pledges to correct errors called to its attention in subsequent editions.

Photo locators denoted as follows: Top (T), Center (C), Bottom (B), Left (L), Right (R), Background (Bkgd).

Opener: Science Museum, London/DK Images; 3 Nimatallah/Art Resource, NY; 9 (CR) GC Minerals/Alamy Images; 12 (BL) Getty Images; 13 (BC) Lester V. Bergman/Corbis; 15 (BC) Science Museum, London/DK Images; 16 (C) Andrew Lambert Photography/Photo Researchers, Inc., (BR) sciencephotos/Alamy Images; 20 (BC) ©Astrid & Hanns-Frieder Michler/Photo Researchers, Inc.; 22 (BL) ©Prof. P. Motta/Photo Researchers, Inc., (CB) ©Richard Megna/Fundamental Photographs, (CRB) ©F. Krahmer/Zefa/Masterfile Corporation; 23 (CLB) ©Michelle Garrett/Corbis, (CRB) ©Scott T. Smith/Corbis, (CB) ©Mark A. Johnson/Corbis, (BL) ©ER Productions/Corbis.

Unless otherwise acknowledged, all photographs are the copyright © of Dorling Kindersley, a division of Pearson.

ISBN: 0-328-14010-4

Copyright © Pearson Education, Inc.

All Rights Reserved. Printed in the United States of America. The blackline masters in this publication are designed for use with appropriate equipment to reproduce copies for classroom use only. Scott Foresman grants permission to classroom teachers to reproduce from these masters.

2 3 4 5 6 7 8 9 10 V004 13 12 11 10 09 08 07 06 05

Glossary

compound
a substance composed of two or more elements that are chemically combined to form a new substance with different properties

concentration
measure of the amount of solute dissolved in a solvent

element
a substance made of only one type of atom

mixture
a combination of substances in which the atoms of the substances are not chemically combined

periodic table
table that has organized all the known elements

solubility
maximum amount of solute that can be dissolved in a solvent at a particular temperature

solute
a substance that is dissolved in a solution

solution
a combination of substances where one substance dissolves in another

solvent
a substance in which the solute is dissolved

Structure of MATTER

by Colin Kong

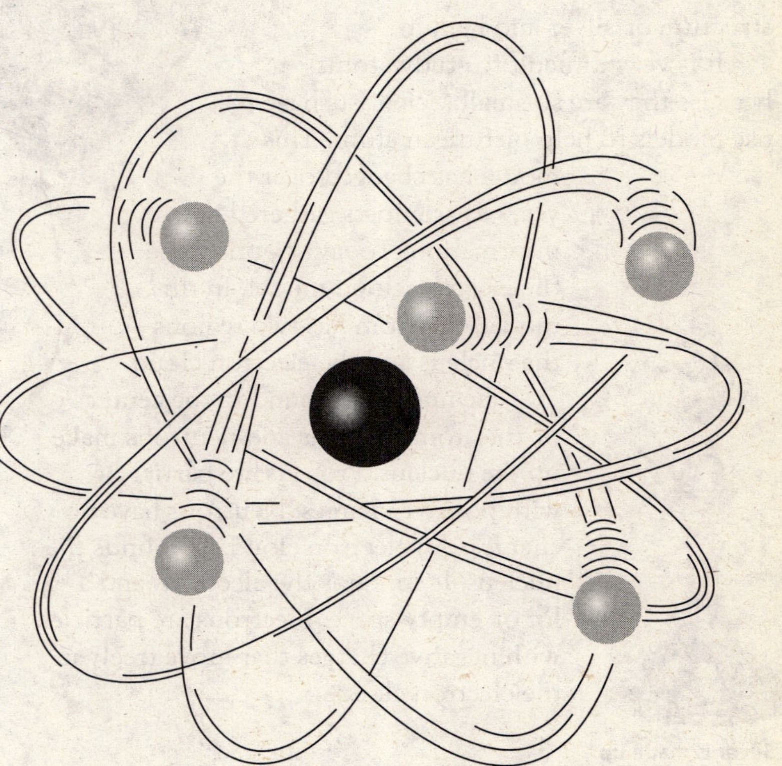

How did we learn about atoms?

The Atom

Do you know what silver has in common with the helium in a balloon? They are both made up of tiny particles called atoms. An atom is the smallest whole piece of matter. Tiny atoms are joined together to make the structure of silver and helium.

It is very difficult to study atoms because they are so small. Scientists have to use models to help picture an atom. This model has changed over the years as scientists gathered new information. Today scientists use the electron cloud model. In this model, the atom has two regions— the nucleus and the electron cloud.

The nucleus is found in the center of the atom. Protons and neutrons make up the nucleus. Protons are particles with positive charges. Neutrons have no charges. An electron cloud surrounds the nucleus. It contains the electrons and a lot of empty space. Electrons are particles with negative charges that move freely in the electron cloud.

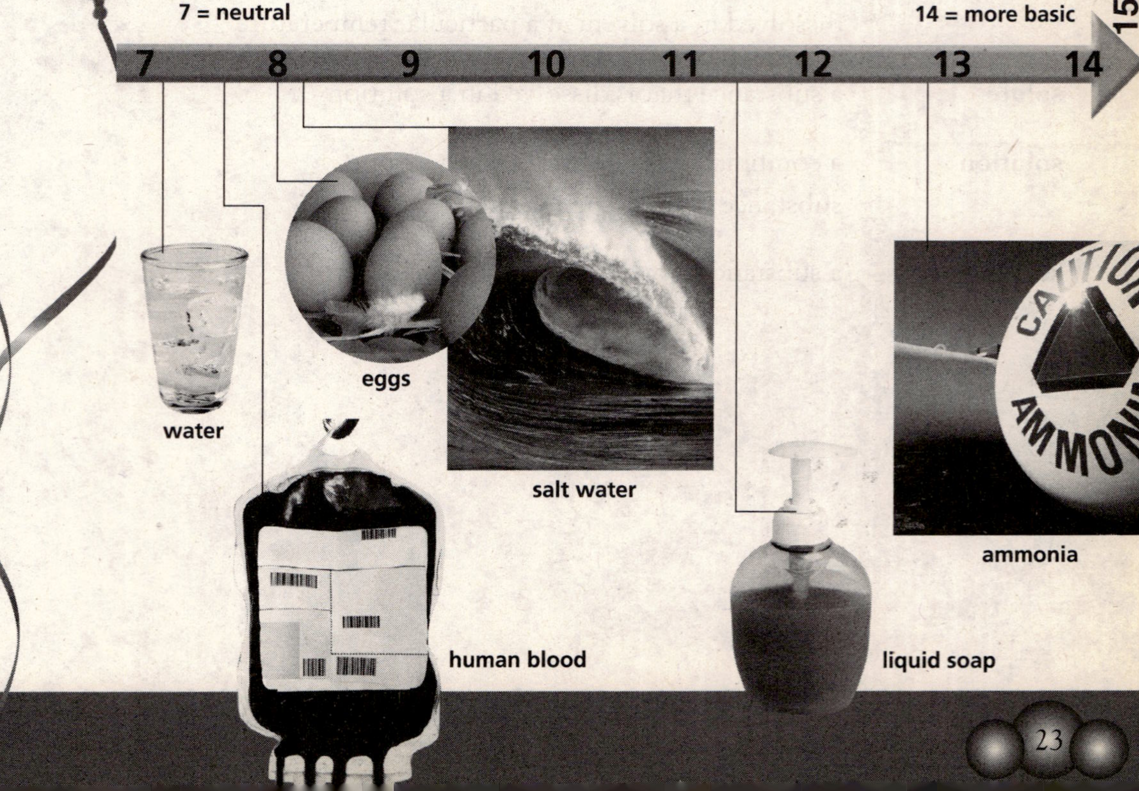

Silver is made up of tiny atoms.

Many things you use contain bases. For example, shampoo, bleach, and soap have bases. Strong bases can react strongly just like acids can. These strong bases can also burn your skin. They are poisonous. Red litmus paper will turn blue when you dip it in a base.

The pH Scale

A pH scale tells you the strength of acids and bases. The scale ranges from 0 to 14. Acids have a pH between 0 and 7. As their pH increases, their strength decreases. Bases have a pH between 7 and 14. The strength of a base increases as the pH reaches closer to 14. The pH of 7 is neutral.

158

Acids and Bases

You may think that acids are liquids that burn holes through everything. But not all acids are that strong. Many of the foods you eat contain acids. Oranges, lemons, pickles, soda, and milk are some examples. They contain weak acids. Even the cells in your body have weak acids to keep you healthy and alive.

There are also some very strong acids. They are poisonous, and they can burn your skin. You should never touch an acid to see how strong it is. You can use an indicator. It is a compound that changes color in acids or bases. Litmus paper is an indicator that changes from blue to red when you dip it in an acid.

Acids

- Taste sour (Never taste a substance to test for the presence of acids.)
- React strongly with some metals to form new compounds
- Change litmus paper from blue to red

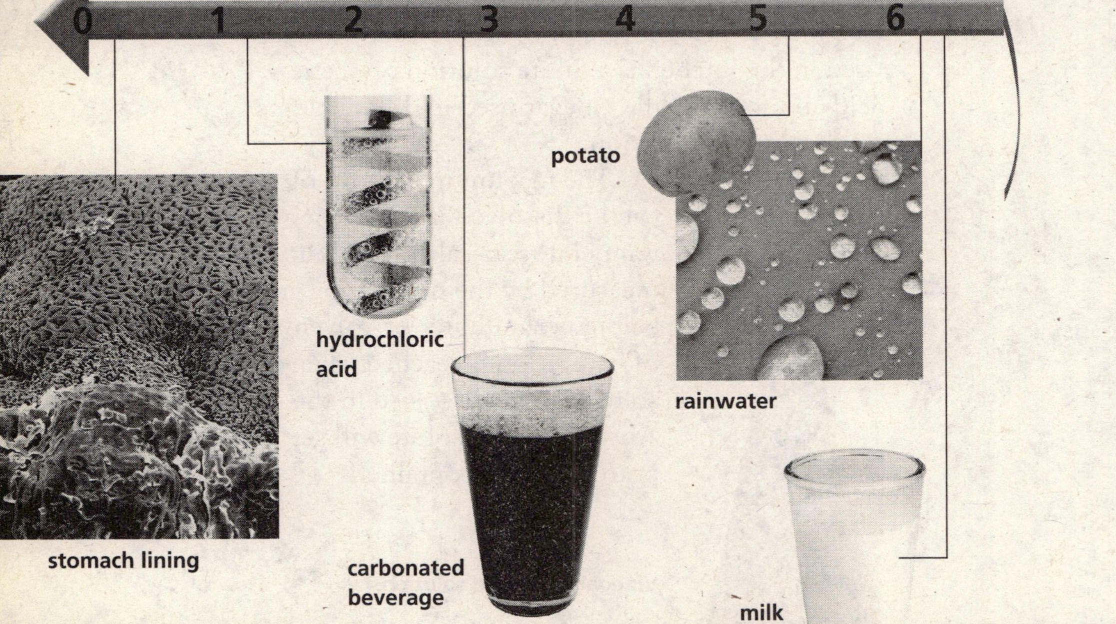

History of the Atomic Model

Scientists did not always know that atoms were made of smaller particles of protons, neutrons, and electrons. It took more than two thousand years to develop today's model of the atom.

A Greek philosopher named Leucippus first came up with the idea that matter is made of smaller particles. His student Democritus further developed the idea. He named the particles *atomos*, meaning "indivisible." Democritus believed that atoms were hard solids that could not be destroyed. He also described them as being completely full, which meant they had no empty space inside. Democritus also believed all atoms were made of the same material in many different sizes and shapes.

Aristotle, another Greek philosopher, did not agree with Democritus's model. He believed that matter could be divided and subdivided indefinitely. Aristotle did not believe in atoms. He proposed that everything on Earth was made up of a combination of earth, wind, fire, and air. Aristotle's theory was more popular than Democritus's theory. Many scientists challenged Aristotle's ideas, but their theories were also rejected. Among them were Galileo Galilei (1564–1642), and Robert Boyle (1672–1691), who claimed that everything was composed of tiny but not indivisible particles. Aristotle's theory remained popular until the 1800s.

Democritus (460–370 B.C.), a Greek philosopher, proposed that all matter consisted of an infinite number of small particles.

Today's Atomic Model

In 1808, John Dalton made the first modern atomic model that was widely accepted. He used scientific experiments to prove that atoms were real. Dalton believed that the atoms in an element are exactly the same size and weight. In his atomic model, Dalton suggested that atoms are similar in appearance to billiard balls. He also believed that atoms of two or more elements unite chemically to make compounds.

By the end of the 1800s, it was generally accepted that matter is composed of atoms that combine to form molecules. In 1897 Joseph John Thompson proposed that atoms were spheres with negatively charged particles surrounded by an area of positively charged particles. He described the negatively charged particles as "plums" surrounded by a soup of positive material he described as "pudding." He called it the plum pudding model. Thompson also discovered the electron.

Dalton used these billiard-ball-shaped models to explain his theory of the atom.

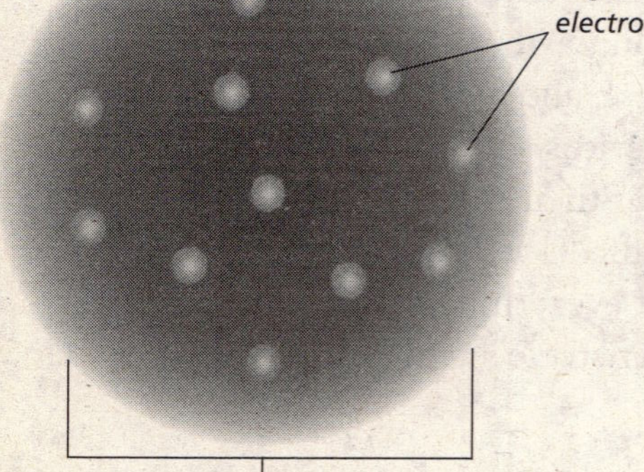

In Thompson's "plum pudding model," negative particles are surrounded by a "soup" of positive particles.

Solutions

It is easy to see the individual components in a pizza. But some mixtures look the same. These mixtures are solutions. A **solution** forms when one substance dissolves into another.

The **solute** is the substance that is dissolved. The **solvent** is the substance in which the solute is dissolved. If you dissolve salt in water, the salt is the solute. The water is the solvent.

Solutions can be solid, such as stainless steel—a solution of chromium, nickel, and iron. They can be liquid, like vinegar—a solution of water and acetic acid. They can be a gas, like air—a solution of nitrogen, oxygen, and other gases.

The **concentration** of a solution is the amount of solute dissolved in a solvent. Solutions can be classified as being dilute or concentrated. Vinegar used in the kitchen is a dilute solution of acetic acid and water, while vinegar used in dill pickles is a concentrated solution.

The maximum amount of solute that can be dissolved in a solvent at a particular temperature is called **solubility.** It is measured by the number of grams of solute per milliliter of solvent. The point of saturation is reached when no more solute can be dissolved in the solution. Any additional solute will settle at the bottom of the container.

Stainless steel is a solid solution.

Vinegar is a liquid solution.

160

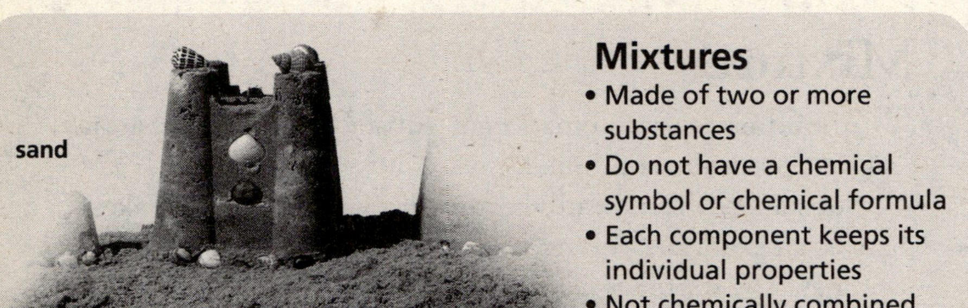

Mixtures

- Made of two or more substances
- Do not have a chemical symbol or chemical formula
- Each component keeps its individual properties
- Not chemically combined
- Can be separated by physical means

Compounds

- Made of two or more elements
- Have a chemical formula
- Properties of a compound differ from the properties of elements that form it
- Elements are chemically combined together
- Can be broken down into simpler substances

Elements

- Made of only one kind of atom
- Have a chemical symbol
- Called a pure substance
- Cannot be divided into simpler substances

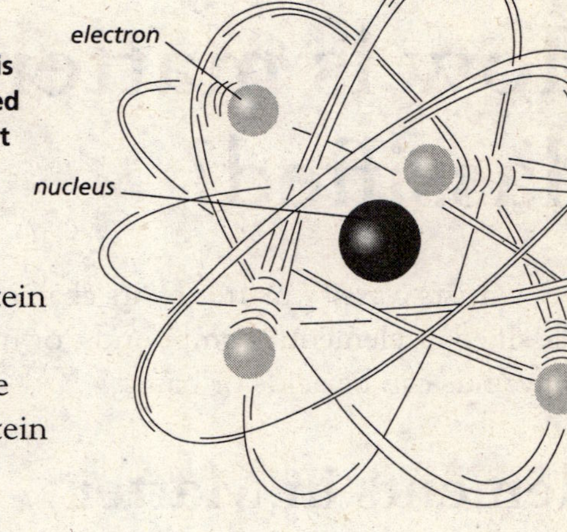

Ernest Rutherford proposed that most of the atom's mass is located in its positively charged center, and that electrons orbit the nucleus.

In 1905, Albert Einstein wrote a paper that gave scientific evidence for the existence of atoms. Einstein also provided a way to count atoms by using an ordinary microscope.

In 1911, Ernest Rutherford discovered the nucleus of the atom. He developed the first explanation of the structure of an atom. He found that most of the mass is located in the center of the atom, or the nucleus. He also found that the nucleus was positively charged and that negatively charged electrons orbit the nucleus.

In 1913, Neils Bohr proposed that electrons could circle a nucleus, moving in orbits called shells. As electrons move from one shell to another they gain or lose energy.

In the 1920s Erwin Schrodinger and Werner Heisenburg proposed the electron cloud model for the atom. In the electron cloud model, the nucleus is the center of the atom. The cloud-like area represents where the electrons are likely to be found.

Today the electron cloud model is widely accepted. It is a good model of the atom. But it does not mean that this model will not change in the future as scientists learn new information.

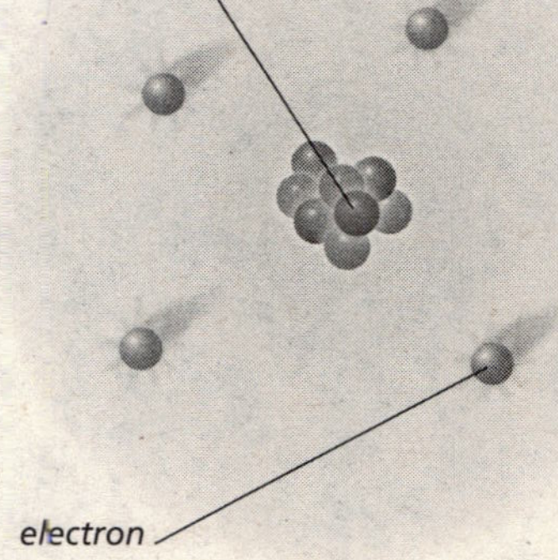

In the electron cloud model the nucleus is surrounded by an electron cloud.

How is matter classified?

Scientists classify matter by its characteristics. Matter is classified as elements, compounds, or mixtures. Some compounds can be acids or bases.

Elements in Matter

Can you believe that all matter around you is made of tiny atoms? Most things are made up of more than one type of atom. But there are some substances called **elements** with only one kind of atom. An element cannot be broken down into simpler substances by physical or chemical means. Some elements are gold, silver, aluminum, and silicon. Since they are made of only one kind of atom, elements are called pure substances.

Silicon is a pure substance. It only has one kind of atom. Silicon is used for making computer components.

Chlorine is an element used to clean swimming pools. It is also used in bleach to wash clothes.

Mixtures

A **mixture** is a combination of substances where the atoms are not chemically combined.

Substances in a mixture keep their own properties. Take a pizza as an example. You may see olives, pepperoni, and other toppings. The toppings can be separated out easily. They are not chemically combined. Components of a mixture also do not have a defined ratio. Two pizzas may not have the same amount of olives or pepperoni, but they are still pizzas.

Separating Mixtures

Mixtures can be easily separated. It is only difficult when the substances in the mixture are small in size. Let's separate a mixture of sugar, iron filings, and sand. Components in a mixture keep their own properties. The iron filings are magnetic, so remove them with a magnet. Next, separate the sugar from the sand. If you add water to the mixture, the sugar will dissolve. Pour the water-sugar-sand mixture through filter paper. Sand will collect on top of the filter paper. Finally, evaporate the water from the sugar water. You will have the solid sugar particles.

A magnet can be used to separate iron filings from a mixture.

Chemical Formulas

Just as symbols are used for elements, scientists also use symbols for compounds. They use a chemical formula for each compound. A formula contains both the symbols for the elements and subscripts. A chemical symbol is listed out for every element that is present in a molecule of the compound. Then the subscripts tell you how many atoms of each element are present in the molecule. Let's look at the chemical formula for water, H_2O. The formula shows that both hydrogen and oxygen elements are present in water. The subscript number 2 shows that two atoms of hydrogen combine with one atom of oxygen. The subscript always follows the chemical symbol of the element it refers to. The subscript 1 is never written out in a formula. If there is no subscript written, then there is only one atom of the element in the compound.

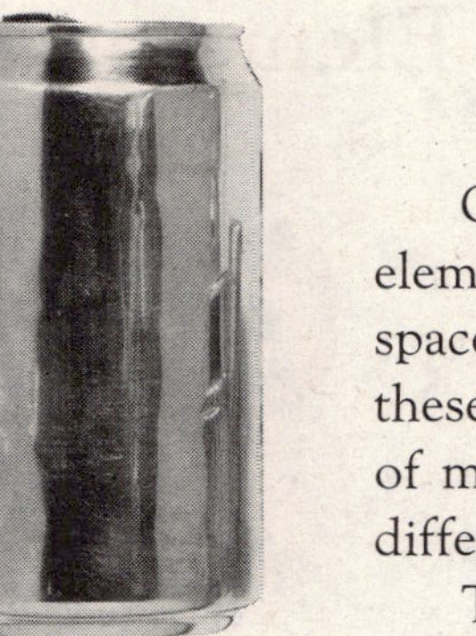

Sucrose is a type of sugar used to sweeten ice tea. It has a chemical formula of $C_{12}H_{22}O_{11}$. Sucrose is a compound with 12 atoms of carbon, 22 atoms of hydrogen, and 11 atoms of oxygen.

Aluminum is a lightweight metal used to make drink and food cans.

Currently there are about 112 different elements. All matter found in nature and space is made of these elements. How can these 112 elements make up the great variety of matter? Elements can combine in many different ways to form all types of matter.

The atoms of one element are not the same as the atoms of other elements. For example, the atoms of gold are not the same as the atoms of silver or the atoms of aluminum. Each element can be identified by the number of protons it has in the atom's nucleus. All matter that has twenty-nine protons in its nucleus is copper. All matter with thirteen protons in the nucleus is aluminum, and so on. An element's atoms have no electrical charge. Its atoms have the same number of protons and electrons. It means they have the same number of positive charges and negative charges. The overall charge of the atom is zero.

Rust forms when iron reacts with the oxygen in air or water. It has a chemical formula of Fe_2O_3. It is a compound of two iron atoms and three oxygen atoms.

The element mercury is a metal. It is the only metal that is in liquid form at room temperature. Mercury is a toxic substance.

Shorthand Names for Elements

Each element has a unique chemical symbol made of one, two, or three letters. The chemical symbol is usually the first letter of the element's name. If two elements have the same first letter, then another letter is added. Some elements' symbols come from their Greek or Latin names. For example, gold has Au as a symbol. It is from the Latin name *aurum*. Elements newly discovered have temporary three-letter symbols, such as Uuu, Uub, and Uuq. These letters correspond to the Latin name for the number of protons found in the nucleus—111, 112, and 114, respectively. These chemical symbols are used by scientists throughout the world. This allows scientists to write formulas that others can understand.

Gold is considered a precious metal. It is often used in jewelry. The chemical symbol for gold is Au.

A particle of a compound is called a molecule. These molecules are always made of the same ratio of elements. For example, a molecule of water contains one oxygen atom combined with two hydrogen atoms. It is always that one-to-two ratio of atoms for water.

Compounds do not have the same properties as the elements that make them. Water has a very different characteristic than oxygen or hydrogen. Water is a liquid. The oxygen and hydrogen elements are gases. But when they both combine, you get water!

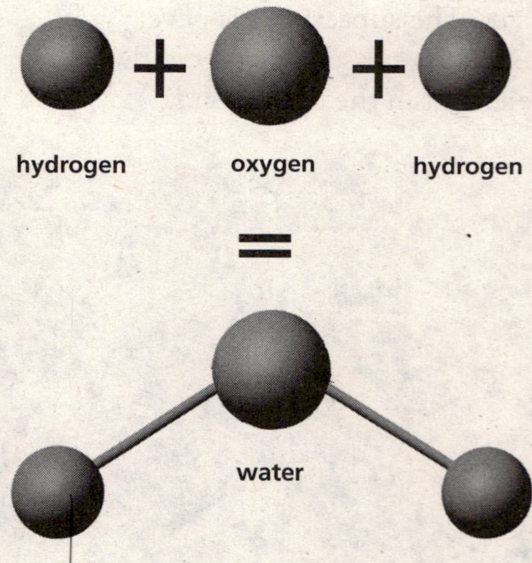

Combining oxygen and hydrogen, both gases, does not produce another gas compound. Instead, it makes water. Water has very different characteristics than either oxygen or hydrogen.

Neon, Ne, is used to make colorful and fluorescent signs.

What are mixtures and compounds?

Elements combine in exact ratios to make compounds. Compounds do not have the same properties as the elements that make them. Substances, which do not combine in exact ratios or undergo chemical changes, form mixtures. These substances retain their own properties even when they are in a mixture. They can be separated by physical means.

Building Blocks of Matter

Most matter in nature is not found as elements. It is found as compounds. A **compound** is a substance composed of two or more elements that are chemically combined. As a result, a new substance with different properties is formed.

Sodium chloride is a common compound. You probably know it as table salt. Atoms of sodium and chlorine combine to form this common seasoning. But sodium's properties are very different from that of sodium chloride. Sodium chloride can be mixed into water to form salt water, but pure sodium reacts violently with water.

When sodium is combined with water, you get a violent reaction. Sodium hydroxide and hydrogen gas are formed.

Grouping Elements

Each element has a unique set of properties and a unique number of protons and electrons. Based on their properties, elements can be divided into three groups. They are metals, nonmetals, and metalloids.

Metals are elements that are usually hard and can be hammered into sheets. They are good conductors of heat and electricity. They can be drawn into wires. Nonmetals are usually brittle, and they are poor conductors. They cannot be hammered into sheets or made into wires. Metalloids are elements with some properties of metals and some properties of nonmetals.

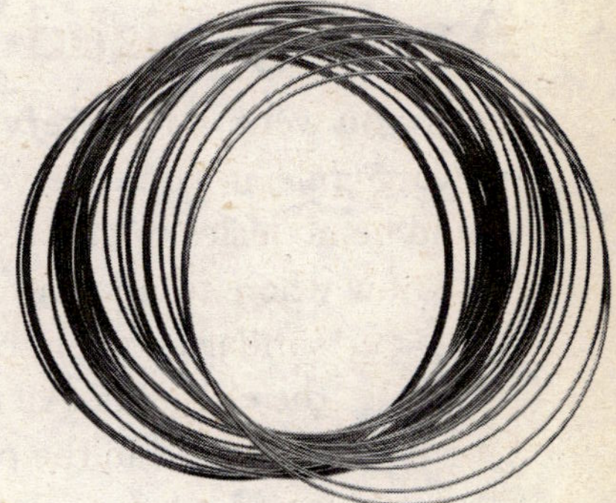

Copper is a metal. Like other metals, it can conduct electricity and heat.

Sulfur is a nonmetal. It is a soft, light substance that melts easily and doesn't conduct heat or electricity.

Boron is a metalloid. It is a semiconductor. This means that it can conduct electricity only when certain elements are added to it.

An Organized Table of Elements

If you went to a grocery store and found all of its items in one large pile, it would be very difficult to find anything. There would be no aisles or shelves to separate the items. You would not know where to find the eggs or the bread. Scientists had a similar problem before they found a way to organize the elements. All the known elements have been organized in the **periodic table.**

Elements in Groups 1–2 and 13–18 have similar chemical properties with other members of their groups. This means that oxygen and sulfur in Group 16 have similar chemical properties. The only exception to the rule is hydrogen. It has a similar atomic structure as other elements in Group 1. But hydrogen does not have similar chemical properties.

A row on the periodic table is called a period. Unlike the elements in a group, elements in a period do not share similar properties. As you move across a period, elements adjacent to one another have similar mass but the properties of elements change quite a bit. This is because you move from properties of a metal to properties of a nonmetal.

Phase at room temperature

- Gas
- Liquid
- Solid
- Not found in nature

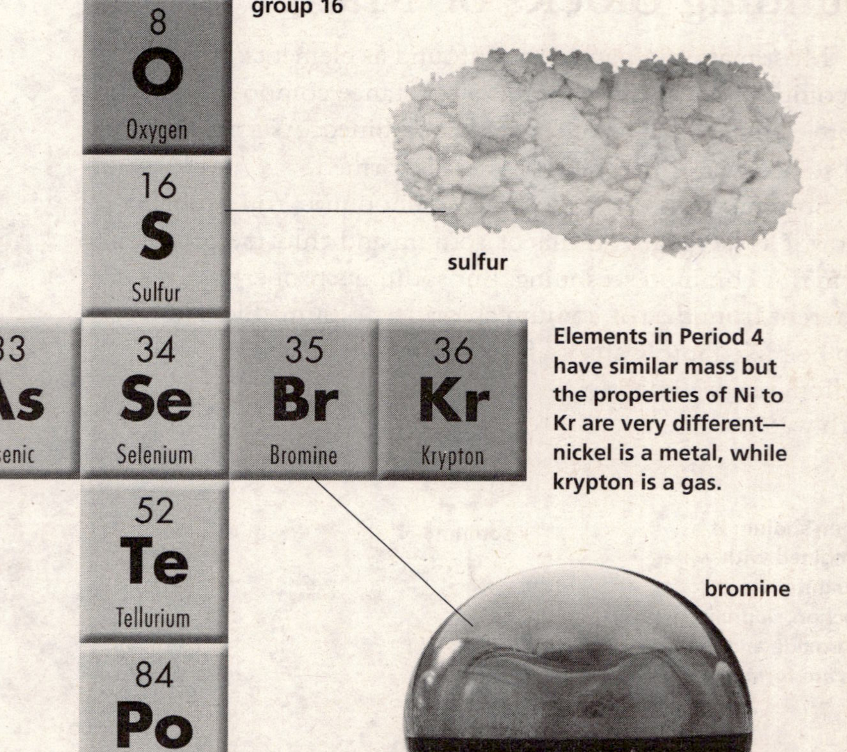

The periodic table contains a lot of information about the elements. Each individual block from the periodic table contains different information about a particular element. Specialized periodic tables may even provide additional information about each element.

The location of the element in the table also can tell you a lot about it. For example, elements found in the same vertical line, or column, have similar properties. The columns of a periodic table are called groups. Presently, there are eighteen groups in the periodic table.

The periodic table is the work of Dmitri Mendeleev and J. L. Meyer. The different elements were arranged in order of increasing atomic weight so that elements with similar chemical properties fell into the same group.

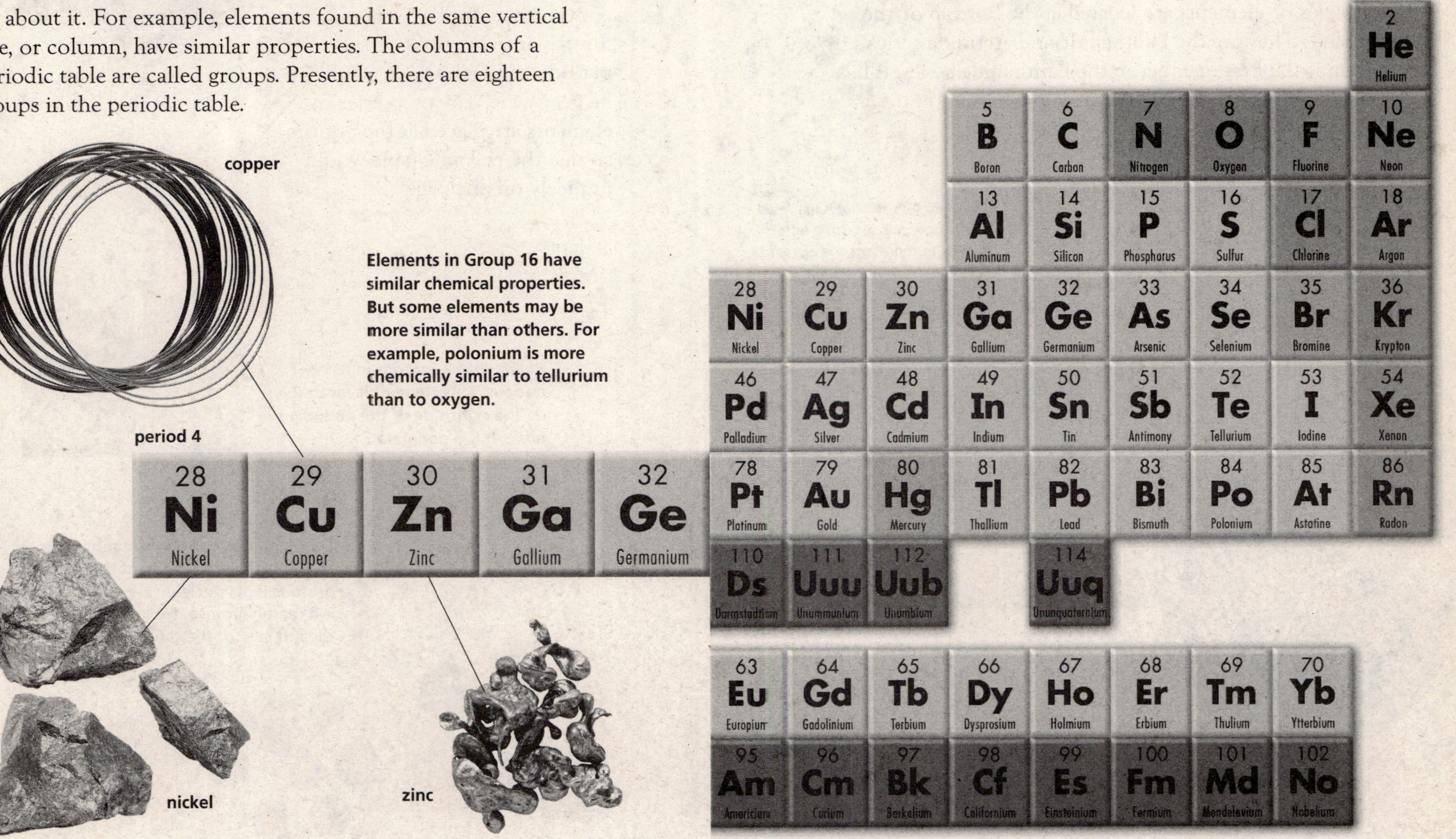

There are different patterns to look at when studying the periodic table. When looking across the rows from left to right, all the elements are listed in order of increasing atomic number. The atomic number is the number of protons in the nucleus of an atom. Elements listed on the left side of the periodic table are metals. The nonmetals are listed on the right side of the table.

Two series of elements are located at the bottom of the periodic table. They are the Lanthanide and Actinide series. Lanthanum is the first member in the Lanthanide series. It has the atomic number 57, and it should follow barium in the periodic table.

Actinium is the first member in the Actinide series. It has the atomic number 89, and it should follow radium. The elements of these two series are only put at the bottom of the periodic table for convenience. If they were put directly into the rows of the periodic table, the table would be very wide. The two series of elements are placed at the bottom so that the periodic table would fit nicely on one page.

The atomic number is 26. This means an iron atom has 26 protons in its nucleus.

The element's symbol is made up of the one, two, or three letters chosen to represent the element. Fe comes from *ferrum*, the Latin name for iron.

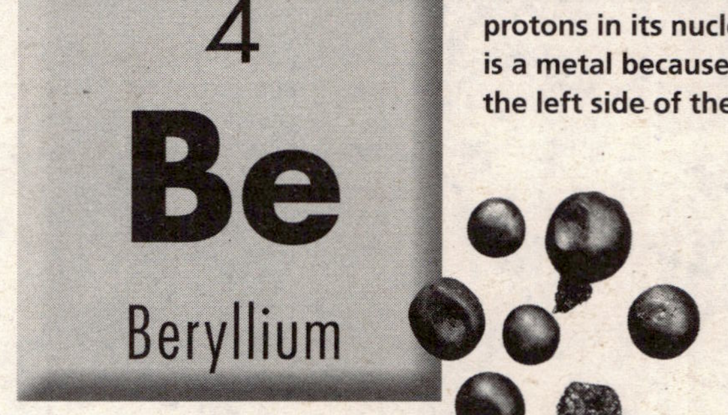

26 Fe
Iron

The color shows that the element Iron is a solid at room temperature.

Helium has 2 protons in its nucleus. This element is located on the right side of the periodic table. It is a nonmetal.

2 He
Helium

Beryllium has an atomic number of 4. It means this element has 4 protons in its nucleus. Beryllium is a metal because it is located on the left side of the table.

4 Be
Beryllium

The Effect of Forces

by Natalie Rompella

Genre	Comprehension Skill	Text Features	Science Content
Nonfiction	Predict	• Captions • Charts • Diagrams • Glossary	Forces and Motion

Scott Foresman Science 6.15

PEARSON
Scott Foresman

scottforesman.com

ISBN 0-328-14013-9

What did you learn?

1. **Put the planets in order by gravitational force,** starting with the least gravitation.

2. A woman is driving a car. She then fills her car with heavy boxes. It now takes more force for the car to accelerate. This is an example of which of Newton's laws of motion?

3. Why is there high tide on the side of Earth facing the Moon?

4. **Writing** in Science Is it harder to stop your bike on concrete than on ice? Why?

5. **Predict** Choose a sport to discuss how it uses gravity, speed, velocity, friction, and acceleration as part of the game.

Picture Credits
Every effort has been made to secure permission and provide appropriate credit for photographic material.
The publisher deeply regrets any omission and pledges to correct errors called to its attention in subsequent editions.

Photo locators denoted as follows: Top (T), Center (C), Bottom (B), Left (L), Right (R), Background (Bkgd).

1 ©Rubberball Productions; 3 (CR) Getty Images; 6 (B, CR) ©Rubber Ball Productions; 10 ©Comstock Inc.;
12 John Shaw/NHPA Limited; 15 Getty Images; 17 Royal Society/Eileen Tweedy/The Art Archive; 18 (TR) Dean Conger/
Corbis, (B) Pete Stone/Corbis; 20 Srdjan Mihic/Alamy Images; 21 (TR) Getty Images; 22 Getty Images.

Scott Foresman/Dorling Kindersley would also like to thank: 23 NASA/DK Images.

Unless otherwise acknowledged, all photographs are the copyright © of Dorling Kindersley, a division of Pearson.

ISBN: 0-328-14013-9

Copyright © Pearson Education, Inc.

All Rights Reserved. Printed in the United States of America. The blackline masters in this publication are designed for use with appropriate equipment to reproduce copies for classroom use only. Scott Foresman grants permission to classroom teachers to reproduce from these masters.

2 3 4 5 6 7 8 9 10 V004 13 12 11 10 09 08 07 06 05

Glossary

acceleration	rate at which velocity changes
force	a push or pull
friction	force that keeps objects from moving past one another
gravitational force	attraction between any object and every other object in the universe
inertia	tendency of an object to remain at rest or in constant motion unless a force acts on it
momentum	product of an object's mass multiplied by its velocity
speed	measure of how fast an object is traveling
velocity	speed plus direction of an object

The Effect of Forces

by Natalie Rompella

The Nature of Forces

How many objects do you apply force to every day? Do you ever push a door open? Do you grab or pull any objects? When you push or pull something, you are applying force. **Force** is a push or pull.

Forces push or pull not only when objects touch, but even when they do not. Have you ever held two magnets near each other and then let go of one? The magnets may have attached to each other. The magnetic pull was the force that pulled and held them together.

When you hit a ball with a bat, you are actually pushing it. If gravity did not pull the ball down, it would never "fall" on the ground, or it would be very difficult to catch.

The Universe in Motion

A force is a push or a pull. We can measure force and identify its direction. Some forces act only if the objects touch, such as when you hold a book in your hand. Other forces act even if the objects do not touch. Earth's gravity pulls you down when you jump. Friction is the force that resists the movement of an object over the surface of another.

Gravitational force is the force of attraction between objects in the universe. Every planet and moon has a different gravitational force. The force depends on the size and mass of the object. Gravity on the Moon is much less than on Earth because the Moon is smaller.

Motion is described using a frame of reference. You are not in motion relative to Earth when you are sitting quietly. But because Earth moves in space and also rotates on its axis, you are moving with Earth relative to the Sun.

If an object moves faster or slower, the change in velocity is called acceleration. Motion can be described by specific laws. Newton's laws explain how things move in the universe.

Though we do not notice it, the Earth moves through space at a speed of 29.8 kilometers per second.

Momentum

After a batter hits a baseball, the player's body continues to swing around. Why? The amount of force needed to stop the ball and make it go in the opposite direction takes momentum. **Momentum** depends on the mass and velocity of an object. The mass of the bat and the direction and speed of the hit need to be greater than the mass and velocity of the ball. When objects collide, the total momentum before the collision equals the total momentum afterward, known as the law of conservation of momentum. The total momentum before the batter hits the baseball equals the total momentum after. The more momentum the ball being pitched has, the harder it is for the batter to hit the ball to make it first stop, and then change its direction.

The law of momentum can be seen in action when a baseball player hits a ball.

Applying Forces

Objects receive force from many different directions. They also apply force on other objects. What determines how something moves? The greater force causes an object to move. If it receives the same amount of force in opposing directions, it will not move.

If two people of the same mass push with the same force on opposing sides of a box, the box will not move. If one of the two people applies more force, measured in newtons (N), the box will move away from him or her.

If you have ever built anything with wood, you may have held the pieces together with nails. As you applied force to the nail with a hammer, the force pushing the nail down was greater than the force of the wood pushing back, and the nail moved into the wood.

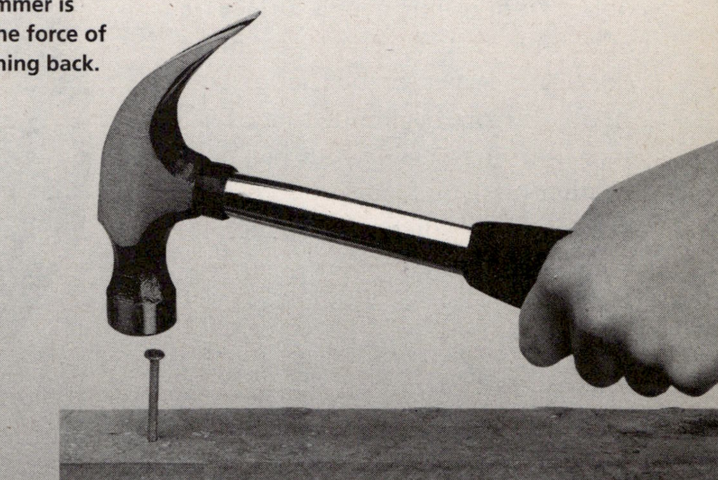

exerting a force on a tennis ball

The force exerted on the nail by the hammer is greater than the force of the wood pushing back.

Understanding Friction

Let's say you take off your shoes before going into the kitchen. As you walk over to the refrigerator in your socks, you slip on the floor. Why? The flat surface of the kitchen floor and the smooth surface of your socks cause little friction with each other. **Friction** is the force that keeps objects from moving past one another. Now think what it would be like to ski with too much friction. Your skis would not slide past the snow easily and you would not ski very quickly.

What happens if you decide to walk in your socks on the carpet? You probably will slide less than you did on the smooth kitchen floor. The carpet's rougher surface creates more friction with your socks. The type of friction that the carpet and your socks make with each other is called sliding friction.

There are two other types of friction: rolling friction and static friction. Rolling friction resists an object from rolling over a surface or other object, such as trying to inline skate on a carpet. Static friction resists an object from beginning to move, such as trying to slide your bed or another piece of furniture across a room. Once you get it moving, it becomes easier.

Friction is essential for ice skating.

Basketball players also use this law to help them slam-dunk. They run, bend their knees, jump, and go soaring toward the basket. The basketball, too, is an example of the third law of motion. As the player dribbles the ball (applying force to it), the ball rebounds off the floor and bounces back up to the player's hand.

This law is also called the law of action and reaction. An action, such as throwing a ball at a brick wall, causes a reaction: the ball bounces back. Because the wall has a greater mass than the ball, the ball bounces back and the wall hardly moves. If a ball is thrown at a glass bottle, such as at a carnival event, the glass bottle may be knocked down if the ball has a greater mass than the bottle.

Basketball players use the third law of motion to help them jump high into the air.

The law of action and reaction can be seen when a basketball player dribbles the ball.

174

Third Law of Motion

What makes trampolines so much fun? They put into practice Newton's third law of motion. When a force is applied to an object, the object exerts an equal force in the opposite direction. You push down on the trampoline, and then bounce back up in the opposite direction. Stretching a rubber band and releasing it is another example of this law. As you pull the rubber band, you are exerting a force on it. As you let go, the rubber band flies off in the opposite direction from which you pulled it.

Try to jump straight up in the air without bending your knees. Were you able to jump very high? Now bend your knees before jumping. Did you get any higher? Dancers know the importance of the third law of motion. Before they jump high into the air, they bend their knees. This force in the opposite direction helps them jump higher.

Bending your knees before jumping will help you jump higher.

Using and Avoiding Friction

You rely on friction every day. When you wash your hands, the soap helps to kill germs, but the motion of rubbing your hands together also creates friction, which helps to get rid of germs.

People who play stringed instruments, such as violins and cellos, know that friction can be a good thing. Before playing the instrument, they rub a special substance, called rosin, on the bow. Rosin is made from tree sap and makes the bow stickier, creating more friction with the strings. Gymnasts also use rosin on their hands to help keep their grip, especially on the uneven bars, balance beam, and parallel bars.

Can friction be harmful? Did you ever get a blister from a pair of shoes? The shoes rubbing against your feet, or the friction between your shoes and skin, caused the blister. Have you ever seen potters making a clay pot? They allow the clay to spin as they work it with their hands. They keep their hands moist with water to avoid friction. They want their hands to easily slide across the surface of the clay to smooth it into a particular shape.

This potter is keeping his hands moist to avoid friction.

Gravitational Force

The force of attraction that is experienced by all the objects in the universe is **gravitational force.** Gravity is the gravitational force on Earth. Jump up. If you try to stay up in the air, you can't. Why? Gravity pulls you toward the surface of Earth. Gravity holds the water in the oceans and holds the air near Earth. Gravity has an effect on the growth of plants. Life depends on gravity in many ways. Earth is not the only source of gravity, however; there are other gravitational forces in the universe.

In the 1600s, Sir Isaac Newton discovered the properties of gravity. He explained that gravity depends on the masses of the objects. Objects with greater mass exert more gravity on objects that have smaller mass. The magnitude of the force not only depends on the mass of the objects, but also on the distance between the two objects. When you jump up into the air, you pull on Earth with gravitational attraction. The Earth is also pulling on you. Because Earth has a much greater mass than you do, its gravitational attraction is stronger, pulling you back to the ground. At a higher altitude, gravity is slightly less.

When you jump, Earth's gravity pulls you back down.

Using an Equation

To find the acceleration of an object, divide the force by the mass. Force can be measured in newtons.

Acceleration = Force/Mass

If a child uses a force of 10 newtons to pull a wagon with a mass of 23 kilograms, the acceleration would be 0.43 m/s^2. The direction of the acceleration depends on where the unbalanced force is coming from.

In a game of tug-of-war, each team depends on its collective mass and force to help pull the opposite team forcing it to cross the line dividing them. Whichever team exercises a much greater force will achieve a greater acceleration, which will cause the other team to move in the direction of that unbalanced force and cross the line.

176

Second Law of Motion

A child can easily pull a wagon. What if the wagon were filled with heavy rocks? It would be more difficult for the child to pull it. This is Newton's second law of motion. The acceleration of an object depends on the mass of the object and the amount of force applied. In the wagon example, the mass of the wagon changes when rocks are added. To move the wagon, more force is needed. If an adult helped to pull the wagon, more force could be applied, increasing the acceleration of the wagon.

More force is needed to move heavy objects, such as this jeep stuck in snow.

The team causing the greatest acceleration forces the other team to cross the line.

Universal Force

Newton was the first to realize that the force holding any object to Earth is the same as the force holding the universe together.

Which do you think has a greater gravitational force, Earth or the Moon? Because Earth has a larger mass, the Moon is pulled toward Earth and orbits Earth. Which do you think has a greater gravitational force, Earth or the Sun? The Sun has a much greater mass than Earth and all of the other planets in the solar system. That is why the planets revolve around the Sun. They are being pulled toward the Sun as they orbit it.

Also, each of the planets has a specific gravitational pull. Although your mass would not change if you traveled to different planets, your weight would. That is because weight is a measure of a planet's gravitational pull on you. Weight in the metric system is measured in newtons. If your mass is 50 kilograms, your weight is 490.3 newtons on Earth.

The Moon is pulled toward Earth because Earth has a greater mass.

Journey to the Planets

Planet	Weight in Newtons (N)	Weight in Pounds (lb)
Mercury	185.3	41.7
Venus	444.7	100
Earth	490.3	110.2
Mars	184.9	41.6
Jupiter	1,159.1	260.6
Saturn	521.7	117.3
Uranus	435.9	98
Neptune	551.6	124
Pluto	32.9	7.4

The table above shows the weight of a child who has a mass of 50 kilograms. The differences in weight are due to the fact that every planet has a specific gravitational force. If she could weigh herself on each of the planets, her weight in newtons would change due to the differences in gravitational force on each planet. If walking on the Moon, she would weigh 83.5 newtons, or 18.8 pounds! The Moon's gravity is about one-sixth the gravity on Earth.

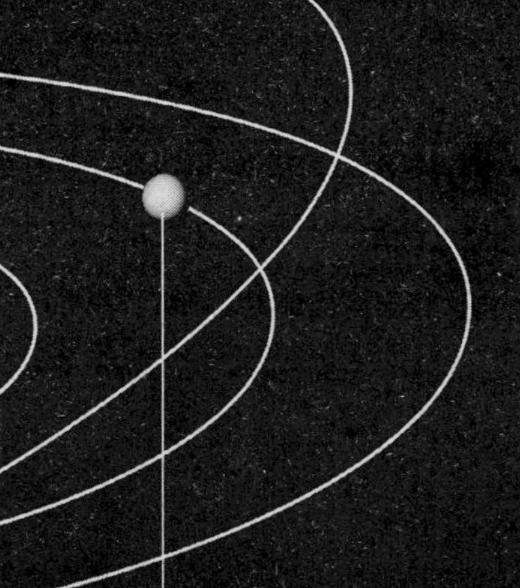

This suitcase would weigh six times less on the Moon!

First Law of Motion

If you set a book on a stationary surface, such as a table, it will remain there (assuming no other forces act on it). If you push the book with your hand, the book will move across the table. This is what Newton named the first law of motion. An object will remain at rest unless acted on by an unbalanced force.

The opposite is also true. An object will remain in motion unless acted on by an unbalanced force. A child on a swing will keep swinging until a force, such as gravity, stops the swing. Another force that can change the motion is friction.

Inertia is another name for the first law of motion. Inertia is the tendency of an object to remain at rest or in a continuous motion unless a force acts upon it.

The mass of an object can affect its inertia. If you set one textbook on your desk, you can easily push it to the other side of your desk. If you were to stack ten textbooks on top of one another and try to push them, it would be more difficult. The stack of ten textbooks has a greater inertia, making it harder to move.

178

Studying Motion

During the second century A.D. an astronomer named Claudius Ptolemy believed that the planets and the Sun circled around Earth. It was not until the 1500s that another scientist, Nicolaus Copernicus, came up with a different theory. He believed that the planets, including Earth, circled around the Sun.

Through the years, scientists have studied force and motion. Many scientists have conducted experiments to help figure out their theories. Some of the major scientists who have worked on force and motion are Galileo Galilei and Isaac Newton. Galileo studied the properties of gravity. Newton is known for the three laws of motion.

Earth and other planets revolve around the Sun due to the Sun's gravitational attraction.

The Effects of Gravity

Have you ever looked at the shoreline by the ocean? Sometimes there is a lot of beach and other times at the same place there is less. This is because the level of the ocean water varies over the course of a day. This is due to gravity.

Both the Earth and the Moon have strong gravitational attraction. The Moon's gravitational attraction causes water to be pulled away from the Earth toward the Moon. When this happens, we experience high tide on that side of the Earth. At the same time, the side of Earth opposite the Moon also experiences high tide. The Moon does not have as strong a pull on the opposite side of the Earth; rather, this bulge of water is caused by the movement of the Earth. While the sides toward the Moon and opposite the Moon are experiencing high tide, the two sides in between are experiencing low tide.

Tides are caused by the Moon's gravity pulling on Earth's water.

Describing Motion

Have you ever been sitting in a car at a stoplight when the car next to you slowly starts to move, and it's hard to tell whether you are in motion or the other car is in motion? If you look at a nearby tree or street sign, you can tell which is really moving. An object that can be used to detect motion is called a frame of reference.

Usually, Earth is used as the frame of reference for motion. When on Earth, one can tell which object is moving in relation to Earth. But isn't Earth moving? It is, but we are moving with it.

At dusk many people will sit outside to watch the Sun "set." In reality, Earth is rotating away from the direction of the Sun, making the Sun seem to disappear and then reappear at dawn.

Although it may appear that the Sun is setting, Earth is actually rotating away from the Sun.

Acceleration

Do you like to ride your bike? As you begin pedaling, you apply force to the pedals, and you begin to accelerate. **Acceleration** is the rate at which the velocity changes. Acceleration can be both increasing and decreasing velocity.

You come to a busy street, so you apply the brakes, causing friction between your brakes and the tires and between the tires and the road. As the bike slows down, your velocity decreases over a period of time. A decrease in velocity is called deceleration.

The velocity of an object only changes if a force acts on the object. If you roll a ball across a floor, eventually the velocity and speed of the ball will decrease. Gravity and friction, among other forces, will slow the ball down. If you roll a ball down a hill, the velocity will change, and the ball will accelerate due to the force of gravity.

When you apply force by pedaling, you are accelerating.

Finding Velocity

Many objects can move at many speeds and in many directions. **Velocity** is the speed and direction of a moving object. A car traveling from New York to California may have a velocity of 80 km/h west. On the return to New York, it may have a velocity of 80 km/h east.

The velocity of an object not traveling in a straight line will constantly change. Think of a snake that slithers in a curvy line. Although its speed remains constant, its velocity changes each time it switches directions.

The wind can change the velocity of an object. If you've ever flown a kite, you've seen how both the speed and direction of the kite can change. Sailors rely on the wind to navigate their sailboats across the water. They need to know the direction and speed of the wind to arrive at their destination.

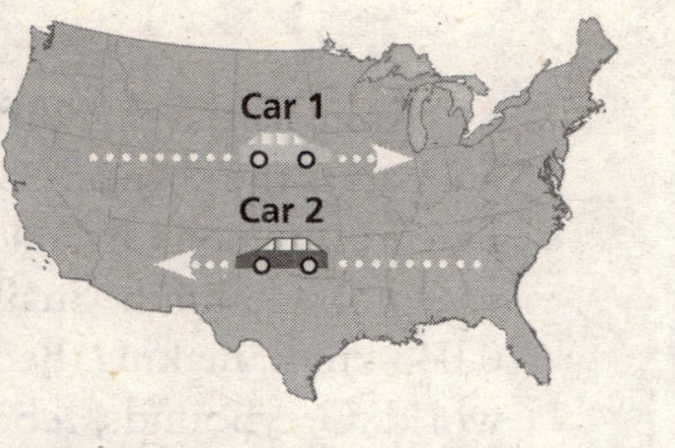

The force of the wind against the sail helps the sailboat to move through water. By rotating the sail, the sailboat's direction and speed can be changed.

Kinds of Motion

Objects can move in many directions. Motion can be straight, zigzag, curvy, or even up and down. Trains and airplanes move mostly in straight lines. Many sports use straight motion. Golfers usually try to hit the ball so that its motion is straight. When you bowl, the ball rolls down the lane in a straight line too.

A zigzag motion is moving in a line that sharply and repeatedly changes direction. Some skiers train to move very fast through gates that are positioned in a zigzag pattern. Some skillful skiers are able to do this easily.

A curvy motion is traveling in a line that is not straight, but moves in a smooth, continuous fashion, such as walking up a spiral staircase. If you've ever watched cars race on a circular track, you may have described the cars' motion as curved. However, from the frame of reference of the drivers in the car, they would probably describe the road's motion as curved.

Think of a child on a seesaw. The movement is up and down. To the child on the seesaw, the ground is moving up and down. To someone watching the child on the seesaw, the seesaw is moving up and down.

Skiers move in a zigzag motion.

12

Calculating Speed

An object in motion moves at a certain pace in a given time. **Speed** is a measure of how fast an object is traveling. If you run one kilometer in ten minutes, your speed would be calculated by dividing the distance by the time. Usually speed is measured in kilometers per hour (km/h). To calculate speed in kilometers per hour (km/h), first calculate the speed in kilometers per minute (km/min) and then multiply by 60.

Distance (1 km)/Time (10 min) = Speed (0.1 km/min) x 60 = 6 km/h

Your average speed would equal 6 km/h. However, you probably would not run at a constant pace of one kilometer for every ten minutes. There would probably be points when you would run a little faster or slower. The speed that you are traveling at the exact moment is your instantaneous speed.

Animals travel at different speeds. One of the fastest land animals is the cheetah. Cheetahs can run as fast as 100 km/h. Peregrine falcons are able to dive down to catch prey at a top speed of 440 km/h. Snails, on the other hand, travel only 0.048 km/h, making them one of the slowest animals in the world. Greyhounds, zebras, ostriches, and gray foxes all move at about the same speed of 64 km/h. Although cockroaches are small, they are known for being quick. They can travel 5 km/h.

Some of the fastest humans are able to run at speeds of 37 km/h. Through the years, humans have tried to decrease the time it takes to travel by creating machines with faster speeds. More than two hundred years ago, the first steam locomotive was invented. Since then, automobiles, airplanes, and rockets have been created. One of the Wright brothers' original airplanes flew at a top speed of 68 km/h. Today airplanes are able to travel at speeds of more than 1,000 km/h.

Cheetahs can run very fast, but only for a short amount of time.

Science

13

Physical Science

The Use of MACHINES

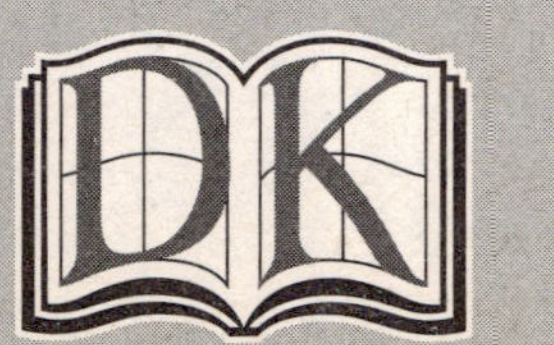

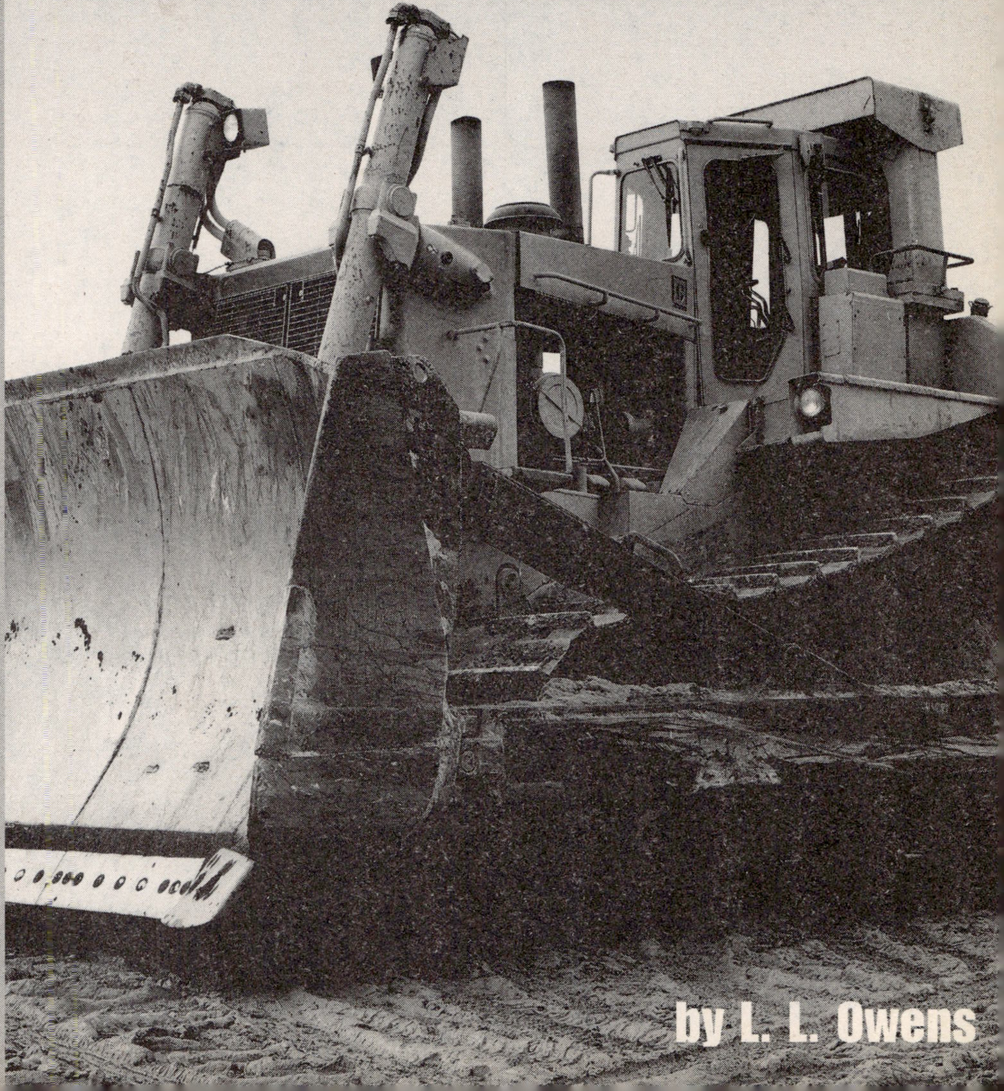

by L. L. Owens

Genre	Comprehension Skill	Text Features	Science Content
Nonfiction	Cause and Effect	• Captions • Charts • Diagrams • Glossary	Simple Machines

Scott Foresman Science 6.16

PEARSON Scott Foresman

scottforesman.com

ISBN 0-328-14016-3

9 780328 140169 90000

What did you learn?

1. What is the scientific definition of work?

2. What type of simple machine is the Ferris wheel?

3. What are some examples of the simple machine called the wedge?

4. **Writing** in Science All machines help people do work. Write to explain the difference between simple machines and compound machines. Include details from the book to support your answer.

5. **Cause and Effect** What would be the effect of friction when moving a heavy object, such as a piano, over wheels, as opposed to moving it without wheels?

Picture Credits
Every effort has been made to secure permission and provide appropriate credit for photographic material.
The publisher deeply regrets any omission and pledges to correct errors called to its attention in subsequent editions.

Photo locators denoted as follows: Top (T), Center (C), Bottom (B), Left (L), Right (R), Background (Bkgd).

5 Jeffrey Greenberg /Photo Researchers, Inc.; 6 ©The Science Museum, London /DK Images; 8 Felicia Martinez/ PhotoEdit; 10 (T) ©Conrad Zobel/Corbis. (BL) Brian Mitchell/Alamy Images; 12 Brand X Pictures; 15 (BR) ©The Science Museum, London /DK Images.

Scott Foresman/Dorling Kindersley would also like to thank: 11 (BL) Stephen Oliver/DK Images.

Unless otherwise acknowledged, all photographs are the copyright © of Dorling Kindersley, a division of Pearson.

ISBN: 0-328-14016-3

Glossary

compound machines	machines consisting of many parts and two or more simple machines
effort force	force applied to a machine
fulcrum	a fixed point or support on which a lever turns or moves
load	the resistance of an object that must be overcome by a machine
machine	a device that helps people do work
simple machine	a machine with just one or two parts
work	the use of force to move an object by pushing or pulling, in order to move it a certain distance

The Use of MACHINES

by L. L. Owens

Work and Machines

Defining Work

What do you think about when you hear the word *work*? Do you think of chores you do around the house, such as taking out the garbage, setting the table for dinner, or making your bed? Do you think of different jobs that adults have, such as truck driver, computer programmer, or nurse? All of these examples fit the meaning of work as we use it in our daily lives. We're going to take a closer look at another way to think about work.

In science, **work** is the use of force to move something a certain distance. The force—or pushing and pulling—is applied to an object. You can tell that work has occurred when an object moves. If the object doesn't move, no work has occurred.

If you use a wheelbarrow to move a heavy load across your yard, you have done work. Work was done because the load moved. Suppose you tried to lift the load out of the wheelbarrow but it was too heavy. No matter how hard you push or pull, you cannot move the load. In this case, you have not done work because the load did not move.

When you lift and push a wheelbarrow, work is occurring.

pulley
The winch is a type of pulley. The rope end hoists weights and raises or lowers the sail.

lever
The boom is a lever with a fulcrum at the mast joint. The weight of the sail above it is the load. Force is applied by the guide rope. The rope controls the direction the boom swings.

wheel and axle
The helm is a type of wheel that can change the direction of the rudder.

wedge
The rudder is a type of wedge. It sticks out below the rear of the boat and helps steer it. The keel is another example of a wedge on a sailboat. It keeps the boat moving through the water in a straight path.

screw
The propeller is a type of screw that pushes some sailboats through the water.

Compound Machines

Most of the machines you come across every day are compound machines. That means they are made up of two or more simple machines. Examples include the stapler you use to fasten papers together and the can opener you use in the kitchen. More complicated examples are your watch, the school bus you ride, and the airplanes that buzz overhead. Compound machines can have hundreds or thousands of parts.

Have you ever seen a sailboat up close? It's a great example of a compound machine made up of many simple machines. Here are examples of all six types of simple machines in a sailboat.

A sailboat is a compound machine made up of many different simple machines.

inclined plane
The jib sail, or jib, is an inclined plane. It directs the wind to the bigger mainsail.

Work Can Be Measured

You can find out how much work is done for a given task. All you need is to know the formula that scientists use to measure work:

> **work = force x distance**

Work is measured in a unit called the joule. The abbreviation for the joule is J.

> **1 joule (J) = 1 newton (N) x 1 meter (m)**

Let's use the formula to measure some work. You moved a wheelbarrow a distance of 20 meters. You pushed with a force of 10 newtons. The wheelbarrow moved 20 meters. The work done was 10 N x 20 m, or 200 J.

The amount of work that occurs when you push a wheelbarrow depends on how much force you push with and how far you push it.

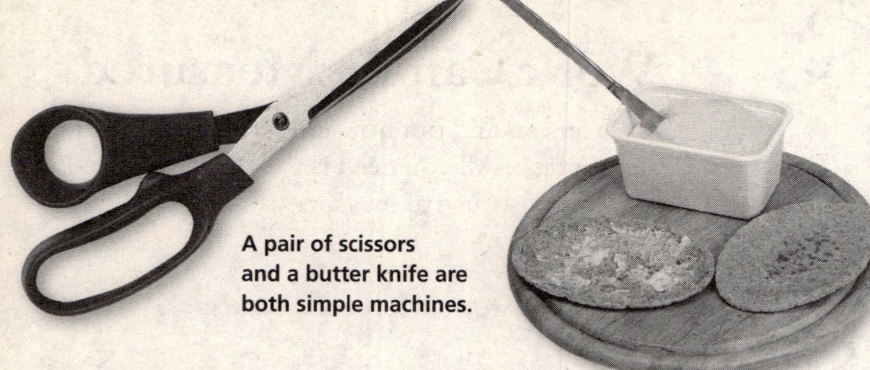

A pair of scissors and a butter knife are both simple machines.

Machines: The Basics

What do you think of when you hear the word *machine*? Something big and noisy, such as a bulldozer—or even bigger and noisier, such as an airplane? Both of these machines are made up of hundreds, or even thousands, of moving parts. Did you know that some machines don't have any moving parts? It's true. By definition, a **machine** is any device that helps people do work.

A **simple machine** is a tool or device made up of just one or two parts. Think about some everyday objects, such as a butter knife, a hammer, and a pair of scissors. These are all good examples of simple machines. They have one or two parts, and they help you do work, such as spreading peanut butter, removing a nail from a wall, and cutting paper.

Bulldozers and airplanes are **compound machines.** They're made up of many parts, including two or more simple machines. Other common compound machines include an electric pencil sharpener, a lawn mower, a car, and a steamboat.

A bulldozer is a compound machine because it is made up of many simple machines.

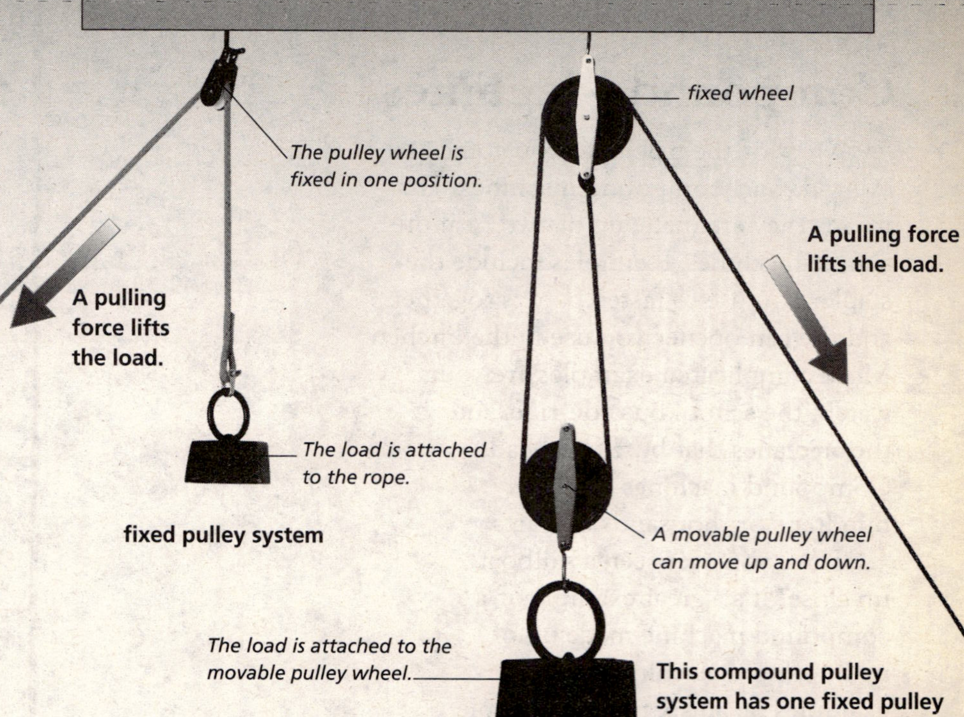

Pulley

Have you ever seen a crane lifting large objects at a construction site? That's an example of the simple machine called the pulley. A pulley is a grooved wheel with a rope, belt, or chain around it. You attach a load to one end of the rope and apply effort force to the other end. In other words, you pull on the rope, causing the wheel to turn and the load to move. The point is to make moving the load easier.

Pulleys can be fixed or movable. As the wheel turns, a fixed pulley stays in one position. Think about seeing a flag raised on a flagpole. You pull down on the rope to move the flag up. The fixed pulley doesn't move or reduce the effort force needed to raise the flag. It simply changes the direction of the force.

A movable pulley is attached to the object being moved. It decreases the effort force, but you must apply the force over a greater distance.

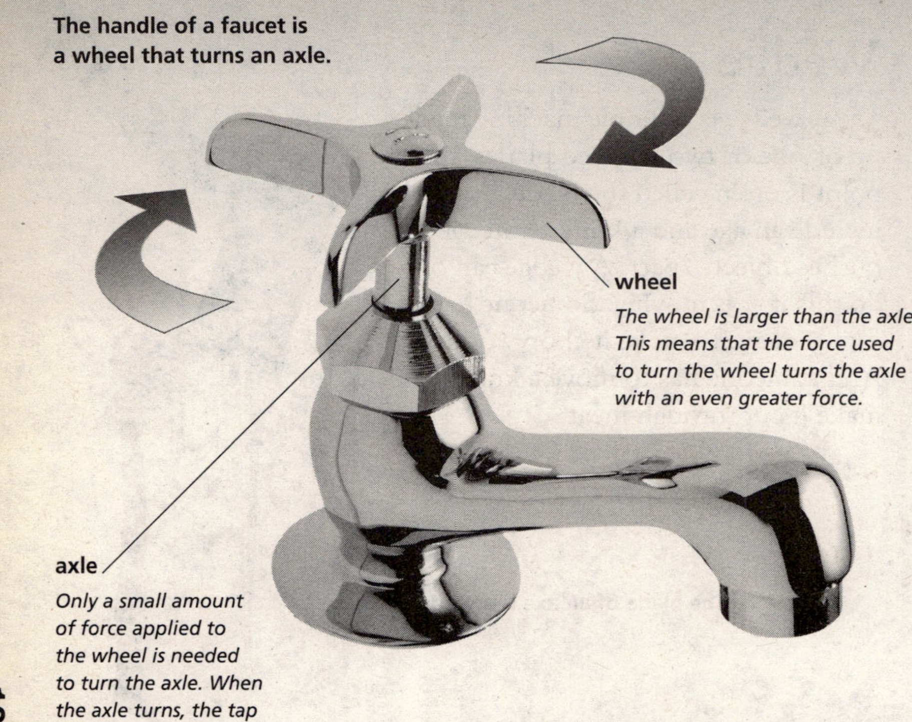

Loading and unloading a
truck is easier with a ramp.

Wheel and Axle

A wheel and axle is a wheel with a rod, called an axle, through its center. A Ferris wheel is an example of a big wheel and axle—you've probably ridden on one at a carnival or fair. A smaller example of a wheel and axle is something you use every day—a doorknob.

How does a wheel and axle do work? The axle attaches the wheel to the object it is moving. The axle turns when force is applied to the wheel, and it is more powerful than the wheel. So when you turn a faucet, the force you apply turns into a greater force in the axle inside the knob. The force from the axle is what operates the tap and opens the faucet.

Other examples of the wheel and axle can be found in cars, bicycles, clocks, roller skates, and faucets.

Machines Make Doing Work Easier

Machines help people do work by reducing the amount of force needed to complete a task. You have probably seen a ramp attached to the back of a truck. It is a simple machine that makes the work of loading objects into the truck easier. The force needed to push objects up the ramp is less than the force needed to lift the same objects. Because less force is required, the task is easier.

A ramp reduces the force needed to lift an object by increasing the distance over which the force is applied. When you push something up a ramp into a truck, you cover more distance than the distance from the ground to the truck. Still, the task is much easier to complete.

Friction and Machines

For a machine to do its job, work must go into it. Work comes from you when you carry your books upstairs. It also comes from you when you sweep the floor. Work can sometimes go into a machine from a different energy source. Some machines, such as the washing machine that cleans your clothing, are powered by electricity.

Do you think the amount of work a machine does is the same amount of work that goes into it? Actually, a machine does less work than the amount put into it. The main reason for this difference between input and output is friction. Most machines generate heat when they are operated. Most machines have many movable parts. Heat is the result of friction between the many parts of the machine.

Many of a car's moving parts wear out because of friction.

Wedge

A wedge is a simple machine made up of one or two inclined planes. Its point is often called the blade. Examples include an axe and a knife. A wedge pushes objects apart. A wedge can only do this if it is moving. Someone has to swing an axe to make it chop wood. And someone has to move a knife to make it cut through meat.

The blade of an axe is a wedge.

Screw

A screw looks a lot like a nail with ridges. Those ridges are called threads. A screw is actually an inclined plane that wraps around a cylinder. That is what forms the ridges. A screw works by increasing distance and decreasing force. You can put a light bulb securely into a socket by screwing it in. The ridges let you fasten it tightly with less force than if you pushed directly, but you have to apply the force over a greater distance.

The ridges on this light bulb form a screw.

For example, machines with many moving parts, such as cars, lose a lot of the input work to friction. This is one of the reasons the car's engine and its other moving parts need to be properly lubricated. Lubrication reduces friction. People who design machines try to reduce friction and the loss of work as much as possible. Reducing friction saves energy and decreases the amount of work that must go into a machine.

Oil reduces friction between the moving parts of a car's engine. This increases the amount of work that the car can do.

A road that twists and turns up a mountain is an inclined plane.

Inclined Plane

Remember how a ramp attached to the back of a truck helps people do work? A ramp is a type of simple machine called an inclined plane. It's a slanted surface that makes moving a load from a low place to a higher place easier.

Other examples of inclined planes are the slide you see at many playgrounds and the wheelchair access ramp you can find at many public buildings. Yet another example is a road system that winds up a steep mountainside. You have to travel a greater distance to get to the top of the mountain than if you had gone straight up. But less force is needed to move the car along the twisting road, so it makes the work easier.

An access ramp for a wheelchair-user is also an inclined plane.

Types Of Simple Machines

Let's take a look at how the different types of simple machines help you do work. There are six basic types.

This hammer is acting as a lever.

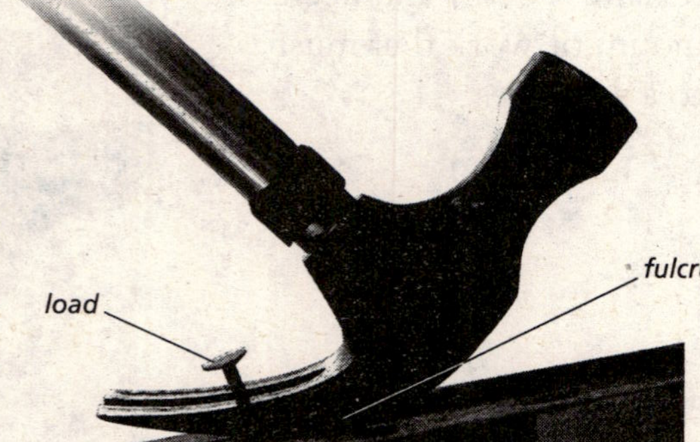

Lever

A lever is one or more bars resting on a support, or **fulcrum.** The lever is used for applying force, such as lifting a weight. Recall that a hammer used to pry a nail out of a wall is a simple machine. It is one example of a lever. The curved part of the hammer's head is the fulcrum. The nail, or **load,** creates a force on the hammer. The force applied to the end of the hammer's handle is called the **effort force.** When effort force is applied to the handle it pulls up on the load. This pulls the nail out of the wood. It is much easier to pry a nail out of wood with a hammer than by hand.

A fulcrum can occur in different positions on a lever. The closer the fulcrum is to the load, the less force is needed to move the load. The closer the fulcrum is to the effort force, the more force is needed to move the load. When the fulcrum is close to the load, the load won't be lifted very high. But when the fulcrum is close to the effort force, the load will be lifted higher.

Levers fall into the following categories:

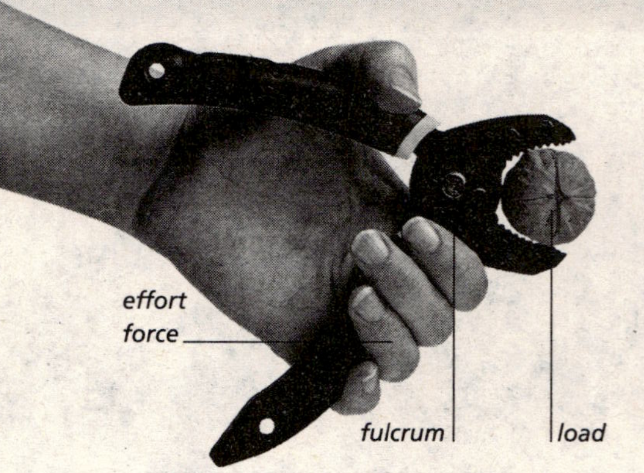

A pair of pliers is a first-class lever.

First-class Lever

In a first-class lever, the effort force is located at one end, the load is at the other end, and the fulcrum is in the middle. A pair of pliers is an example of a first-class lever.

Second-class Lever

An example of a second-class lever is a nutcracker. The fulcrum is at the closed end. You apply the effort force to the handles, and the load is the nut you're cracking.

This nutcracker is a second-class lever.

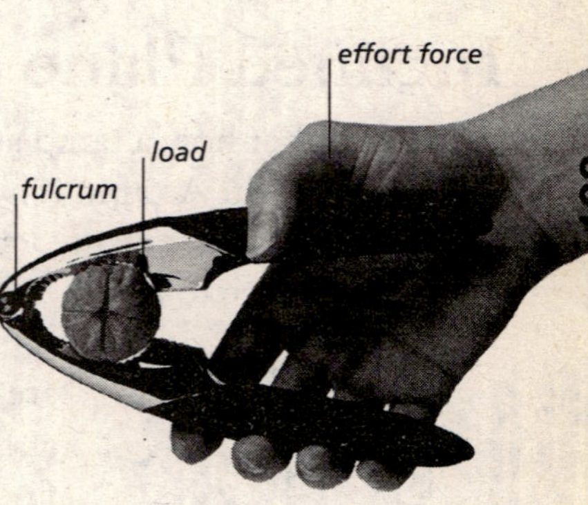

A pair of chopsticks is a third-class lever.

Third-class Lever

In a third-class lever, the fulcrum is at one end and the load is at the other. The effort force is in the middle. A pair of chopsticks is a third-class lever.

192

Energy

by Peggy Bresnick Kendler

Genre	Comprehension Skill	Text Features	Science Content
Nonfiction	Sequence	• Captions • Charts • Diagrams • Glossary	Forms of Energy

Scott Foresman Science 6.17

What did you learn?

1. Describe the difference between potential energy and kinetic energy.

2. What discoveries made scientists give up on the law of conservation of energy? What law has replaced it?

3. Based on what you have read, explain how a magnet and a coil can produce an electric current.

4. **Writing** in Science Energy has many forms, and it can change from one form to another, such as when spotlights change electrical energy into light. Write to explain some other ways energy changes from one form to another.

5. **Sequence** Describe the steps needed to produce an electric current.

Vocabulary

electric circuit
electric current
electric motor
energy
generator
kinetic energy
magnetic domain
potential energy

Picture Credits
Every effort has been made to secure permission and provide appropriate credit for photographic material.
The publisher deeply regrets any omission and pledges to correct errors called to its attention in subsequent editions.

Photo locators denoted as follows: Top (T), Center (C), Bottom (B), Left (L), Right (R), Background (Bkgd).

10 Alex Bartel /Photo Researchers, Inc.; 11 Dr. Jeremy Burgess /Photo Researchers, Inc.;
12 Michael Melford/Getty Images.

Scott Foresman/Dorling Kindersley would also like to thank: 6 (BR) Stephen Oliver/DK Images.

Unless otherwise acknowledged, all photographs are the copyright © of Dorling Kindersley, a division of Pearson.

ISBN: 0-328-14019-8

Glossary

electric circuit — a closed path along which current can flow

electric current — the flow of electrical charges through a material

electric motor — a device that changes electrical energy into kinetic energy

energy — the ability to do work or cause change

generator — a device that transforms mechanical energy into electrical energy

kinetic energy — the energy of something that is moving

magnetic domain — a large number of atoms that have their magnetic fields pointing in the same direction

potential energy — stored energy that is determined by an object's position

Different Kinds Of Energy

Energy is defined as the ability to do work or cause change. Energy is found in many sources in nature, including sunlight, wind, water, plants, and animals. We use energy every day. You get energy from the food you eat. We use energy to light and heat our homes. Cars, trucks, planes, and trains all need fuel for energy.

There are many different forms of energy, including mechanical energy, electrical energy, nuclear energy, thermal energy, and solar energy. In photosynthesis, green plants convert the solar energy of light from the Sun into chemical energy. Each type of energy shares the ability to cause some kind of change or to do work. In fact, nearly anytime something moves or changes at all, energy is used.

What sources of energy can you see in these pictures?

Electricity is a form of energy that we use every day to power everything from pocket calculators to trains. We generate electricity by harnessing other forms of energy, such as the burning of fuels, nuclear reactions, wind, or flowing water.

All things possess some type of energy. Even inanimate objects have energy. Energy moves waves to the shore and pushes sailboats through the water. Energy is what bakes our cookies in the oven. It heats and lights our homes, and runs our radios, televisions, and computers. It is the ever-changing nature of energy that makes our lives on Earth possible.

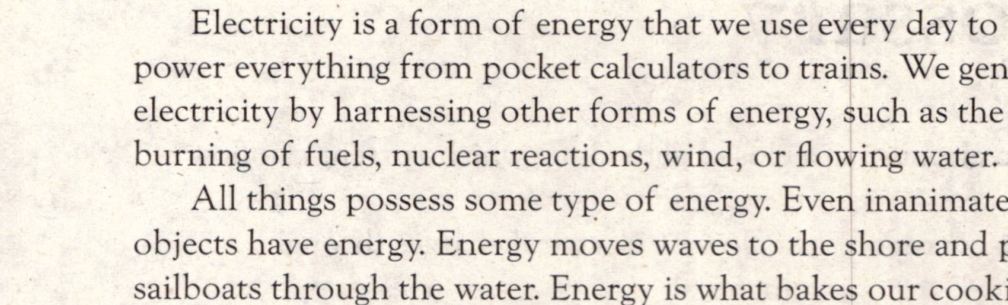

The electricity supplied by this power plant is just one form of energy. There is some form of energy in every living and nonliving thing on Earth.

There is a fixed amount of energy in the world. Energy is constantly being transferred from one object to another. Energy is also constantly changing from one form to another.

A car's engine burns gasoline. The engine converts the fuel's chemical energy into mechanical energy to make the car run. Solar energy panels convert the Sun's radiant energy into electrical energy. Your body has chemical energy that it gets from the foods you eat. You expend that energy through your muscles. This energy allows your body to do work.

When we use energy, it doesn't get used up and it doesn't disappear. We simply change it from one energy form to another. Any time one object does work or has an effect on another object, energy is being used.

The Different Forms of Energy

Kinetic energy is the energy an object possesses because it is moving. **Potential energy** is stored energy determined by an object's position.

A tennis ball thrown through the air has kinetic energy because it is moving. So does a dog when it jumps to catch the ball.

A tennis ball placed on a shelf has potential energy. If the ball falls from the shelf, its potential energy will be changed into kinetic energy because it will be moving. At the very top of its leap the dog also has potential energy. It is no longer moving up, and pauses slightly before falling back to the ground. In that short pause, the dog has potential energy. This potential energy changes into kinetic energy as the dog moves back toward the ground.

A dog has kinetic energy when it runs or jumps to catch a ball in its mouth.

Energy and Change

Almost all energy on Earth comes from the Sun. Plants convert the Sun's light energy into chemical energy when they make and store food. This stored energy is transferred to animals that eat plants, and then to animals that eat plant eaters. Fossil fuels come from the remains of organisms that got their energy from the Sun. They also store the Sun's energy.

Objects can be changed in many ways. A pile of books or magazines can be moved onto a tall shelf. A sculptor can take a slab of clay and mold it into a statue.

Each of these changes requires one thing: energy. When you change an object, you do some sort of work on it by transferring energy to that object.

The energy in the wind can blow objects around in the air.

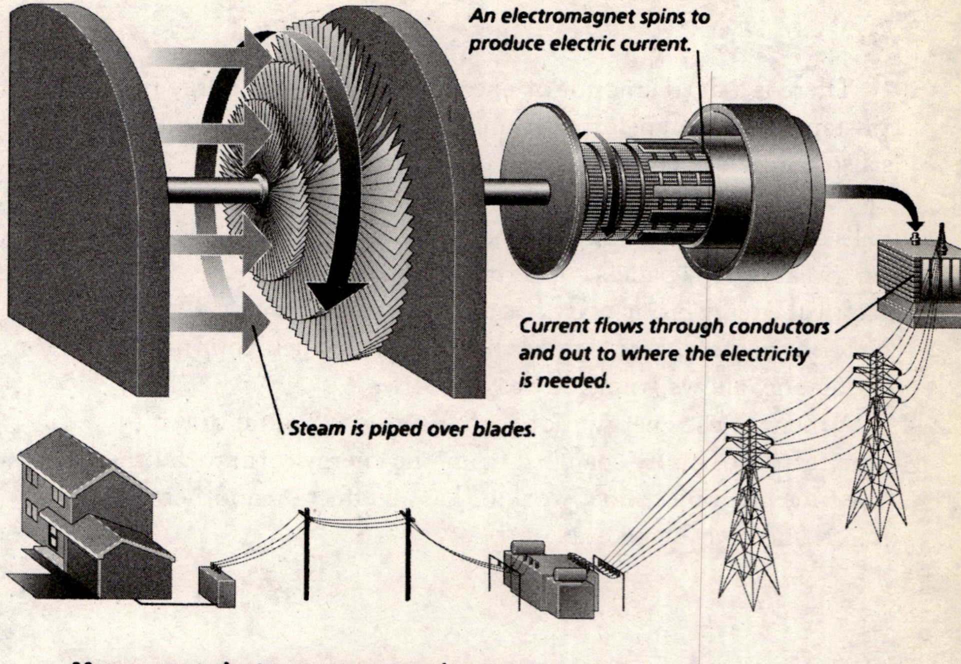

Many power plants use steam to spin generators. The steam pushes on the blades of a turbine, which spin to turn the generator.

A device that transforms mechanical energy into electrical energy is called a **generator.** The generator is based on the principle of electromagnetic induction.

Electric generators, which work with magnets, produce the electricity that we use in our homes and schools. Generators create an electric current by spinning a magnet inside a coil of wire. They can also work by moving a coil of wire inside a magnetic field.

In order to produce electricity, a generator needs more than a wire coil and a fixed magnet. It also needs something to provide the spinning motion. Usually power plants use a device called a turbine. Steam, water, or wind pushes on blades in the turbine, causing them to spin. The spinning motion turns the generator. Most power plants in the United States burn fossil fuels to generate steam.

Changing Magnetism Into Electricity

An English scientist named Michael Faraday found that a magnetic field can be used to produce electricity. Faraday knew that when an electric current flows in a wire, it makes a magnetic field. He found that if a wire was moved into a magnetic field, an electric current would be generated in the wire. A current is also generated if a magnet is moved across a piece of wire. Moving the wire or the magnet faster will produce a stronger current. This is called electromagnetic induction.

generators inside a hydroelectric power plant

Conservation Laws

Energy is changed and transferred all the time, but it is never lost. A piece of wood has a certain amount of chemical energy. When the wood burns, this energy is changed into heat and light energy. The energy changes form, but the same amount of energy is still present.

For hundreds of years, scientists believed there were no exceptions to this rule. They called it the law of conservation of energy. A similar rule, called the law of conservation of mass, stated that matter was never lost or gained, only changed.

But in the early 1900s, scientists found that these laws were not exactly correct. The famous scientist Albert Einstein came up with the idea that under certain conditions matter could change directly into energy, and energy could be changed into matter. For example, inside the Sun, nuclear reactions turn hydrogen into helium. But not all of the hydrogen is changed into helium; some of it is converted directly into energy. A new rule stated that although matter can change into energy and energy can change into matter, the total amount of matter and energy never changes. This is called the law of conservation of mass and energy.

A car converts chemical energy into mechanical energy.

Electricity And Magnetism

Electric Current

Hardly a moment goes by when we are not using electricity. Whether you are watching television, riding in a car, or simply checking your watch, electricity is at work. But what exactly is electricity? Electricity is the movement of charged particles.

Atoms have a central nucleus surrounded by moving electrons. An atom's nucleus has protons that have positive charges, and neutrons that have no charge. The atom also has electrons that have negative charges. These negative charges hold them near the nucleus. Most atoms have no charge, since their positive and negative charges cancel each other out.

In some materials, the electrons are not tightly held to the atoms and can move from one atom to another. The flow of these electrons from atom to atom causes an electrical charge. Since all electrons have negative charges, they repel each other. As they repel each other, the electrons flow from one nucleus to the next, producing an **electric current.** Materials that allow current to flow through them are good conductors of electricity.

The voltage of a battery or other electrical source measures the force of the electrons as they are pushed. It takes a source of energy, such as a battery, to make the electrons leave their nucleus and force them along a wire.

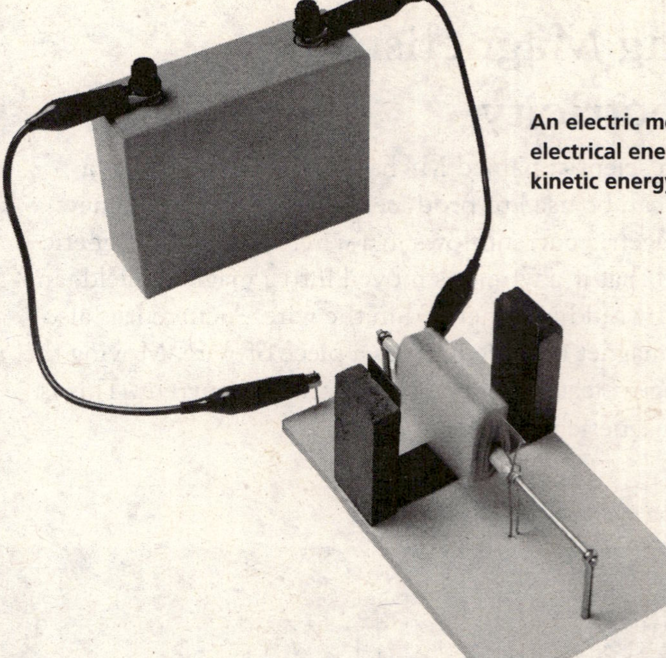

An electric motor converts electrical energy into kinetic energy.

A device that changes electrical energy into kinetic energy is called an **electric motor.** An electric motor has a permanent magnet, an electromagnet, and a device that changes the direction of the current that flows through the electromagnet. When current passes through the electromagnet, each pole is attracted to the opposite pole of the fixed magnet. This attraction causes the electromagnet to spin. The current is then reversed so the poles of the electromagnet are flipped, causing the electromagnet to move again. This happens over and over, producing a constant spinning motion.

We use electromagnets in our everyday life. The speakers in a stereo use rapid electromagnetic movements to produce sound vibrations. When the electric current is turned on, it flows at a very fast rate, producing a magnetic field. This magnetic field causes a cone in the speaker to move back and forth. If you look at the cone of a speaker playing loud, low tones, you can see it moving.

Electromagnets

A magnet that works only when electricity is run through it or around it is called an electromagnet. Unlike regular magnets, its magnetism can be switched on and off.

Electromagnets are made from a coil of wire that's attached to a power supply. When current flows into the coil, it becomes a magnet. If you add more coils, you can make the magnetic field stronger. The coils in an electromagnet are usually made out of copper wire. Copper is a good conductor of electricity.

Electromagnets only attract magnetic objects. When the current is turned off, the electromagnets are not magnetic.

This powerful electromagnet is used to pick up scrap metal. The operator can turn the electromagnet on to lift the metal and turn it off to drop the metal.

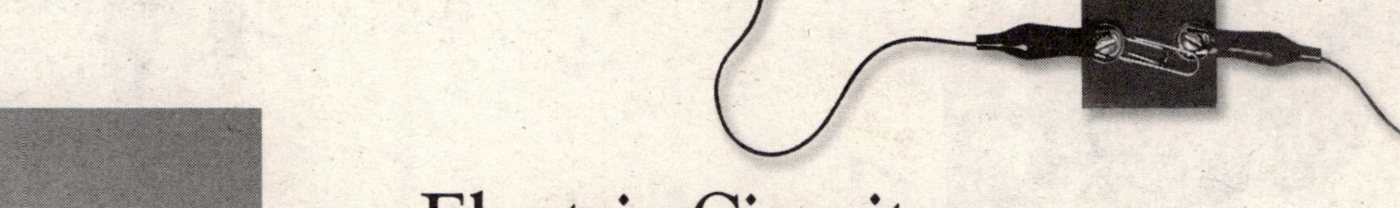

a series circuit

Electric Circuit

A closed path along which current can flow is an **electric circuit.** A circuit must have a source of electrical energy, a wire through which current can flow, and a device that can change the electrical energy into a useful energy form.

The device can be any type of object that runs on household electricity or batteries, such as a flashlight, a refrigerator, or a computer. Wires inside the appliance slow the flow of the electrons and the resistance causes electrical energy to change into other types of energy. In a flashlight, for instance, the resistance turns the electrical energy into light energy and thermal energy.

Circuits can be set in series—with one path along which current can flow—or in parallel—with more than one path along which current can flow. In a parallel circuit, if you remove one bulb, the others will still work; in a series circuit if one bulb burns out, the rest will not light up until that one is replaced.

8

Magnetic Fields

All magnets have their power concentrated in their two ends, called poles. One pole is called south and the other is called north. The north pole of a magnet is always attracted to the south pole of another magnet. Two north poles or two south poles always repel each other. However, the entire magnet attracts objects containing a lot of iron, such as pins or paper clips.

The area around a magnet that attracts other magnets is called a magnetic field. The magnetic field is strongest at a magnet's poles.

A magnet attracts metal paper clips.

9

Many materials can never be magnetic. The magnetic fields within these materials face in different directions and cancel each other out. In other materials, such as iron, cobalt, and nickel, the atoms line up in groups called domains. A large number of atoms with their magnetic fields pointing in the same direction is called a **magnetic domain.** When a piece of metal becomes magnetized, all of its magnetic fields are pointed in a single direction.

Earth's Magnetic Field

Earth acts as a giant magnet and is surrounded by a magnetic field. Scientists think this is the result of Earth spinning on its axis and the movement of hot iron in its core. The poles of this giant magnet are located near, but not exactly at, Earth's geographic poles. You can use a compass to point in the direction of Earth's magnetic north pole.

Earth's magnetic poles, which are shown by the red line, are not the same as its true poles.

Energy Heat from Light and Light

by L. L. Owens

Genre	Comprehension Skill	Text Features	Science Content
Nonfiction	Compare and Contrast	• Captions • Charts • Diagrams • Glossary	Light and Heat

Scott Foresman Science 6.18

What did you learn?

1. What is thermal energy?

2. What is radiation?

3. What are some examples of insulators?

4. **Writing** in Science Two types of waves are transverse waves and compressional waves. Write to explain the difference between them. Include details from the book to support your answer.

5. **Compare and Contrast** Explain how conduction and convection are alike and how they are different.

Vocabulary

conduction
conductor
convection
heat
insulator
radiation
reflection
refraction
thermal energy

Picture Credits
Every effort has been made to secure permission and provide appropriate credit for photographic material.
The publisher deeply regrets any omission and pledges to correct errors called to its attention in subsequent editions.

Photo locators denoted as follows: Top (T), Center (C), Bottom (B), Left (L), Right (R), Background (Bkgd).

Opener: Mark Romanelli/Alamy Images; 5 (TR) Mark Romanelli/Alamy Images; 6 (T) Willie Sator/Alamy Images;
9 (T) Tom Vezo/Nature Picture Library; 13 (TR) Digital Vision.

Unless otherwise acknowledged, all photographs are the copyright © of Dorling Kindersley, a division of Pearson.

ISBN: 0-328-14022-8

Glossary

conduction	the transfer of thermal energy between two objects that touch
conductor	a material that easily transfers thermal energy
convection	the transfer of thermal energy by the movement of a fluid
heat	thermal energy that moves from one substance to another
insulator	a material that does not easily transfer thermal energy
radiation	the transfer of thermal energy as waves
reflection	the bouncing of light rays off a surface
refraction	the change in direction of light when it moves from one material to another
thermal energy	the total kinetic and potential energy of the particles in a substance

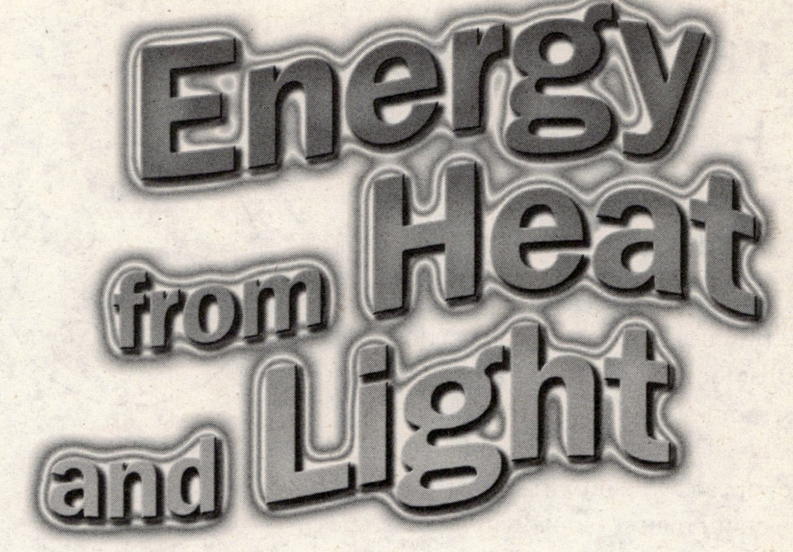

by L. L. Owens

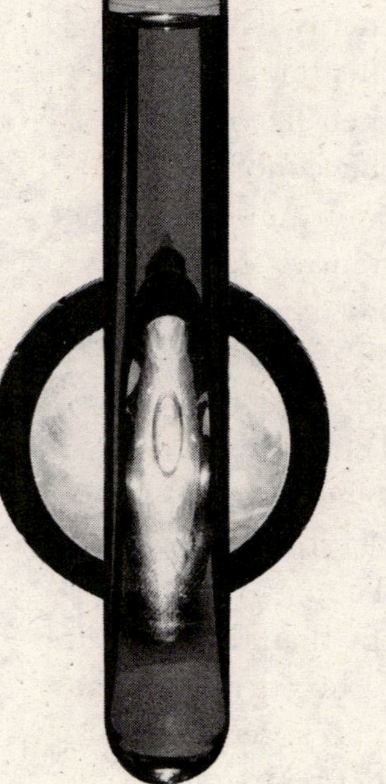

Transferring Thermal Energy

Thermal Energy

Thermal energy is the total kinetic and potential energy of the particles in a substance. If you could see the particles in steam you would see that they move quickly. The particles that make ice might not appear to be moving, but they are. In fact, all matter is made up of particles that are always moving. The energy that results from the movement is called kinetic energy.

Particles in a solid have a small amount of kinetic energy. That energy causes them to vibrate, but the particles cannot move from their fixed position. Particles in a liquid have more kinetic energy. They can flow around each other. Particles in a gas can move freely. They have even more kinetic energy than particles in a liquid. Particles in a substance always pull on each other. They have potential energy, which is stored energy due to position.

Thermal energy is affected by temperature. A cool cup of water has more potential energy than the same size cup of warm water. The warm water has more kinetic energy because particles move faster at a higher temperature.

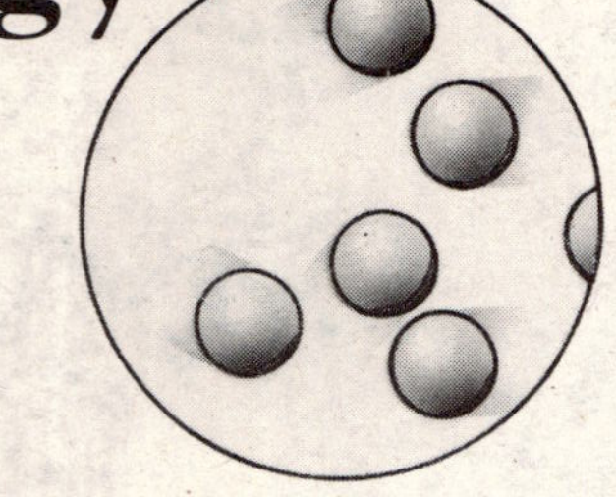

gas particles

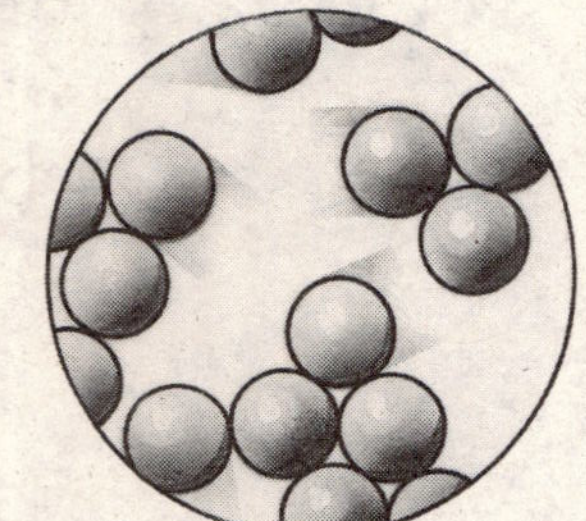

liquid particles

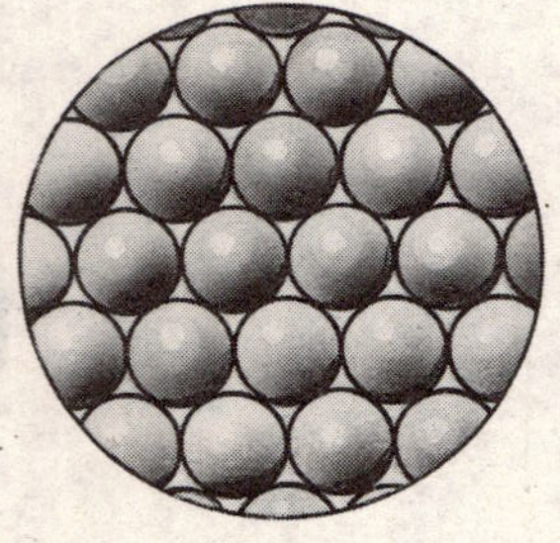

solid particles

All matter is made up of particles that are always moving.

The Color of Things

Have you ever thought about why you see things in color? The color of any object depends on the wavelengths of light that it absorbs and reflects.

A black object absorbs almost all the light that hits it. When you look at a black bowling ball, very little light reflects back to your eyes.

White is made up of a combination of all wavelengths of light. This white dog reflects almost all of the light that hits him.

When you look at a red apple, you see the red light that reflects off it. Red objects absorb all light wavelengths except red.

Green objects, such as this clover, absorb all light wavelengths except green. That means they reflect the green wavelengths of light.

These blue gloves reflect only blue wavelengths of light. All other wavelengths of light are absorbed.

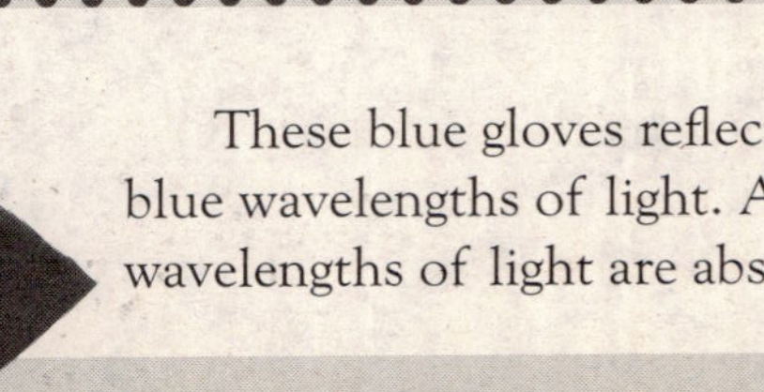

Heat

If you have ever taken your temperature, you've measured your own kinetic energy. A thermometer measures the average kinetic energy of particles in your body, which is your temperature. Temperature and thermal energy are not the same thing. Recall that thermal energy is the total kinetic and potential energy. Temperature is a measure of the average kinetic energy. It does not depend on how much of a substance there is.

Heat is the transfer of thermal energy from one substance to another. It always moves from a warmer substance to a cooler one. When something gets warmer, that means thermal energy has moved into it. You see this when you toast a slice of bread. The energy from the toaster moves into the bread and warms it up. It causes the average kinetic energy of the bread's particles to rise.

The thermal energy from the toaster moves into the slices of bread.

A mirror's smooth surface allows light to reflect back.

Reflection

The bouncing of light rays off a material's surface is called **reflection.** Reflection happens when light does not pass through a material and it also is not absorbed. A mirror's smooth surface allows light to reflect back so you can see your image, or your reflection. You can also see your reflection in some other smooth-surfaced materials.

Surfaces such as walls, tabletops, and book covers appear to be smooth, but do not reflect well enough for you to see a reflection. If you look very closely at them, you will see that their surfaces contain bumps and holes. Light bounces off of these surfaces in many different directions. For you to see your reflection, a surface must be so smooth that light bounces back to your eyes.

Conduction

There are three types of transfer: conduction, convection, and radiation. **Conduction** is the transfer of thermal energy between two objects that touch. An example is ice cubes dropped into a glass of water. The water has a higher temperature, so its particles are vibrating faster than those in the ice. When the cooler ice touches the warmer water, the water's particles bump against the particles in the ice. The ice particles start moving faster. Energy transfers from the water to the ice. Conduction has made the water cooler and the ice particles warmer.

Conduction does not cause the particles in the substances to change location. Instead, energy moves from particle to particle. This happens as the particles bump against each other. It can occur between a warmer object and a cooler one. It can occur between the warmer part of an object and a cooler part of the same object.

ice cubes

Thermal energy moves from the liquid to the ice by conduction.

Refraction

Refraction is the change in direction of light as it moves from one material to another. Light changes speed as it moves through different materials. If a light beam strikes the border of two materials at an angle, this will change the speed. The change in speed then changes its direction.

An example of refraction is when a ray of sunlight hits a glass prism. The light is made up of various wavelengths. It appears to be colorless. But when it enters the prism, the light changes direction. The different wavelengths refract at a variety of angles and give off a rainbow effect. In fact, that is exactly what happens when it is raining and the Sun comes out again. Where it is still raining, some of the raindrops act like little prisms. Light from the Sun refracts at various angles, and you can see a rainbow!

Raindrops act like little prisms and split light into different colors.

A prism splits white light into different colors.

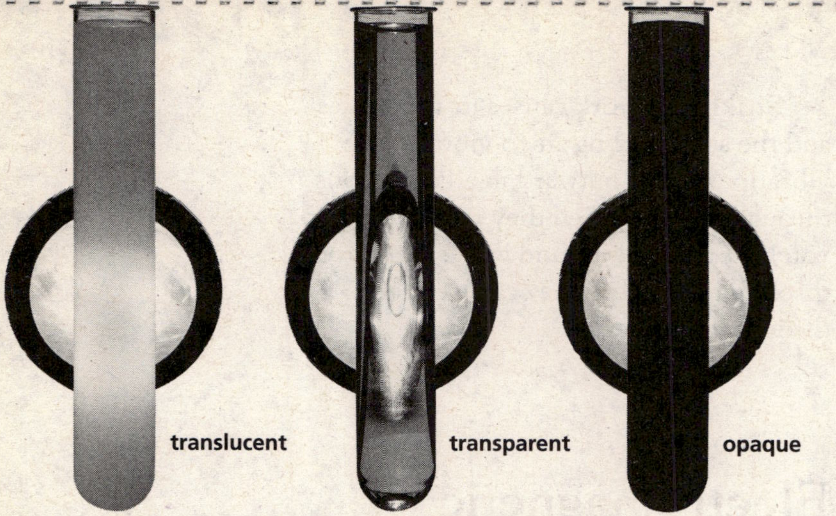

Light cannot travel through all objects. Some materials take in or absorb light, while some materials let some or all light pass through.

Light Absorption

If you were to shine a flashlight on a window, would the light travel through the glass? Yes! Would the same light travel through a metal door? No. Light reacts differently when it travels through different types of matter. Some light is taken in or absorbed by matter. Some of this light energy is converted to thermal energy. Dark-colored materials absorb more light energy than light-colored materials. A black car sitting in hot sunlight will feel warmer than a white car will. Darker objects absorb more light energy and convert it into thermal energy.

Almost all light passes through transparent materials, such as glass and water. Less light passes through translucent materials such as waxed paper. No light passes through opaque materials such as rock and metal.

The speed of light is 300,000 kilometers per second. That's the speed at which all electromagnetic waves travel through empty space. Light travels through matter at slower speeds, and those speeds vary. Light travels the fastest through gases. It moves slower through liquids and slowest through solids.

Convection

Thermal energy can also be transferred by convection. **Convection** is the transfer of thermal energy by the movement of a fluid. A fluid is any gas or liquid. When fluids are heated, they become less dense. This causes warm fluids to rise above cooler, more dense ones. Cool fluids sink. When warm fluids rise, they carry their thermal energy with them, and can then transfer that energy to other materials.

The rising and sinking of fluids often occurs in circular patterns called convection currents. Huge convection currents are generated in Earth's atmosphere, causing wind. Warm land transfers thermal energy up into the atmosphere. There energy is transferred to the cooler surrounding air. When the air cools enough, it sinks back to Earth. It rushes in under other air that is being heated by the land. This cycle happens over and over again.

Hang gliders soar on convection currents.

As hot water rises from the bottom of the pan, thermal energy is transferred by convection.

Crocodiles are cold-blooded and need to absorb energy from the Sun.

Radiation

Radiation is the transfer of thermal energy as waves. This transfer can happen through matter or across empty space. In the picture above, energy from the Sun warms the crocodile through radiation. Solar energy travels to Earth through space. Some solar radiation is absorbed into Earth's surface. The absorbed radiation causes Earth's surface to become warm.

Some solar radiation is reflected back toward space. But gases in the atmosphere can also cause it to be reflected back to Earth's surface again. This is known as the greenhouse effect. The greenhouse effect is crucial to the survival of life on Earth. Without it, Earth would be cold and lifeless. Scientists study whether the greenhouse effect causes such gases as carbon dioxide to trap too much radiation. The concern is that the unnecessary radiation makes Earth's climate warmer.

Striking the fork causes its molecules and the surrounding air to vibrate. The vibrations move outward in all directions through the air. When they reach your ear, you hear a sound. Sound waves can travel through matter, but they can't travel through empty space.

Electromagnetic Spectrum

Light travels as a wave. Unlike sound, light can travel through empty space. One of the many types of waves that travel from the Sun to Earth is visible light. Wavelengths can be long or short. The electromagnetic spectrum is the pattern you would get if you arranged all types of waves from the shortest wavelength to the longest. As wavelengths become longer, frequencies become lower.

A shorter wavelength indicates that a wave has more energy.

The electromagnetic spectrum arranges waves according to frequency and wavelength.

How Waves Carry Energy

Kinds of Waves

Many types of energy move in waves. There are two main types of waves: compressional and transverse. Both move through matter, but they do not carry the particles of the matter along with them. In compressional waves, the particles move back and forth, like the folds of an accordion. In transverse waves, they move up and down, like a cork bobbing on an ocean wave.

Vibrations cause all waves, including sound waves. Sound is an important type of compressional wave. Have you ever seen someone use a tuning fork? It's made up of a handle and only two tines, or teeth. When you strike the tuning fork, the tines vibrate and produce a specific pitch.

Tuning forks always produce a certain pitch.

Insulation

The process of insulation helps stop or reduce energy transfer. A heavy winter coat acts as an **insulator** because it is made of material that does not easily transfer thermal energy. It can help keep you warm on a cold day. On the other hand, a metal flagpole will feel very warm when it's hot outside. Metal is a **conductor,** so it easily transfers thermal energy.

Let's take a closer look at insulators and conductors. Remember that particles in a warmer object move faster than particles in a cooler object. What happens if the two objects touch? The particles in the warmer object bump against the particles in the cooler object. This causes the particles in the cooler object to start moving faster. The kinetic energy rises. Conduction causes the temperature of the cooler object to rise.

Clothes insulate us against the cold.

The Greenhouse Effect

Some solar radiation bounces between the surface of Earth and gases in the atmosphere.

Pollution causes gases to build up in the Earth's atmosphere. These gases trap solar radiation and make Earth's climate hotter and hotter.

Silver and copper are two metals that are good conductors.
Electrons in these metals are not tightly held to the atoms.
These electrons can move easily. They can carry energy from
place to place. If you have ever felt the handle of a metal spoon
that is in a bowl of hot soup, then you have experienced
conduction. The handle feels warm because thermal energy
from the hot soup was transferred into the spoon, and when
you touched it, heat moved into your hand.

If the particles of a material do not easily transfer energy,
that material is an insulator. The particles in fluids are farther
apart. This makes fluids better insulators than solids. Empty
space is another example of an insulator. Energy can only
move through empty space by radiation.

Metal objects, such as this spoon, conduct heat well.

Polar bears have a thick layer of fat and fur, which acts as an insulator against frigid weather.

Use of Insulators

Insulators are an important part of
daily life. You may put extra blankets on
your bed if it is cold. Layers keep you warm.
Air is a good insulator, so the pockets of
air between the layers keep you warm.
Animals living in cold climates have their
own insulation to help them get through
the harshest conditions. They may have
thick layers of fat or fur that trap thermal
energy and keep it close to their bodies.

Insulation helps buildings stay at a
comfortable temperature. You may have
seen insulating materials such as fiberglass,
carpet, double-layer windows, and foam
used in your own home. The many layers
of insulation contain air pockets that slow
the movement of thermal energy out of
the home. This is important on cold winter
days. In warmer weather, the insulation
keeps thermal energy out of the house.

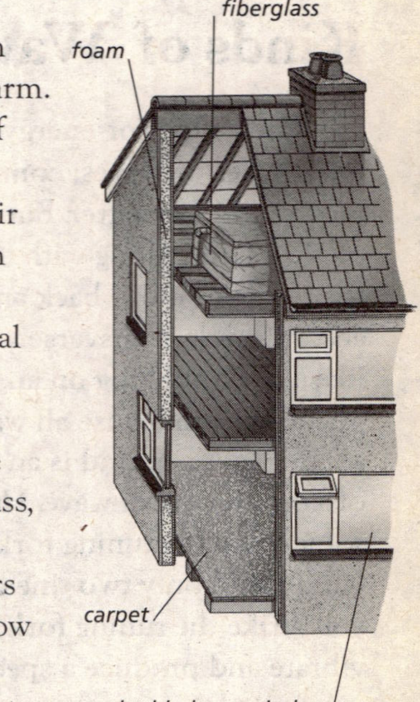

Houses are built using insulating materials, which slow the movement of thermal energy in and out of the house.

Space and Technology

SUN, EARTH, AND MOON

by Mary F. Blehl

Genre	Comprehension Skill	Text Features	Science Content
Nonfiction	Main Idea and Details	• Captions • Charts • Diagrams • Glossary	Earth and Space

Scott Foresman Science 6.19

What did you learn?

1. Describe the surface of the Moon and what it is made of.

2. What causes the seasons on Earth?

3. What were the Apollo missions?

4. **Writing** in Science Write to explain the positions of the Sun, the Moon, and Earth during solar and lunar eclipses.

5. **Predict** Use what you know about velocity to predict the motion of a volleyball during a volleyball game.

Picture Credits
Every effort has been made to secure permission and provide appropriate credit for photographic material. The publisher deeply regrets any omission and pledges to correct errors called to its attention in subsequent editions.

Photo locators denoted as follows: Top (T), Center (C), Bottom (B), Left (L), Right (R), Background (Bkgd).

Opener: Brand X Pictures; 1 Brand X Pictures; 2 (T, B) Brand X Pictures; 4 (B) Brand X Pictures, (CR) Getty Images; 5 (CL) Brand X Pictures; 6 (B) Brand X Pictures, (T) Getty Images; 7 (TR, CR) NASA; 8 (TL, B) Brand X Pictures; 9 (BC) Brand X Pictures; 10 (CR, B) Brand X Pictures; 12 (B) Brand X Pictures; 13 (TL) David Nunuk /Photo Researchers, Inc., (CR) Brand X Pictures, (BC) Dr. Fred Espenak /Photo Researchers, Inc.; 14 (B) Brand X Pictures, (T) Fred Espenak/ Photo Researchers, Inc.; 15 (CR) John Chumack /Photo Researchers, Inc.; 16 Brand X Pictures.

Unless otherwise acknowledged, all photographs are the copyright © of Dorling Kindersley, a division of Pearson.

ISBN: 0-328-14025-2

Glossary

lunar eclipse   an eclipse that occurs when Earth casts a shadow on the Moon

orbit   a path that a body follows in space, usually around another body; for example, Earth moving around the Sun

revolve   to move around an object in space in an orbit; for example, when Earth moves around the Sun

rotate   to move around an axis; for example, when a top spins, or Earth spins in space

solar eclipse   an eclipse that occurs when the Moon passes between the Sun and Earth, blocking the Sun's light

SUN, EARTH, AND MOON

by Mary F. Blehl

PEARSON
Scott Foresman

DK

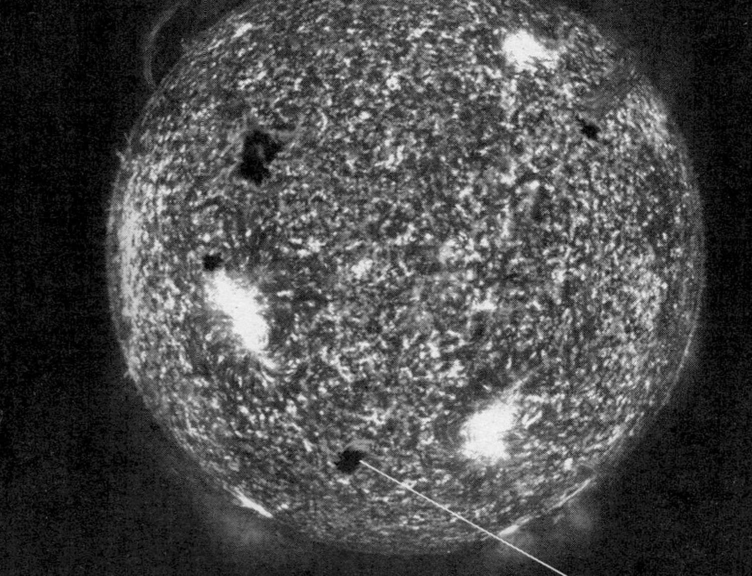

The photographs above show the different stages of a total lunar eclipse.

During a lunar eclipse, the Moon can look reddish.

Features Of
The Sun and Moon

The Sun

The Sun is the nearest star to Earth. It is so huge that a million Earths could fit inside it! The Sun looks like a giant ball of fire in the sky. At one time, people thought it was a huge burning rock, similar to a piece of coal on fire. Actually, the Sun is neither burning nor solid. It is made of a type of super hot matter called plasma, which is similar to a gas. The plasma's heat causes it to glow very brightly. Reactions between particles in the Sun's core cause its intense heat. Temperatures in the core may reach 15,000,000°C.

Lunar Eclipses

Date	Type of eclipse
October 17, 2005	partial
September 7, 2006	partial
March 3–4, 2007	total
August 28, 2007	total
February 21, 2008	total

Lunar Eclipses

At certain times of the year, the Sun, Earth, and Moon can line up to cast a shadow on the Moon. Up to three times a year, the full Moon moves through Earth's shadow. When Earth blocks the sunlight from reaching the Moon, we call this a lunar eclipse. *Lunar* means "related to the Moon." Lunar eclipses can be partial, total, or penumbral.

During a partial lunar eclipse, Earth's shadow covers only part of the Moon. During a total lunar eclipse, the shadow covers the entire Moon. During a penumbral lunar eclipse, the Moon moves through the outer edge of Earth's shadow and its light is only slightly dimmed.

A lunar eclipse can be seen from any part of Earth that can see the Moon at that time. Scientists know when lunar eclipses will occur. In the chart on the opposite page, you can see when the next one will happen.

This is the placement of the Sun, the Moon, and Earth during a total lunar eclipse.

Reactions in the Sun's core release massive amounts of energy. Energy released in the core travels through layers of plasma inside the Sun until it reaches the surface. Some of this energy comes to Earth as light and infrared radiation. Light from the Sun illuminates our days and provides energy for green plants. Infrared radiation provides heat. Without the Sun's heat, Earth would become colder than the North Pole.

The Sun's outer layer, called the corona, is about 8,000,000 miles thick. Solar flares, which are powerful explosions of gases, occur on the Sun's surface. These flares create intense radiation. If some of that radiation reaches Earth, it sometimes causes a magnetic storm. This disrupts radio communications on Earth. Other times the radiation causes auroras, which are colorful lights in the sky.

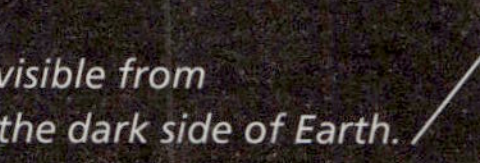

This aurora is caused by solar radiation interacting with Earth's upper atmosphere.

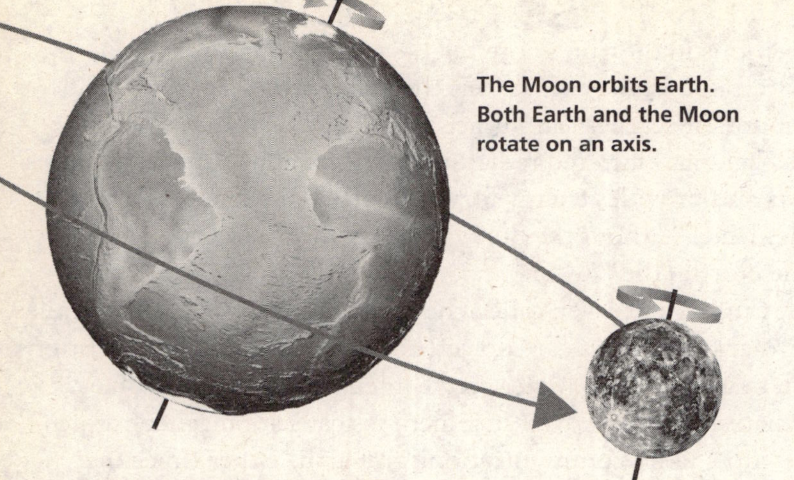

Earth's Satellite

The Moon is the closest body in space to our Earth. It is more than four billion years old! The Moon has no light of its own. Light from the Sun reflects off it, and that is the only way we can see it from Earth.

The Moon is Earth's satellite. That means it revolves in an orbit around Earth. An **orbit** is the path that a body in space follows around another object.

It takes 27.3 days for the Moon to **rotate,** or spin, on its axis. It takes exactly the same amount of time for the Moon to **revolve,** or complete its orbit around Earth. Because of this, the same side of the Moon faces Earth at all times.

Phases of the Moon

As the Moon revolves around Earth, it seems to have different shapes. But the shape of the Moon does not actually change. What changes is the part of the Moon's lighted surface that is visible from Earth. The Sun always lights half of the Moon, but at different places in the Moon's orbit different amounts of the lighted area are visible from Earth. We call the different visible parts "phases."

In an annular eclipse, a small part of the Sun can be seen around the edge of the Moon.

Here you can see the corona of the Sun during a solar eclipse.

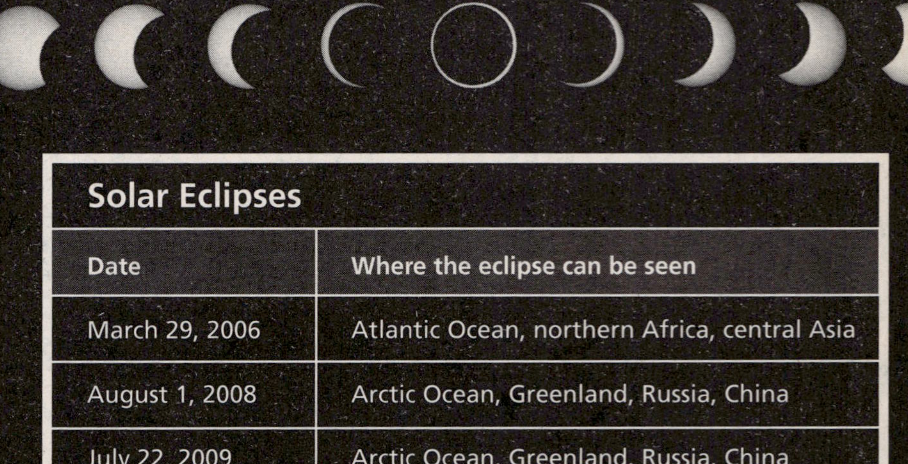

These photographs show the different stages of an annular solar eclipse.

Solar Eclipses	
Date	Where the eclipse can be seen
March 29, 2006	Atlantic Ocean, northern Africa, central Asia
August 1, 2008	Arctic Ocean, Greenland, Russia, China
July 22, 2009	Arctic Ocean, Greenland, Russia, China

Solar Eclipses

The changing positions of the Sun, the Moon, and Earth can cause solar and lunar eclipses. A **solar eclipse** is when the Moon passes directly between the Sun and Earth. Although the two bodies are not the same size, sometimes the Moon will block the Sun's light for a while. The Moon crosses a little above or below the Sun because of the tilt of its orbit. But sometimes the orbit of the Moon crosses exactly between the Sun and Earth. When the three bodies are in line, the Moon casts a shadow on Earth, blocking the Sun. The shadow has a small, dark center called the umbra, and a lighter outer part called the penumbra. When the Moon seems to block all the sunlight, we call it a total eclipse. Total eclipses are seen only in areas covered by the umbra. If the Moon blocks only part of the sunlight, we call it a partial eclipse. Partial eclipses can be seen in areas covered by the penumbra.

When the Moon gets into position for an eclipse, sometimes we see only the Sun's corona. It looks like a bright glow around the Moon. At other times, the Sun is closer than usual, and the Moon is farther away than usual. Then the whole Sun does not seem to be covered by the Moon. This is called an annular eclipse. You can see the Sun in the shape of a ring!

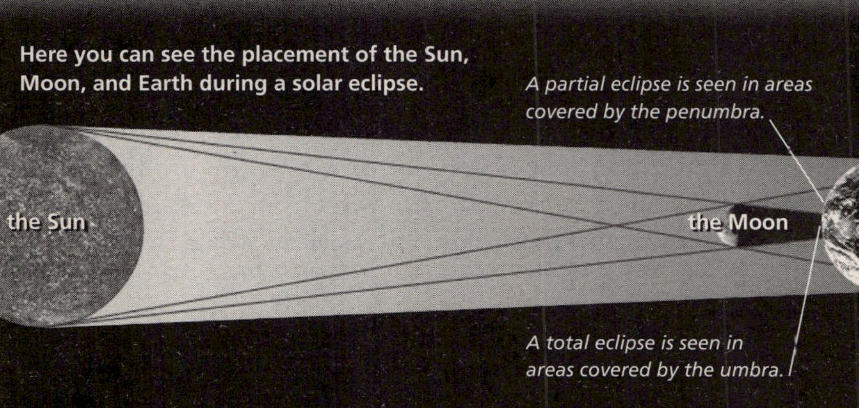

Here you can see the placement of the Sun, Moon, and Earth during a solar eclipse.

Waning and Waxing

Just like Earth, one half of the Moon is always lighted by the Sun, while the other side is not. When none of the lighted part is visible from Earth, we call it a new moon. As the Moon keeps moving in its orbit, we see more of the part that is reflecting sunlight. This is called *waxing*, which means "growing larger." The Moon waxes until we see its entire lighted half, called a full moon. As the Moon continues in its orbit, the phases reverse. It appears to be getting smaller, or waning, until it becomes a new moon again. It takes about 29.5 days for the cycle of Moon phases to be completed.

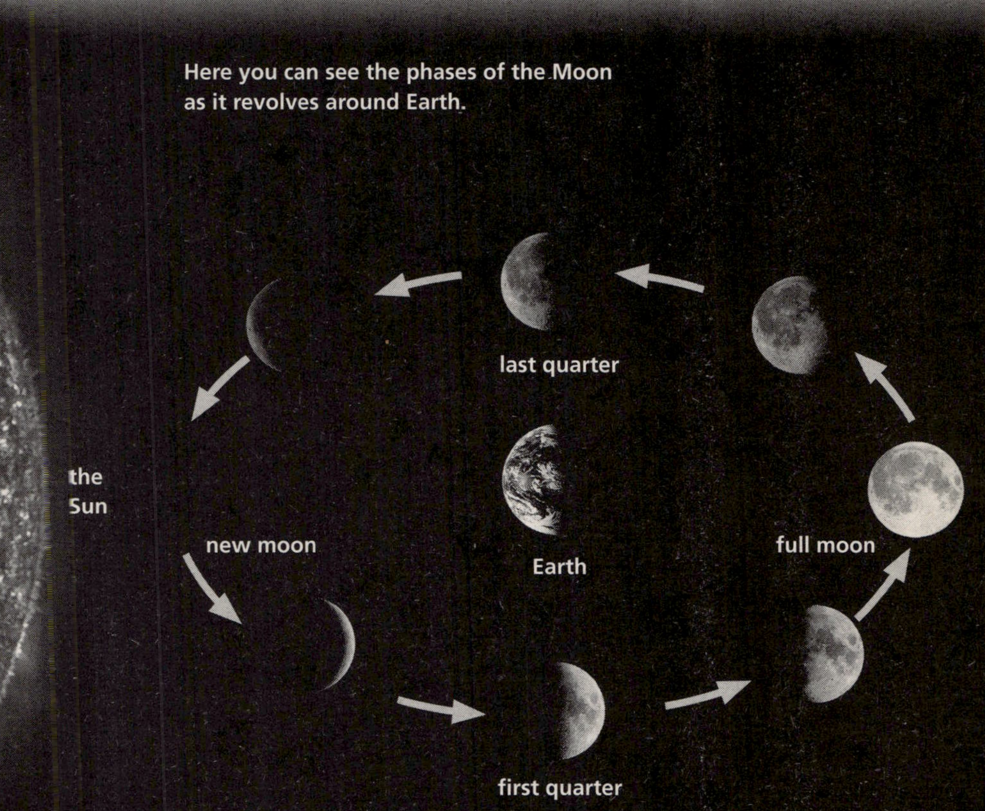

Here you can see the phases of the Moon as it revolves around Earth.

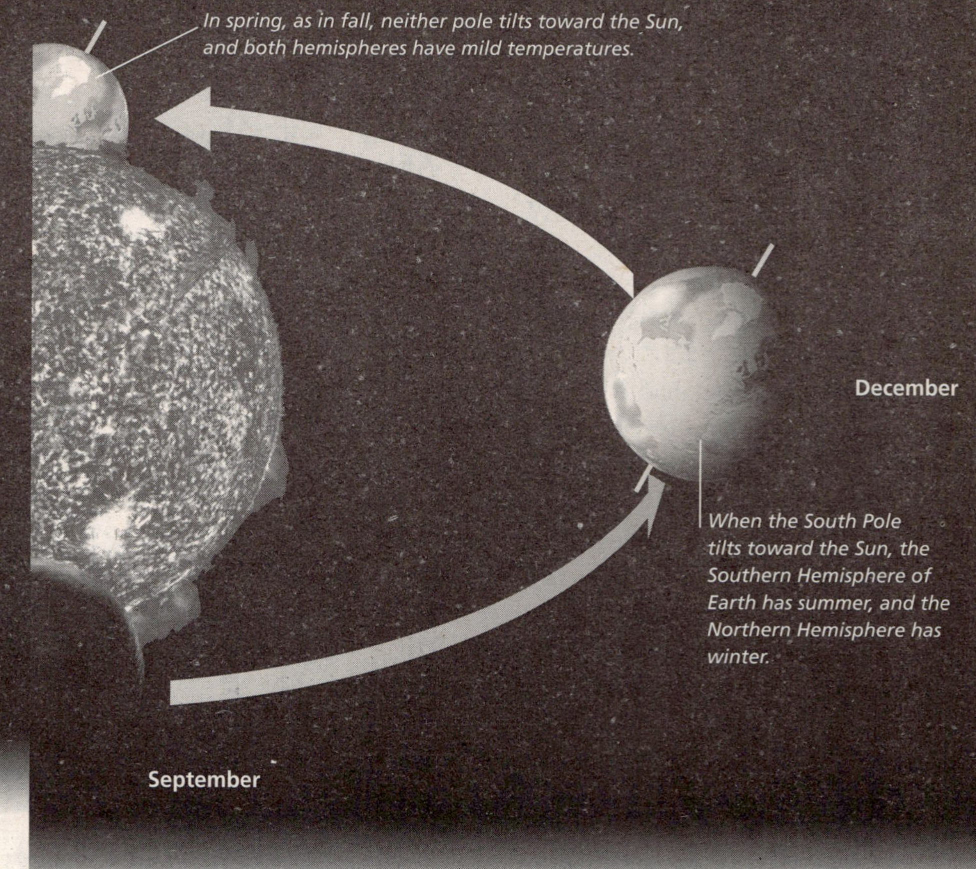

Studying the Moon

The surface of the Moon is mostly dust and rock. There is almost no atmosphere on the Moon. Without atmosphere to protect it from the Sun's radiation, it can get very hot in sunlit areas. Also, without much atmosphere, very little heat is absorbed, so dark areas of the Moon are extremely cold.

On the Moon's surface, we can see dark gray plains. Early astronomers named these areas *mare*. *Mare* is a Latin word for *sea*. Early astronomers thought these areas were seas. We now know they are flat plains of cooled lava, but the name stayed. There are highlands around the craters and the seas. Craters are indentations of different sizes left by meteorites that hit the Moon.

The seasons are caused by the tilt of Earth's axis. The Sun warms the part of Earth that is tilted toward it more than it does the side that is tilted away. The part that is tilted toward the Sun has summer, while the other part has winter. The tilt causes the temperature to change by changing the angle at which the Sun's rays hit Earth. When part of the planet is tilted toward the Sun, that part receives sunlight at a direct angle, delivering lots of heat. When part of Earth is tilted away from the Sun, the angle is less direct. The Sun's rays are more spread out, so they do not warm that part as much.

The direction of Earth's tilt on its axis causes the seasons.

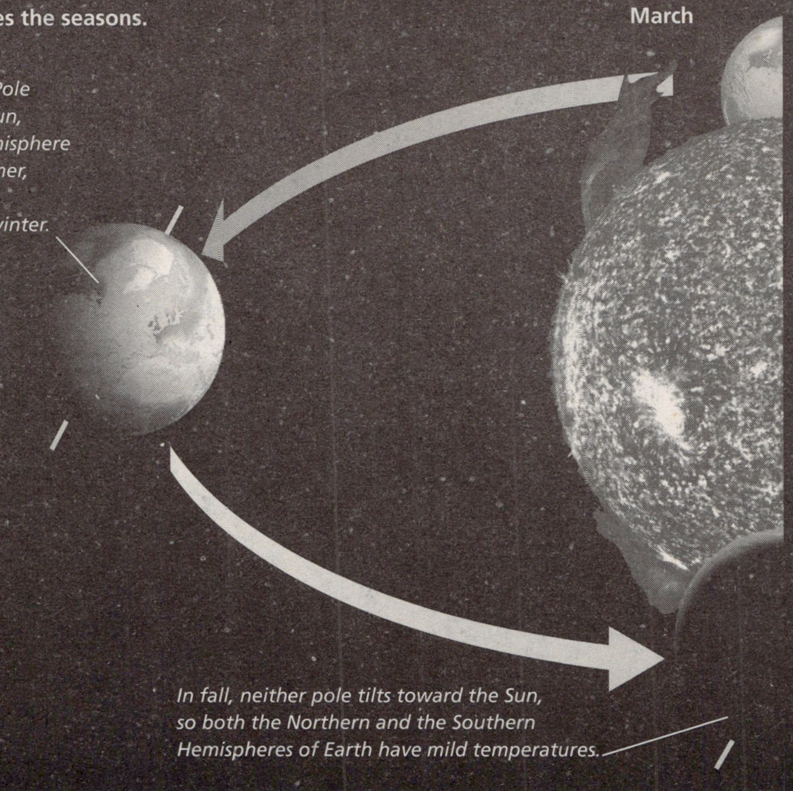

When the North Pole tilts toward the Sun, the Northern Hemisphere of Earth has summer, and the Southern Hemisphere has winter.

In fall, neither pole tilts toward the Sun, so both the Northern and the Southern Hemispheres of Earth have mild temperatures.

Seasons Change

Days, years, and seasons are caused by Earth's motion. Days and nights are caused by Earth's rotation on its axis. A day, about 24 hours, is the total time Earth takes to make one full rotation. A year, about 365 days, is the amount of time it takes Earth to complete one revolution around the Sun.

Earth revolves around the Sun following an elliptical path. Because Earth's path is an ellipse, it is sometimes slightly closer to the Sun than at other times. People think that summer occurs when Earth is closer to the Sun. But this has nothing to do with the seasons.

In 1959 the first spacecraft landed on the Moon. This Soviet vehicle, named *Luna 2*, did not have any humans on board. In 1969 Neil Armstrong was the first person to step on the Moon. As he did it he said, "That's one small step for man, one giant leap for mankind." Armstrong and Edwin "Buzz" Aldrin brought back the first samples from the Moon's surface. Michael Collins, the mission's pilot, remained in the spacecraft, orbiting the Moon.

From 1969 to 1972 there were six Apollo missions altogether. Twelve astronauts took pictures there and brought back rock and soil samples. During the last mission, the men stayed on the Moon for three days.

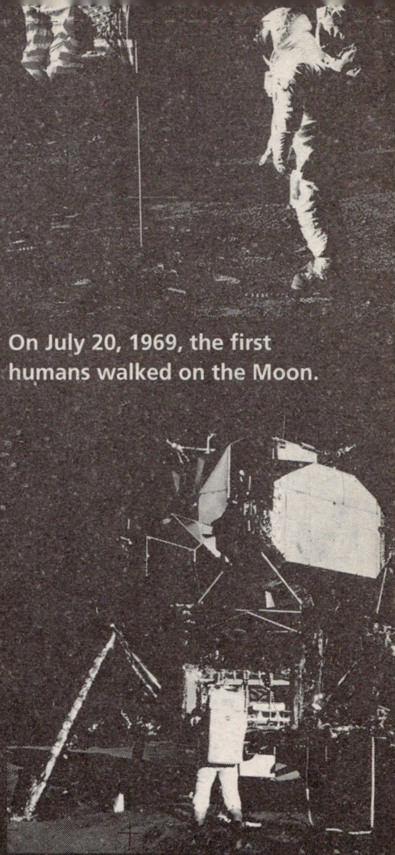

On July 20, 1969, the first humans walked on the Moon.

The lunar lander separated from a larger spacecraft and landed on the Moon's surface.

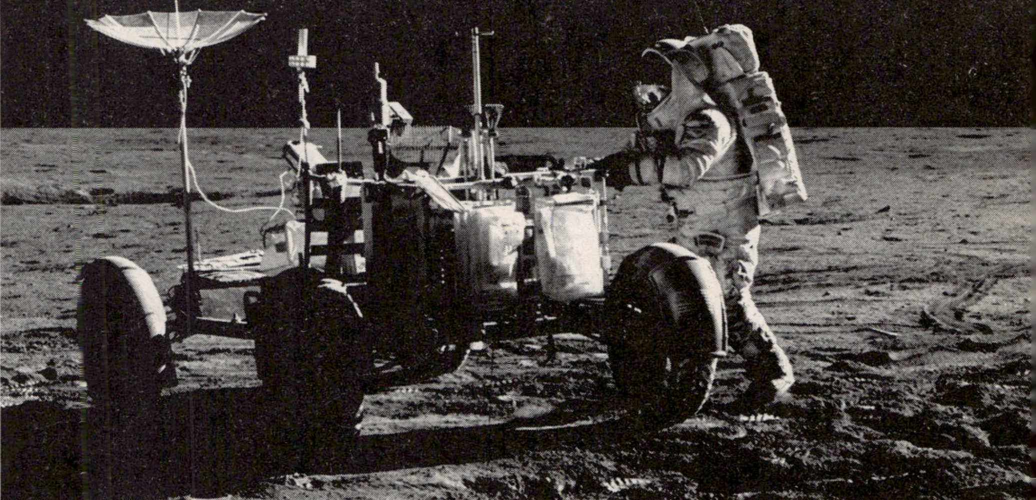

The lunar rover let astronauts explore large areas of the Moon.

The Moon and Earth In Motion

Earth's Rotation

As ancient people watched the sky from Earth, it looked as though the Sun was moving around our planet. The Sun seemed to rise in the morning, travel across the sky, and set in the evening. Eventually, people learned that Earth orbits the Sun, not the other way around!

Earth revolves around the Sun in an orbit, and it also rotates on its axis. It rotates every twenty-four hours. This rotation is what causes us to have night and day.

Earth always rotates in the same direction. This is why the Sun appears to rise in the east and set in the west. Earth rotates from west to east. We see the Sun first in the east because Earth is turning toward that direction.

In most places on Earth, there are more hours of daylight during the summer than there are during the winter. This is caused by Earth's tilted axis. Look at the diagram on page 8. Notice that the southern part of the planet is tilted toward the Sun, while the northern part is tilted away. The parts of Earth that are tilted toward the Sun have more daylight hours. The parts that are tilted away have fewer.

This effect is greatest at the poles. When the North Pole is tilted toward the Sun, it gets sunlight twenty-four hours a day. The Sun is up all day for six months! When the North Pole is tilted away from the Sun, it is dark all the time.

Have you ever seen the Moon during the day? Although we usually see the Moon only at night, it is often on your side of Earth during daytime.

Exploring the Universe

Space and Technology

by Jane Green

Genre	Comprehension Skill	Text Features	Science Content
Nonfiction	Draw Conclusions	• Captions • Charts • Diagrams • Glossary	Stars and the Solar System

Scott Foresman Science 6.20

ISBN 0-328-14028-7

9 780328 140282

90000

PEARSON

Scott Foresman

scottforesman.com

223

What did you learn?

1. The nine planets in our solar system have different characteristics. Name the two groups scientists use to describe the planets and how they differ.

2. Describe the difference between the rotation of a planet and the revolution of a planet.

3. What is the difference between the apparent magnitude and absolute magnitude of a star?

4. **Writing** in Science Stars produce huge amounts of energy. Write to explain the process by which stars produce energy. Use details from the book in your answer.

5. **Draw Conclusions** Navigators at sea have used constellations to guide their ships. Why is it important for navigators to take note of the season when they use constellations to guide them?

Picture Credits
Every effort has been made to secure permission and provide appropriate credit for photographic material. The publisher deeply regrets any omission and pledges to correct errors called to its attention in subsequent editions.

Photo locators denoted as follows: Top (T), Center (C), Bottom (B), Left (L), Right (R), Background (Bkgd).

Opener NASA/Photo Researchers, Inc.; 2 (Bkgd) Getty Images; 11 (BL) Jason T. Ware /Photo Researchers, Inc., (BCL) John Chumack /Photo Researchers, Inc., (BR) Eckhard Slawik /Photo Researchers, Inc.; 15 Larry Landolfi /Photo Researchers, Inc.

Scott Foresman/Dorling Kindersley would also like to thank: Opener (B), 4 (TL), 5 (C), 6 (TL), 7 (T) NASA/DK Images; 10 (CL) NASA/JPL/DK Images.

Unless otherwise acknowledged, all photographs are the copyright © of Dorling Kindersley, a division of Pearson.

Glossary

astronomical unit	the average distance between Earth and the Sun, about 149.6 million kilometers
constellations	groupings of stars, often named after mythological people, events, animals, or objects
galaxy	a massive grouping of stars and other matter that make up part of the universe
light-year	the distance that light travels in one year, about 9.46 trillion kilometers
magnitude	the brightness of a star
nuclear fusion	the process in which the nuclei of two or more atoms join, releasing huge amounts of energy
solar system	a star and all of the objects that orbit it
star	a huge ball of hot, glowing gases

Exploring the Universe

by Jane Green

Where in the universe is Earth?

A satellite orbits Earth, collecting information about our solar system.

This photograph shows the way stars appear to move over several hours.

Space

People studied the sky and the objects in it as far back as 3,500 B.C. In 1609 the Italian scientist Galileo Galilei became the first scientist to observe the stars through a telescope. It allowed people to see even farther into space than they could with just their eyes. His theories and findings about the universe changed astronomy forever.

Scientists have developed many other technologies to help answer questions we have about the universe. Recent technological advances, such as more powerful telescopes and probes launched into space, have further contributed to what we know about our solar system and our galaxy, the Milky Way.

Movement of Constellations

As Earth rotates on its axis, the nighttime sky appears to change. The positions of the stars look different in the early evening than they do just before the Sun rises.

The positions of the stars in the night sky change also because of Earth's movement around the Sun. The night sky changes during the year, just as seasons change. As Earth revolves around the Sun, the constellations that you see appear in different places in the sky throughout the year.

Constellations

Constellations are groupings of stars in the night sky. Constellations were first identified by ancient civilizations. The Babylonians identified the twelve star constellations that make up the zodiac around 450 B.C.

The ancient Greeks identified and named forty-eight constellations. They named these constellations after mythological people, events, animals, or objects. The constellation Orion was named after a hunter who fell in love with the goddess Artemis. According to the myth, after Artemis accidentally killed Orion, she put him in the sky.

The Big Dipper is one of the most well-known constellations. It is part of the Ursa Major constellation, which means "big bear." The North Star is found in a straight line from the end of the bowl of the Big Dipper and has been used as a point of reference by navigators for centuries.

Orion

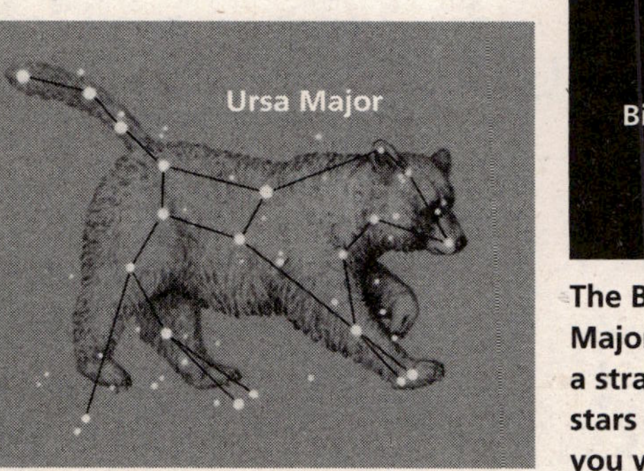
Ursa Major

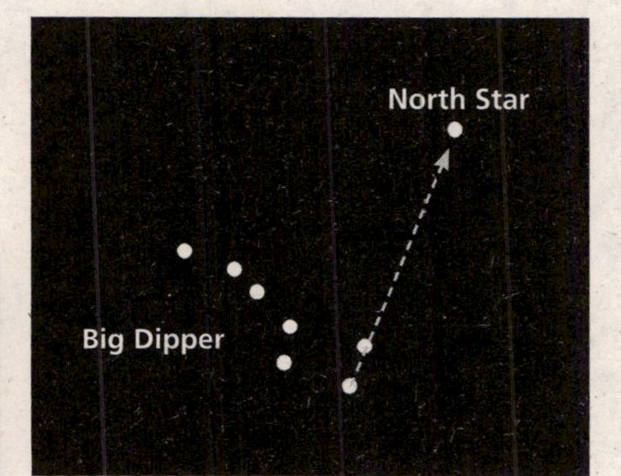

The Big Dipper is part of the Ursa Major constellation. If you look in a straight line from the last two stars of the Big Dipper's bowl, you will see the North Star.

spiral galaxy

elliptical galaxy

irregular galaxy

A **galaxy** is a huge grouping of stars. Galaxies are found throughout the universe and can have different shapes. The Milky Way Galaxy is shaped like a pinwheel and is known as a spiral galaxy. Some galaxies are elliptical, or oval-shaped. Irregular galaxies have no particular shape.

The Sun is in one of the "arms" of the spiral, and is only one of at least 100 billion stars in the Milky Way. The galaxy spins within the universe, and makes one complete rotation once every 200 million years.

Earth and Mars are two of the inner planets, which are made of rock and metal.

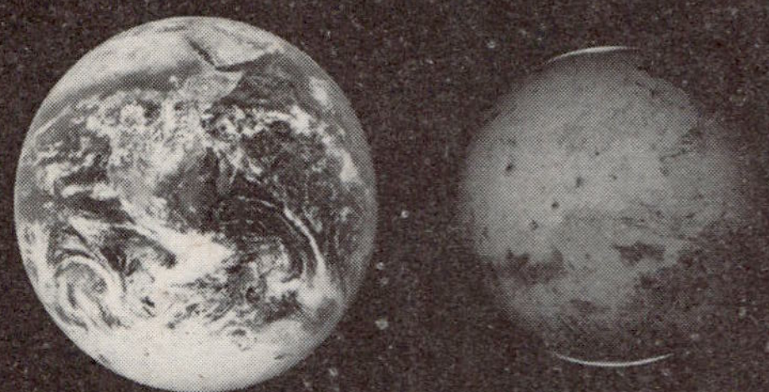

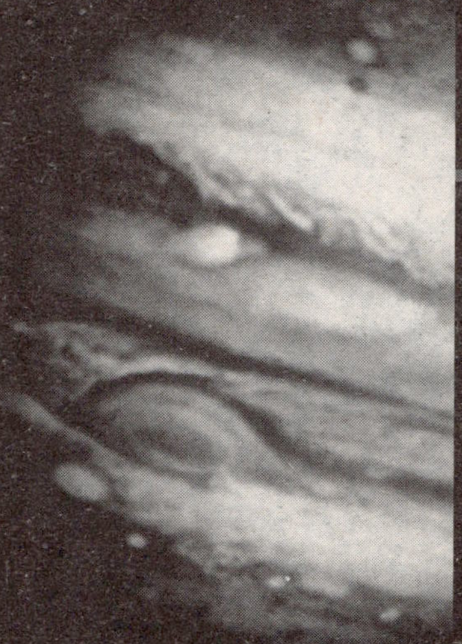

The Solar System

Our solar system is made up of the Sun and nine planets, including Earth. These nine planets orbit the Sun. The Sun's gravity keeps the planets in their orbits. The orbits of all of the planets, except Pluto, are almost circular. Natural bodies called moons orbit most planets in the solar system. Some planets have only one moon, while others have many. Mercury and Venus do not have any moons.

Other objects also orbit the Sun in our solar system. More than 100,000 asteroids orbit the Sun. Asteroids are small bodies made of rock and metals. Comets orbit the Sun in long, narrow, oval paths. Comets are made of ice. When a comet goes past the Sun, some of the ice turns into gas, forming the tail of the comet. One of the most famous comets is Halley's comet. It passes close to Earth once every seventy-six years.

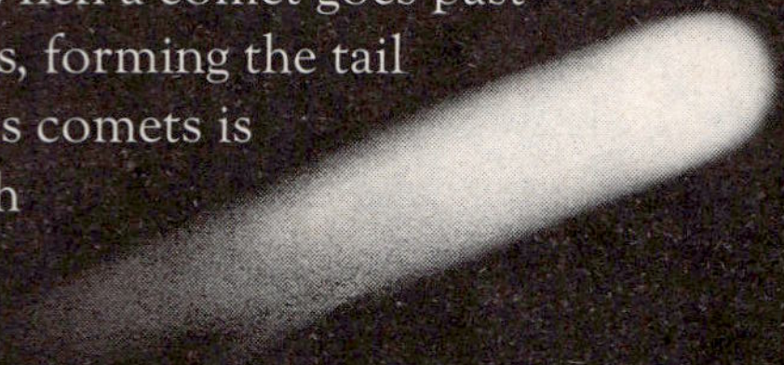

The tail of a comet is made of gas and dust.

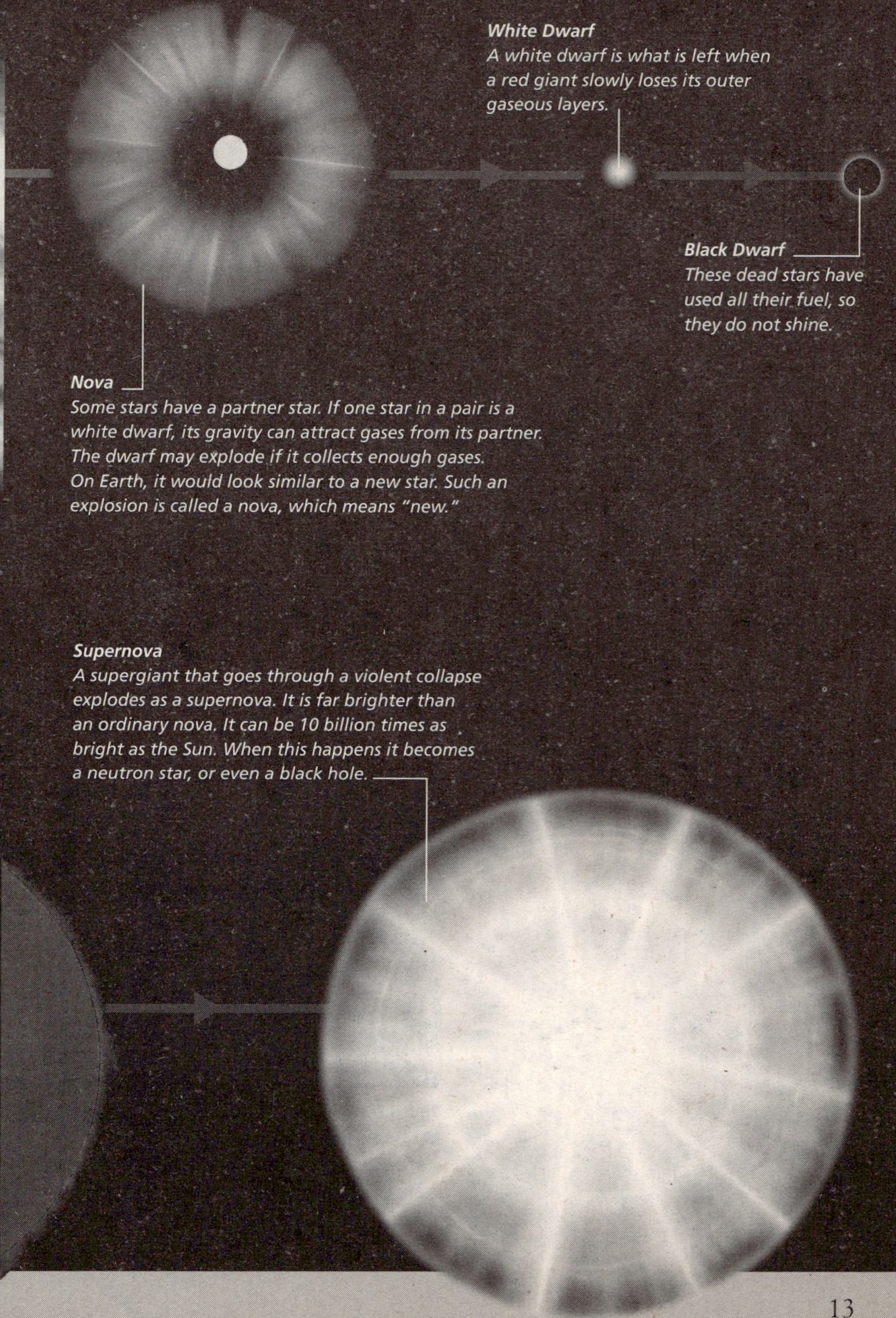

Life Cycle of Stars

Stars shine for billions of years, but they eventually stop shining. They change throughout their lives in many ways. A star forms inside a nebula, which is a cloud of hydrogen and other gases. Gravity holds the gas particles together and pulls in more gas particles. Nuclear fusion begins when the inside of the star reaches about 10,000,000°C. Fusion produces hot gases that push away from the center of the nebula. Gravity pulls these gases back. When the push of these gases becomes stronger than gravity's inward pull, a new star is formed.

Great distances separate the objects in our solar system. Scientists use a measurement known as an astronomical unit (AU) to measure these distances. An AU is about 149.6 million kilometers. It is about the same as the average distance between Earth and the Sun.

Scientists classify the planets into two different groups. Mercury, Venus, Earth, and Mars are called inner planets. They are closer to the Sun, and have solid, rocky surfaces that resemble the surface of Earth. Jupiter, Saturn, Uranus, Neptune, and Pluto are outer planets. They are farther away from the Sun. With the exception of Pluto, the outer planets are mainly composed of gases and are extremely large. Pluto, the planet that is farthest from the Sun, is different from the other outer planets. Pluto is small, solid, and more like the inner planets.

The Planets of the Solar System

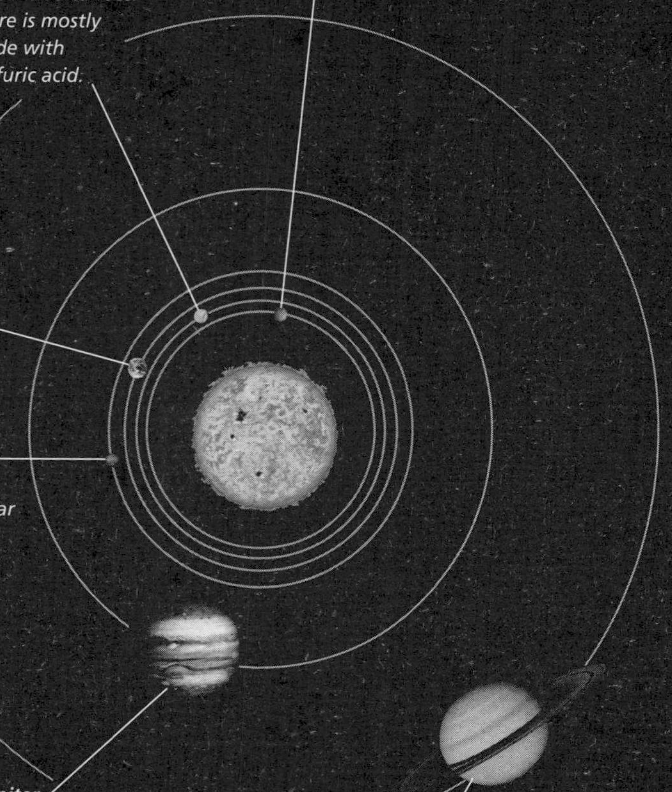

Venus
Very hot and mostly rock with craters, Venus may have some active volcanoes. Its atmosphere is mostly carbon dioxide with clouds of sulfuric acid.

Mercury
This planet is rocky with craters formed by meteorites. There are traces of hydrogen and helium in the atmosphere.

Earth
Mostly water-covered, Earth is the only planet known to support life.

Mars
This planet has craters in its southern part and white polar ice caps. The atmosphere contains mostly carbon dioxide. Strong winds blow red surface dust, which makes the sky pink.

Jupiter
Jupiter is covered by liquid hydrogen and is very cold. Its atmosphere is mostly hydrogen with clouds of ammonia crystals.

Saturn
Ice and liquid hydrogen surround a core of rock and metal. Saturn is very cold. In the atmosphere, there are strong winds and swirling clouds of ammonia.

Brightly Glowing Stars

Astronomers use the term magnitude to describe the brightness of a star. The term apparent magnitude is used to describe the brightness of a star as we view it from Earth. The Sun is the star with the greatest apparent magnitude. It appears the brightest to us. Absolute magnitude is another way astronomers measure star brightness. It is the measure of how bright stars would appear if they were all the same distance from Earth. Some stars that look tiny and dim from Earth are actually more than 150,000 times brighter than the Sun. Their absolute magnitude is much greater than their apparent magnitude.

The Color of Stars

Some stars appear to be different colors. If you look through a telescope at night, you may be able to see red, yellow, white, or blue stars. The surface temperature of a star determines its color.

Red stars have temperatures between 2,000°C and 5,200°C. These are the coolest stars.

Yellow stars, such as our Sun, have temperatures that range from 5,300°C to 7,000°C.

White stars are even hotter, with surface temperatures of 7,200°C to 9,500°C.

The hottest stars burn blue. Their surface temperatures can range from 10,000°C to 50,000°C.

Stars Shining Far Away

Stars

A star is a huge ball of hot, glowing gas. The intense heat and pressure at the center of a star cause the atoms there to crash into each other at extremely high speeds. The nuclei of two or more atoms may join during this process to form a larger nucleus. This process is called nuclear fusion, and it gives off huge amounts of energy. Some of this energy produces radiation and light energy, which allows us to see stars that are very far away.

Star Distances

We use astronomical units to measure distances within our solar system. Distances in the vast universe are even greater. An AU is too small, so light-years are used instead. A light-year is the distance that light travels in one year in a vacuum. It is equivalent to 9.46 trillion kilometers.

The light from the Sun—the closest star to Earth—takes about eight minutes to reach Earth. The next closest star to our galaxy is Proxima Centauri. The light from Proxima Centauri takes about four years to reach Earth! The light from most of the other stars we see can take millions or billions of years to reach Earth.

An eruption of very hot gas on the surface of our star, the Sun, is called a solar flare.

Neptune
This planet is possibly covered by liquid hydrogen and helium. The atmosphere is mostly hydrogen and helium. Neptune appears pale blue in color.

Uranus
The atmosphere is made up of mostly hydrogen and helium. Uranus appears blue-green in color. It is the only planet that rotates on its side. This makes it appear to roll through space.

Pluto
This tiny planet is made mostly of frozen methane, ice, and small amounts of methane gas. There is an ice cap at its north pole.

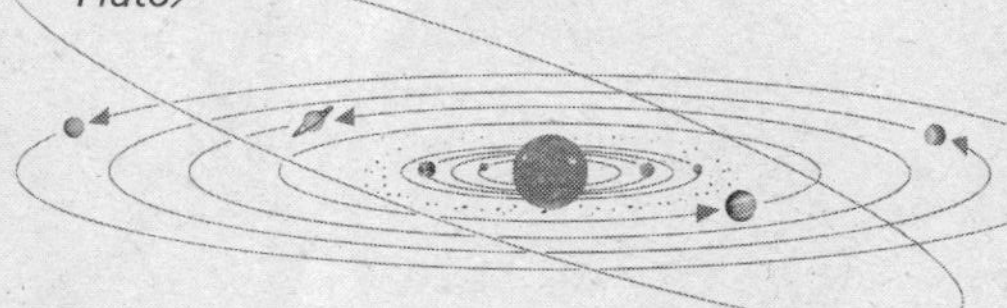

The orbits of all the planets are roughly level, except for Pluto's, which tilts at a different angle. Pluto's orbit is also more elliptical—the orbits of the other planets are almost circular. All the planets orbit the Sun in the same direction.

How Planets Are Arranged

The distances between the planets in our solar system are so great that it would be difficult to show a scale model in this book. In the previous two pages, you saw the arrangement of the planets, but not the actual distance between them.

The chart below shows what the relative distances between the planets in our solar system would be if Earth were 1 millimeter wide at the equator. The sizes of the planets relative to Earth are also listed. If you looked at a ruler, you would see that 1 millimeter is very small. Now look at how far Earth is from the Sun using these scale sizes—11.7 meters. If Earth were the size of a marble, the Sun would be about 100 meters away. That is longer than a football field!

Planet	Size (millimeters)	Distance from Sun (meters)
Mercury	0.4	4.5
Venus	1.0	8.5
Earth	1.0	11.7
Mars	0.5	17.9
Jupiter	11.3	61
Saturn	9.4	112
Uranus	4.1	226
Neptune	3.9	354
Pluto	0.2	463

The images below show the approximate relative sizes of the planets.

Planets Are Unique

The distance between a planet and the Sun can affect the temperature of a planet. For example, Venus is twice as close to the Sun as Mars, so it is much warmer. But distance is not the only thing that determines its characteristics.

Based on distance from the Sun, you might expect Venus to be a little warmer than Earth, but not as warm as Mercury. This is not exactly true. Temperatures on Mercury range from about 467°C during the day to −183°C at night. Average temperatures on Earth range from 36°C to −13°C. The average temperature on Venus is 453°C. It does not change through seasons or from day to night. These differences occur because a planet's atmosphere also affects its temperatures.

Although Venus and Earth are about the same size, and their orbits around the Sun are close to each other, Venus is surrounded by an atmosphere of carbon dioxide and clouds of sulfuric acid. This sort of atmosphere traps heat. Mercury has a very thin atmosphere that does not protect it from the Sun's powerful rays. Because of this, days on Mercury are very hot. But the atmosphere is too thin to trap heat as well, which is why Mercury's nights are so cold.

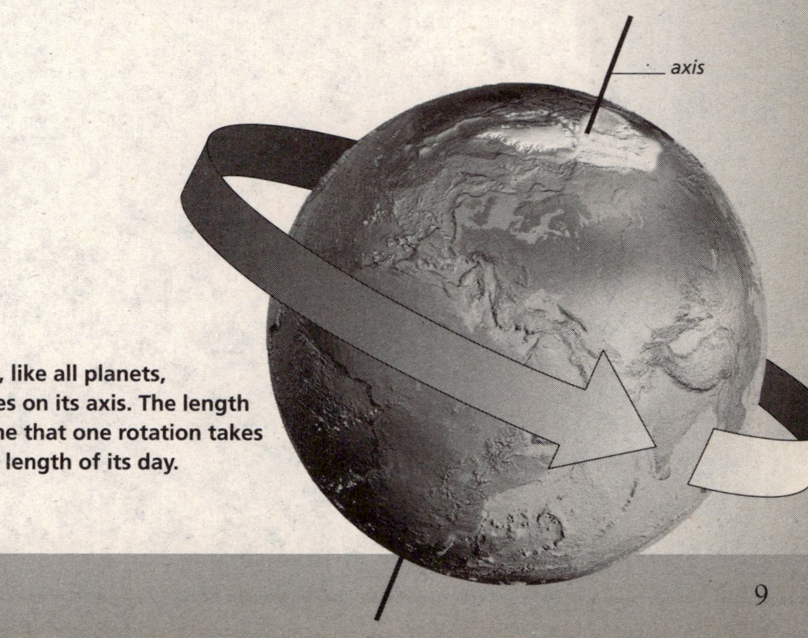

Earth, like all planets, rotates on its axis. The length of time that one rotation takes is the length of its day.

The Uses of Technology

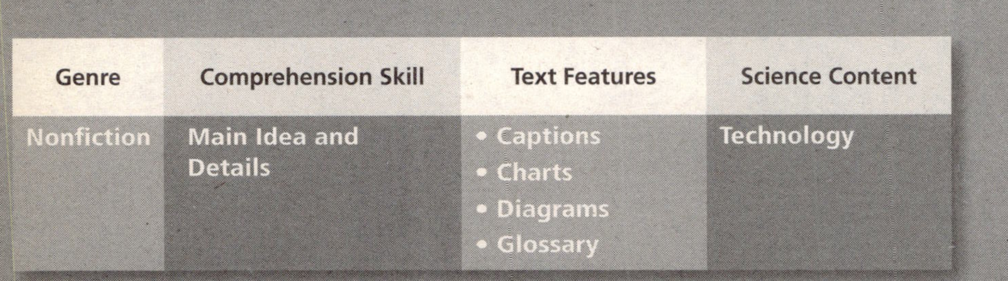

by Natalie Rompella

Genre	Comprehension Skill	Text Features	Science Content
Nonfiction	Main Idea and Details	• Captions • Charts • Diagrams • Glossary	Technology

Scott Foresman Science 6.21

What did you learn?

1. What are some of the activities that can be automated and performed by robots?

2. Why are robots so useful to people?

3. List some places or situations that are too dangerous for humans, but where robots can be sent instead.

4. **Writing** in Science   After hundreds of years a fourth form of the element carbon was discovered. Write to explain what the uses are for this new form of carbon known as carbon nanotube.

5. **Main Idea and Details** Do you think nanotechnology is a good idea? Why or why not? Use information from the book to support your answer.

Picture Credits
Every effort has been made to secure permission and provide appropriate credit for photographic material.
The publisher deeply regrets any omission and pledges to correct errors called to its attention in subsequent editions.

Photo locators denoted as follows: Top (T), Center (C), Bottom (B), Left (L), Right (R), Background (Bkgd).

Opener: ©JPL/NASA; 3 (BR) Mauro Fermariello /Photo Researchers, Inc.; 5 Getty Images; 6 ©JPL/NASA;
8 Volker Steger /Photo Researchers, Inc.; 10 (T) Tatsuyuki Tayama/Fujifotos/The Image Works, Inc.;
11 (Bkgd) Digital Vision; 13 Michael St. Maur Sheil/Corbis; 14 (BL) Dr. Peter Harris/Photo Researchers, Inc.,
(T) ©Science VU/NASA/Ames Research Center/Visuals Unlimited; 15 Volker Steger /Photo Researchers, Inc.

Unless otherwise acknowledged, all photographs are the copyright © of Dorling Kindersley, a division of Pearson.

ISBN: 0-328-14031-7

The Uses of Technology

by Natalie Rompella

Glossary

autonomous robots robots that can act without direct human supervision

carbon nanotubes the most recently discovered form of carbon, with properties far different from those of diamonds and graphite

industrial robots automatically controlled robots that can handle several products at once and can be programmed to complete several different tasks

nanotechnology technology that deals with materials and processes in terms of one-billionth of a meter

robot a machine that is able to get information from its surroundings and do physical work, such as moving or manipulating objects

robotics the technology dealing with the design, construction, and operation of robots

The World of Robotics

Machines can do many activities that once required human effort. Is there a chore you are required to do at home that you dislike? Someday you may have the help of a robot for simple tasks, such as taking out the trash or mowing the lawn. A **robot** is a machine that is able to get information from its surroundings and do physical work, such as moving or manipulating objects. Robots are now used in many places, including hospitals, factories, outer space, and even the military. **Robotics** is the technology dealing with the design, construction, and operation of robots.

There are many kinds of robots. Their design depends on the functions they will perform. Some may need to pick up objects; others may have to locate objects by using sensors.

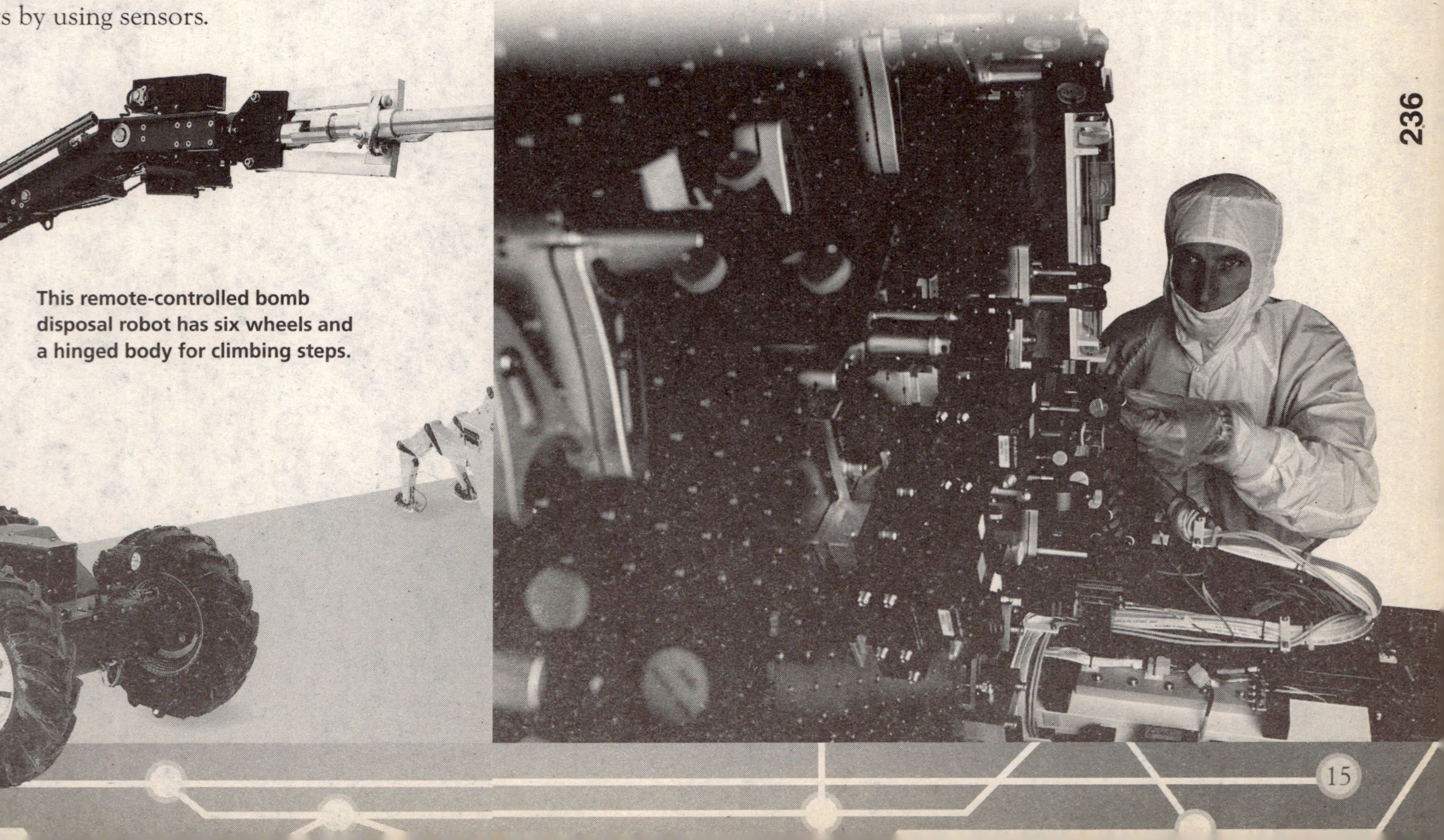

This remote-controlled bomb disposal robot has six wheels and a hinged body for climbing steps.

Benefits and Risks Of Nanotechnology

Most advances in technology have both positive and negative effects. Nanotechnology is no different. It obviously has its benefits. It can have positive effects in agriculture, industry, medicine, and other areas. However, although there are ways that nanotechnology can improve the world, there are also risks involved.

The systems of Earth and of the human body are fragile. Any technology that changes a part of a system must be carefully researched before it is put into use. The costs and benefits of new technologies must be explored before informed decisions can be made about their use.

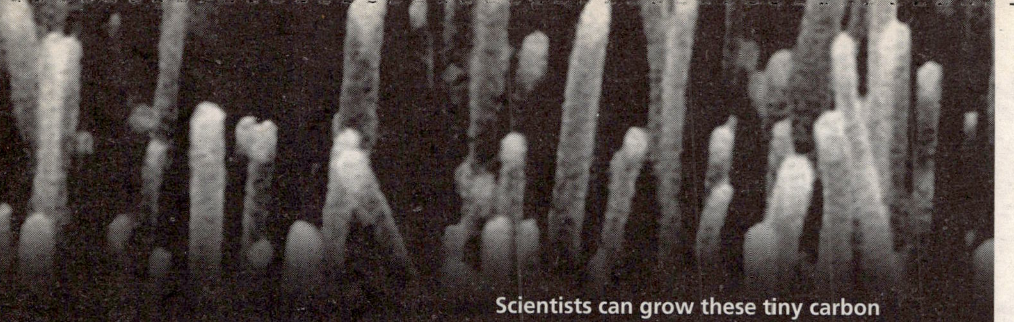

Scientists can grow these tiny carbon nanotubes, here magnified 295 times.

Another Form of Carbon

Carbon forms more chemical compounds than any other element except hydrogen. Diamonds, graphite, and "amorphous" carbon are all forms of carbon. Diamonds are known as the hardest substance on Earth. Not only are they used in jewelry, but they are also used as tools for cutting and grinding other substances.

Graphite is a soft solid. It is used in pencils for what is referred to as "lead." Graphite is also mixed into paints and clays and is used as a lubricant.

When certain organisms decompose, they form amorphous carbon. Coal and charcoal are two forms of amorphous carbon; they can be used as fuel. Amorphous carbon is also used for gunpowder, ink, and paints.

Scientists have found a new form of carbon, called **carbon nanotubes.** The molecules of this form of carbon are about the size of a nanometer and are rolled into a tube shape. Carbon nanotubes are much lighter than a similar amount of steel, but they are much stronger. They can also be used as conductors and insulators.

The structure of a carbon nanotube can be seen through an electron microscope.

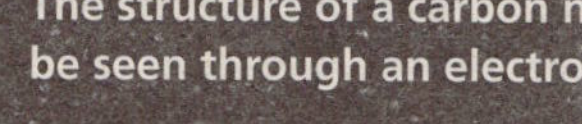

A robotic hand holds a fragile egg.

Not all robots are made to resemble humans. If a robot's job requires it to search for something on the ground, it will be designed to be close to the ground. If a robot is to perform a task of attaching two objects to each other, it may have long "arms" and "hands," but it might not need any parts other than that.

The human body is able to perform many complicated tasks. Even the motion of turning a doorknob is very complicated. Scientists have been able to imitate human arm movements in robots.

Some robots are made to resemble the human form. These robots are sometimes called humanoid, or android robots. Robots that can perform humanlike tasks, such as walking or responding to voices, are more complex. But unless it is necessary, robots usually do not have all these features.

This humanoid robot was built to take part in a robot soccer tournament.

This robot's "legs" each have four joints, allowing the robot to move over uneven terrain.

The History of Robots

Robots date back to about 270 B.C. The Greek scientist Ctesibus invented a water clock called the clepsydra, which used moveable figures to measure time.

The word *robot* was first used in a play by Karel Capek called *R.U.R.*, or *Rossum's Universal Robots*, in 1921. It comes from the Czech word *robota*, meaning "drudgery or forced labor." The robot, as a concept, has been the subject of stories since medieval times. In the 1940s it reached a wider audience through the science fiction stories of Russian-born American author and scientist Isaac Asimov.

Through the years, there have been advancements in the development of robots. New technologies, such as better sensors, smaller and faster computers, and more sophisticated computer programs, have been very useful in designing robots that do more complex tasks. In the future, robots may be used more at home—helping with everyday tasks, such as cooking and cleaning.

Water is necessary for life. Not only do we use it in our homes but also in industries such as agriculture and manufacturing.

Many parts of the world do not have a large enough source of clean water. In other places, oil spills, runoff, industrial wastes, and other forms of pollution have contaminated the water supply. Nanotechnology may also help reduce this problem. Some scientists are currently researching a type of molecule called a nanospore. They have found that nanospores can absorb harmful elements, including lead, mercury, bacteria, and viruses from water sources, making it usable. Scientists are also working on ways to use nanospores to control and aid in the cleanup of oil spills.

Nanotechnology Applications

Nanotechnology has many uses. One use is producing substances by rearranging the atoms in one substance to make another. Diamonds come from carbon, so by changing the atomic structure, a diamond can be constructed from other carbon forms.

Someday nanotechnology may also be able to help the ozone layer. Nanorobots are very small robots. Airborne nanorobots may be programmed to repair the thinning of the ozone layer.

One of the biggest areas in which nanotechnology could be applied is medicine. Viruses and bacteria can make us sick. Nanotechnology could provide a way to help combat viruses and bacteria while not harming healthy cells. With this technology, scientists hope to someday be able to battle diseases such as cancer.

Scientists hope that someday nanorobots will be able to examine blood vessels from the inside.

Nanotechnology may enable physicians to repair any part of a patient's 60,000 miles of blood vessels.

Industrial Robots

Help wanted: Looking for someone to do the same job the same way each time, twenty-four hours a day. Who would do this job? A robot would. Unlike humans, robots do not get tired. They do not need to take breaks to eat or sleep. Robots can do the same task over and over by being programmed to repeat an action exactly. Jobs that involve working with hazardous gases or chemicals are not hazardous to a robot. Robots are not affected by very loud sounds or hot and cold conditions. Lifting heavy materials might hurt a human's back over time. But robots can be built to handle such tasks.

Most robots are used in factories. They assemble parts, inspect products, and test materials. Robots that can handle several products or items at a time and can be programmed to complete several different tasks are called **industrial robots.**

The automobile industry is a major user of industrial robots. Robots can weld, spray paint, and assemble parts.

Robots weld metal parts together in an automobile factory.

Robots for Exploration

Because of robots, we have learned about faraway places. NASA has used rovers to learn more about Mars. Rovers are remote-controlled vehicles. Human controllers decide where and how fast rovers go, as well as what they do. *Sojourner*, *Spirit*, and *Opportunity* are rovers that have been on missions to Mars. Using their robotic hands, they have been able to pick up soil and rock samples. They have taken pictures of various parts of Mars, revealing more than telescopes can.

Other robots, however, are autonomous robots. These robots are able to act without specific instruction or direct supervision. They are not constantly controlled by human operators. They can analyze information and make a choice, such as walking over or around an obstacle.

Opportunity landed on Mars in 2004.

Nanotechnology

Molecules and atoms are so small we cannot see them with the unaided eye. One drop of water contains millions of molecules. Each molecule of water is made of two atoms of hydrogen and one atom of oxygen. Scientists have found ways to manipulate individual molecules and atoms. Advances in this technology will let scientists build things one atom at a time.

Nanotechnology is the technology of materials and processes on a scale best measured in nanometers. A nanometer is one-billionth the length of a meter, or one-millionth of a millimeter.

Nanotechnology may someday allow scientists to build molecules, such as this one, from individual atoms.

Robots
At Home

How would your family react to a housekeeper made of metal and wires? Scientists are developing robots that will do household tasks. Robots are already able to do simple chores, such as vacuuming and mowing the lawn. Some can follow simple verbal commands. Someday robots may be able to perform all the chores that you and your family dislike doing, such as cooking, cleaning the bathroom, and making the beds.

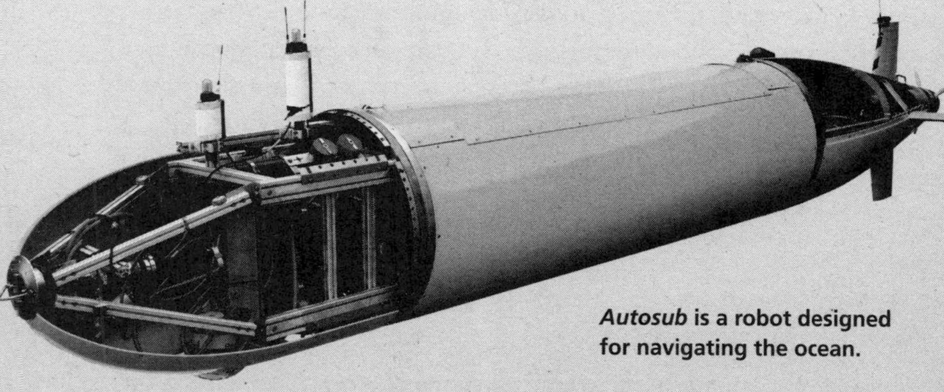
robotic vacuum cleaner

241

Autosub is a robot designed for navigating the ocean.

Robots are also used to explore locations on Earth that are unsafe or not accessible to humans, such as the inside of active volcanoes. Active volcanoes are too dangerous for scientists to explore themselves. But robots are able to collect volcanic samples and various chemical and physical data without the risk of injury.

Robots can also be used to explore the deep, dark, and cold underwater environments at the bottom of the ocean. Since robots' batteries run out, scientists have even found a way for robots to regain their energy by "eating" marine life such as plankton. These robots recharge their batteries through a chemical reaction powered by the remains of decaying plankton. By maintaining their power, these robots are able to stay in the ocean for months.

The military has discovered the advantages of robots for use in the air, on the land, and in the water. Robots search caves and tunnels for hazardous chemicals or explosives, and go places that are too dangerous for humans.

Robotics in Medicine

Does a "surgeon robot" sound impossible? Not anymore. Robots are often used in hospitals. Surgery requires precise movements of surgical tools. One small mistake can be dangerous for the patient. Some doctors are learning how to perform surgery with the assistance of robots. Although the doctor directs the movements of the tools, the robot carries out the actual motion. The benefits of this technology are that robots can be programmed to do exact, small movements with less chance of error, and there is less chance of spreading disease from doctor to patient. Because of this, patients heal in less time.

Robots may help care for patients who need special assistance, such as elderly patients and persons with a disability. Robots could pick up fallen objects, retrieve items, and help the patient get in and out of bed.

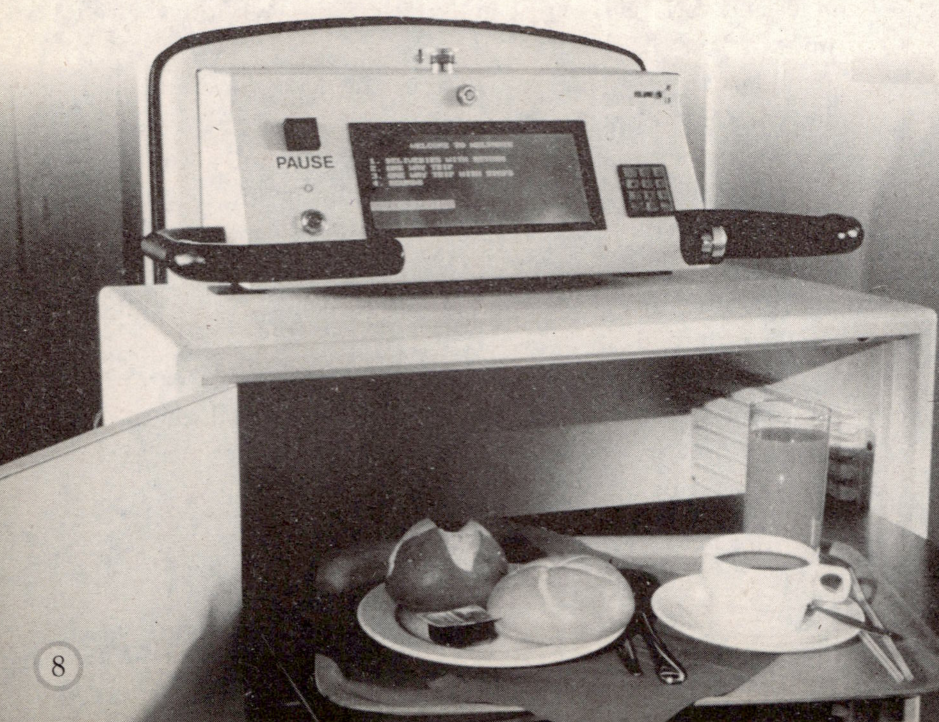
This robot serves food to hospital patients.

Robotics in Farming

Just as farm machines have made farming easier for humans, so have robots. Some countries have begun using robots to milk cows. Others have been developing robots to harvest fruits, such as strawberries and melons. Robots can be programmed to recognize objects of a certain size and color, and then remove only those objects from trees or bushes.

Robot technology is used on fish farms to scare away birds that prey on fish. As birds approach the ponds, these special robots, called scarebots, sense the birds and quickly scare them away. Even jobs such as shearing sheep can be done quickly and efficiently with robots.

A robot shearer can shear the fleece off of a sheep.

fleece